GARDEN POOLS

FOUNTAINS & WATERFALLS

Tall horsetails surround this tranquil koi pond (see page 49).

Water lilies add a burst of color to the pool's surface. For specifics on growing them, see page 50.

Book Editor
Scott Atkinson

Coordinating Editor
Suzanne Normand Mathison

Design
Joe di Chiarro

Illustrations
Lois Lovejoy
Rik Olson

Consulting Editor
Jane Horn

Editorial Coordinator
Vicki Weathers

Cover
Design by Vasken Guiragossian and James Boone. Photography by Van Chaplin. Landscape Architect: Dan Franklin.

Our appreciation to the staff of Southern Living magazine for their contributions to this book.

BY POPULAR DEMAND...

Garden pool technology has taken a great leap forward in recent years. Enthusiasm for water gardening and raising koi have also reached new heights. For these reasons, we decided that the time was right for an up-to-date book on the subject.

We begin with a planning overview, which includes many color photos of contemporary pools, fountains, waterfalls, and streams. The next two chapters focus on water plants and fish, respectively. Finally, we present pool-building and maintenance specifics, including the latest information on liners and shells, masonry, pumps and plumbing, and outdoor lighting.

This edition has benefitted greatly from the input of many professionals in the field. We'd especially like to thank Paul Cowley of Potomac Waterworks, Michael Glassman of Environmental Creations, and Herb Simons of U.S. Koi Sales for reviewing the manuscript and generously offering their expertise. Fred Tonai of Golden State Fisheries also read parts of the book and provided numerous suggestions. We are also grateful to the many homeowners and garden pool lovers who shared with us their knowledge of and enthusiasm for pools, plants, and fish.

Special thanks go to Rene Lynch for carefully editing the manuscript and to Marianne Lipanovich for scouting photo possibilities.

Photographers: Ray Albright: 21 bottom; Ardon Armstrong, 20 top, 36; Scott Atkinson: 56; Van Chaplin: 8 top, 9 left, 18 bottom, 22, 31 top, 43 bottom; Derek Fell: 14 right, 15, 25 center; Richard Fish: 42 top; Mark E. Gibson: 2, 24 center, 25 right, 50 left; Harry Haralambou: 24 right, 48 left; Pamela Harper: 18 top; Saxon Holt: 8 bottom, 20 bottom, 46, 48 right, 49 right, 58, 64; Horticultural Photography: 7 top, 24 left, 50 right; Mary-Gray Hunter: 7; Sylvia Martin: 4, 6, 21 top, 30 top, 33, 41; Jack McDowell: 10; Michael McKinley: 4, 6, 7 bottom; Allen Rokach: 32; Jeff Stone: 3, 25 left; Michael S. Thompson: 12 left, 44 bottom right; Tom Wyatt: 1, 9 right, 11, 12 right, 13, 14 left, 16, 17, 19, 27, 28, 29, 30 bottom, 31 bottom, 34, 37, 38, 39, 42 bottom, 43 top, 44 top and bottom left, 45, 49 center, 61.

Photo styling: JoAnn Masaoka Van Atta: 1, 9 right, 11, 12 right, 13, 14 left, 16, 17, 19, 27, 28, 29, 30 bottom, 31 bottom, 34, 37, 38, 39, 42 bottom, 43 top, 44 top and bottom left, 45, 49 center, 61.

Southern Living® Garden Pools, Fountains & Waterfalls was adapted from a book by the same title published by Sunset Books.

First printing January 1999

ISBN 0-376-09061-8

Library of Congress Catalog
Card Number: 98-87046

Printed in the United States.

CONTENTS

Handcarved lion head spills water into a wall fountain's holding pool (see page 25).

GARDEN POOLS

I f anything in nature can be called magic, it must be *water*. The shimmer and sound of water have cast their spell throughout history. The Chinese, and later the Japanese, perfected the balance of three basic elements: water, stone, and plants. The Romans used fountains and stair-step pools to cool hot summer nights along the Mediterranean. The English Victorians built palatial homes for goldfish, and the French spread out enormous sheets of water in front of their chateaux.

Quiet and reflecting, dancing and image-shattering—water still brings both energy and old-world charm into a garden. Whether it reflects the sky and clouds, a piece of garden sculpture, or the arching branches of a nearby tree, a garden pool presents an ever-changing picture. The cooling effect of a fountain or waterfall on hot, dry summer days and evenings is as welcome as in Roman times. Goldfish or koi dimpling the surface of a fish pond continue to be a captivating sight. For gardeners, a water garden opens up a whole new world.

Emerald Island
Quiet, reflecting water is special, regardless of size. This tranquil diminutive pool is proof, set in an equally tiny sunken garden. A spray fountain looks best when outlined against a flat surface such as this fine-textured lawn. Landscape architects: Hugh and Mary Palmer Dargan.

5

Although few of us have the space or inclination to build a full-scale, traditional pool, water can play a part in many other ways in today's landscaping scene. You can choose from among three basic possibilities: a small accent pool, a formal pool, or a natural or informal pool. Today's do-it-yourselfer also has a choice of materials—from traditional concrete, stone, and brick to easy-to-install liners and shells. In addition, there's an entire realm of pumps, filters, and lighting hardware. Here's a closer look, in words and pictures, at the many possibilities for today's garden pool.

Water as a Decorative Accent

Water in small amounts serves an ornamental purpose in a garden, and it doesn't take much effort or expense to achieve satisfying results. Let the pool draw attention to arrangements of container plants as seasonal blooms appear, or start a tiny water garden (for pointers, see "Tub Gardens" on page 10). Or accent the pool itself, placing a glass float or colorful bloom on the water's surface. The simplest "decoration" of all is to keep the water clear and let birds play in it.

If you want to start small, there are tiny decorative garden pools that have the advantages of being both portable and versatile. You can pick them up at garden supply and statuary stores. Innovative garden decorators have demonstrated that almost any container capable of holding water can—with suitable cleaning and appropriate placement—become an attractive accent pool. Add your own ideas to the following list: bonsai bowls, terra cotta planters, wine barrels, industrial drums, claw-foot bathtubs, laundry basins, cattle-watering troughs, and hot water (or other) tanks. Scout around your house and yard (or grandmother's) for that chipped enameled dishpan, rusty wheelbarrow, or galvanized bucket; you may even find a crock still gathering dust since Prohibition days.

Want to create your own accent pool? Consider freeform concrete—shaped, colored, and textured to resemble a waterpocket in native stone—or a sand-cast circular basin. Waterproofed lumber or marine grade plywood can also fit the bill. Leave the basin in its rough state or paint it, tile it, or line it with a mosaic of pebbles, seashells, or whatever you have available.

Starting Out Small

A tiny accent pool, such as this charming birdbath, is one of the simplest ways to introduce water to your garden. Most feathered bathers prefer 1 or 2 inches of water.

Formal Garden Pools

In a Victorian garden the pool was frequently a generous circle, oval, or rectangle, slightly raised, set in the center of an area, and surrounded by spacious walks so that it could be viewed from every side. But the Victorian garden failed to survive the disappearance of the patient, pipe-smoking professional gardener with quarters above the coach house. A few gardens are still large enough to accommodate such pools, but in most cases the pool has to be set near some border if there is to be enough room for anything else.

If you build a pool of concrete, brick, stone, or tile in a simple shape, you'll succeed in recalling the old style. Classic rectangles or ovals are best and can be scaled up or down to fit the available space and harmonize with the surroundings. Fountains and sculpture are characteristic accessories.

Formal pools can be raised above ground level, semi-raised, or sunken, depending on the site and the border effect you wish. A raised pool takes the most effort and materials but provides surfaces for sitting and sunning, as well as for container plants and decorations.

Formal pools look best when set in formally landscaped areas with adequate elbowroom. Crowding a formal pool into a small area tends to destroy vital esthetics that depend upon proper scale.

Natural Pools

A natural-appearing pool is almost any body of water without square corners, perpendicular walls, or man-made edges in sight. It should have native stone and soil close around it, along with plants common to the area in which you live.

Traditional Ties

For centuries, formal pools were the norm for any proper English garden. To continue the tradition, plan a rectangular or circular shape, either sunken, raised, or semi-raised. This classic fountain is meant to be viewed through a series of rose-covered arbors.

From that point, the variety of choices open to the designer is as wide-ranging as the designs are beautiful. Yours could be an alpine pool, a willow-shaded pond, a tiny spring at some desert oasis, or a water retreat such as one you remember from a vacation. Japanese gardens are an excellent source of natural ideas and techniques.

Most older natural pools are hand-packed shells of reinforced concrete; today, do-it-yourselfers may opt for pool liners or fiberglass shells (see pages 12–13). It's the border that counts: typically, edges are camouflaged with lush plant materials or rocks, soil, and other material so that the pool appears to be the work of nature.

A natural-appearing pool is the most enjoyable to create, but it's also the most demanding. The physical construction is not the difficult part, however; the problem is finding a way to artfully blend your chosen materials.

Unlike formal pools, informal designs seem to fit comfortably in limited space. However, a boulder-framed pool requires ample elbow room. Boulders fill up space quickly, so the shell of the pool itself has to be sizable to remain in scale.

For do-it-yourselfers, the only rule is this: Keep it simple. Complex designs not only are difficult to manage during construction but also rarely achieve the hoped-for effect.

Peaceful Retreat
A placid pond fed by a well stands as the centerpiece of a serene garden in the gentle Virginia countryside. The dark surface of the water reflects the leafy canopy of the surrounding hardwood trees. Landscape architects: Charles Gillette, Ralph Griswold.

Nature Adrift
A natural pool is usually best for mixed plantings and fish. Yellow flag iris and pickerel weed frame this quiet scene, while water lilies and fish share the water rights.

Locating Your Pool

Finding the right location for a garden pool is not always a simple matter. An obvious spot, it seems, is where everyone can enjoy it. If such a location requires renovation of your entire yard, though, it is obviously impractical. Don't hestitate to look beyond the backyard: consider a dramatic entry pond with arched bridge; a quiet sideyard setting outside the study window; an enclosed courtyard pool with lush plant life; even a living room koi pond.

Before you begin, you'll need to check any deed restrictions, setback requirements, and local ordinances that may affect the placement of your pool. Bone up on local building codes as well. Then you'll need access to the site for s⟨...⟩ earth-moving equipment; if plumb⟨...⟩ connections are required, make su⟨...⟩

If you are planning to add plan⟨...⟩ page 11), consider the pool's locatio⟨...⟩ the sun. The site should be protecte⟨...⟩ and situated away from deciduous t⟨...⟩ rain a steady supply of leaves and tw⟨...⟩ water. Drainage is important: *don't ch⟨...⟩* lying or "bottom" area that will constantly overflow in wet weather. Water seeks its own level, so if you can't provide a level site, you'll have to build a retaining wall at one end or design a split-level pond, connected by a waterfall or stream.

A Different Sort of Pond

As this fish pond attests, a garden pool needn't be tucked into a backyard corner. To visually tie the house to the garden, the narrow body of water hugs the house in precisely the same arc as the wall. A black fiberglass liner gives the pond the illusion of depth. Landscape architect: Carol Macht, Anshen & Allen.

Valley Oasis

Tumbling natural falls and a large holding pool (which doubles as a swimming pool in season) create a cool retreat for a hot summer's day; stepping stones lead the way. Tender ferns, rhododendrons, and drought-tolerant valley oaks share the scene; drip irrigation system and mini-sprayers help keep moisture lovers green without wasting water. Landscape designer: Dennis Tromburg/Zierden Landscaping.

TUB GARDENS

If you don't have space for a full-scale water garden, don't despair—instead, plant a tub garden. You'll need only a few springtime hours and some simple ingredients: a suitable container, a sunny site, gallons of water, some bog or aquatic plants (you may have to order these ahead from a specialty catalog), and a few fish to help keep the pool clean.

The container. Searching for the right container is half the fun of tub gardening. If you want a good-size pool, buy at least a 25-gallon container, or build your own; almost any leakproof vessel will do. A wooden half-barrel is an attractive choice, and it's easy to find. For a more ornate pool, use a large decorative tub, such as the one shown in the photo at right. You can always place the main container inside a more handsome—but less seaworthy—barrel or tub.

The site. Because a water-filled 25-gallon container is heavy (over 200 pounds), it makes good sense to set up your water garden in its permanent location. You may prefer to place it on garden ground rather than on a deck or patio: the pool will have to be drained occasionally, and there's always some chance of seepage.

As you evaluate possible sites, remember that it's important to provide plenty of sunshine: most aquatic plants need at least 4 to 6 hours of full sun daily. Keep in mind, too, that your water garden should complement its surroundings; you may want to locate the pool where it will reflect color from blooming trees and flowers, for example.

Sunshine, a small container, and a few water plants are all you'll need to begin tub gardening. Design: Aerin Moore, Magic Gardens.

Filling and planting. Before placing a wooden, metal, or unglazed ceramic container in its permanent location, it's best to coat the inside with epoxy paint or to line it with PVC plastic. A dark-colored coating makes the surface more reflective.

With the exception of plants that simply float free on the water's surface, root aquatic plants before placing them in the pool. Plastic pots are best, since they hold up better than clay when submerged in water. Fill pots with garden loam; an inch-thick layer of sand at the top of each pot helps keep soil particles in place.

Submerge planted pots in the pool, usually positioning them so pot tops are 6 inches or more under water. A few plants do best if containers are only partially submerged; see the listings on pages 52–55. To raise plants to the proper height, set up pedestals made from bricks or overturned pots on the pool's bottom.

Add a goldfish or two, or some mosquito fish, to keep the water free of insects; don't overfeed fish, since this could disturb the pool's ecological balance. A tiny fountain jet, driven by a submersible pump, provides visual interest as well as oxygen.

Once a year, drain the pool and scrub it out thoroughly with a mixture of four parts water to one part household bleach.

Possible plants. Listed below are a few popular water plants. For more complete descriptions and planting details, see Chapter 4, "Water Gardens."

Arrowhead (Sagittaria latifolia)
Cardinal flower (Lobelia cardinalis)
Horsetail (Equisetum hyemale)
Lotus (Nelumbo)
Japanese iris (Iris ensata)
Pygmy cattail (Typha minima)
Umbrella plant (Cyperus alternifolius)
Water hyacinth (Eichhornia crassipes)
Water hawthorn (Aponogeton distachyus)
Water lily (Nymphaea)

Honored House Guests

Something's fishy about the living room shown below—the koi pond, to be exact. Part of a family room remodel, it's plenty deep (about 30 inches) for energetic fish. The construction is concrete, with mortar-embedded stone; the rocks on the bottom are loose to facilitate cleaning. At right, the owner feeds koi from his hand, showing how well these pets have taken to their indoor lifestyle. Landscape contractor: John Nishizawa, Co., Inc.

Plants or Fish?

Before attacking the backyard with pick and shovel, take time to consider the special needs of water plants or fish, if they're to call your garden pool home.

Planning a water garden. Water plants add new colors, shapes, and textures to a garden, especially the hardy and tropical water lilies, oxygenating plants and grasses, and floating plants such as the water hyacinth. A "bog" or border garden adjacent to the pool, receiving some overflow or oversplash, creates a special environment, perhaps with bright blue and yellow irises or papyrus catching the sunlight.

If you want plants in your pool, as you almost certainly will, you'll have to make some design choices. Most plants require at least 4 to 6 hours per day of sunlight, so a sunny site is the number one prerequisite. You'll also probably want a ledge or shelf about 10 inches deep and wide around the pool edges, perfect for many submerged water plants. If you're thinking of raising fish, too, you may wish to build a divided pond, or erect some other type of barrier: fish think nothing of rooting your favorite water plants into oblivion.

For details on choosing and growing water plants, see Chapter 4, "Water Gardens."

Planning for fish. If you're considering the acquisition of a few goldfish or koi, beware! You're almost certain to get hooked and want more. Common goldfish are the patriarchs of ornamental fish; many fancier breeds, suitable for outdoor pools, have come from them. Colorful koi are carp, not goldfish. Larger, spunkier, and longer-living than goldfish, they are known for their outgoing behavior and affection for their owners.

Fish prefer a bit more shade than is optimum for plants, which also discourages the formation of algae. Pool depth is critical: a koi pond should be no shallower than 18 inches and ideally between 24 and 36 inches, or even deeper. It should have shallow places for feeding and fish-watching and deeper water where the koi can go when surface water heats up or starts to freeze—or to escape a raccoon or the family cat. Don't use rough stone below the waterline, because fish can be injured by rubbing against the edges.

A koi pond requires more careful planning than a pool with plants only or no plants; this will almost certainly require some form of pump for aeration and a filtering system for battling ammonia and other impurities in the water. For details, see pages 15–16. If you need additional help with pond design, or with selecting and raising fish, turn to Chapter 5, "Goldfish & Koi."

Pool Materials

At one time, packed bentonite clay and stone were the only choices for a sturdy garden pool. Although many formal pools are still built with masonry materials—concrete, brick, tile, and stone—today's do-it-yourselfer has two handy alternatives: pool liners and fiberglass shells. Here's an introduction to all the commonly used pool materials. You'll find complete installation instructions in Chapter 6, "Building Your Pool."

Flexible liners. These are the big news in garden pools, and you'll find some type of liner in virtually any mail-order catalog. They are not the thin, brittle polyethylene sheets from the hardware store but much stouter sheets—20 to 30 mils and thicker—designed especially for garden pools. Stock sizes range from about 4 by 5 feet to 23 by 30 feet (finished pool size is somewhat smaller); special sizes and shapes may be special-ordered. Installation is straightforward: basically, you dig a hole, drape the liner over the inside, and fill with water. The typical black color allows for maximum water reflectancy; you won't see the liner itself.

PVC plastic is the standard liner material, but it becomes brittle with exposure to the sun's rays. Life expectancy is roughly 10 years. More UV-resistant—but twice the price—are industrial-grade PVC or butyl-rubber liners. Some pool builders prefer EPDM, a roofing material, available in 10- to 40-foot-wide rolls and .045- or .060-inch thicknesses. Most liner materials can be cut and solvent-welded to fit odd-shaped water features.

Fiberglass shells. To picture these fiberglass pool shells, think of a spa or hot tub buried in the ground and filled with plants and fish. They're the easiest pools of all to install; you simply shape a hole that matches the shell's outline, lower the unit into place, and backfill while adding water.

Most shells are treated with gelcoat, a spa material that comes in several colors (again, black usually looks best). A reasonable selection of shapes and sizes is available, but many are too shallow to house fish. Some prefab units can be joined to make larger units; there are also fiberglass streams and waterfalls. Price is about four times or greater than for a comparably sized PVC pool; life expectancy is 20 years plus (although gelcoat is often warrantied for

Easy-to-install Fiberglass

Preformed fiberglass pools are available in a variety of shapes and dimensions and are among the easiest units to install. You can either leave the rolled edges exposed, as shown, or hide them with overhanging rock borders or plantings. Design: Peter Chan.

Riverstones

Ever-popular stone adds the riparian look to this small natural pool. The base of most stone pools is poured concrete or gunite; the stones are then secured in a thin bed of mortar. Landscape designer: Paul Reed.

Dressing Up with Tile

Tile is a sure-fire way to introduce tradition and elegance to your garden pool. This pool doubles as a working spa, with poured-in-place gunite shell and concrete walls capped with hand-painted Spanish tile. Tile inlays in the Mexican paver border echo the cross-shaped motif. Landscape architect: Jeff Stone Associates.

1 year only). Fiberglass shells are available at some garden centers and through mail-order catalogs. Be sure to figure in shipping prices: transporting a large, noncollapsible shell can be quite expensive.

Concrete. Poured concrete has its evident advantages. It is the most plastic of materials, as well as the most impermeable. Its utilitarian character can be disguised with paint or a facing of brick, tile, or stone, and it can also be plastered for greater texture or water protection. The material is normally reinforced with steel to withstand the pressures of soil and water. The amount and size of the steel depend on the geographical location and the structural requirements.

Freeform concrete can be stacked to a slope of about 45 degrees with ordinary mix and can be made steeper with an air-sprayed, professionally applied mixture called gunite or shotcrete. For crisp, perpendicular angles and perpendicular walls, you'll need carpentered forms and poured concrete (see pages 72–73).

Concrete does have some material disadvantages. It is heavy to work with, and forms, if

required, can be time-consuming to manufacture. Concrete also demands considerable post-construction care: the surface must be kept damp for at least a week to allow it to cure. Also, concrete contains lime that has to be neutralized before fish or plants can live in the water.

Concrete blocks sometimes do the job better: their greater size means quick assembly and fewer mortar joints per square foot of surface than other masonry units, and they can be faced with tile, a stone design, or even brick. Concrete blocks are easier to reinforce than brick because of their hollow cores.

Brick. The ruddy face of brick is a warm and familiar friend in both formal and informal gardens. A raised pool with brick walls provides a traditional home for water lilies, goldfish, and koi. Brick serves equally well in a modern context. Brick-in-sand patios with sunken pools appear regularly in contemporary surroundings.

But amateur bricklayers can come to grief with bricks if they use them to form the walls of a pool, as they are too porous to do the job unaided. Some homeowners use poured concrete to form the shell and then face the above-grade portion with brick, or they mount a brick rim atop the concrete walls of a sunken pool. You can also use brick to cap or cover a plastic liner—achieving, in effect, the best of both worlds.

Borders & Edgings

Often, it's the border around the pool that makes or breaks your pool's appearance and harmony within the garden in general.

Your border treatment partially depends on whether your pool is raised or sunken. Sunken pools need some kind of raised border to keep groundwater from running into the pool during rains. In a pool without a drain or overflow, runoff can drown plants near the pool and float fish over-

board with fatal consequences. Even with a drain, the pool water will probably be muddied by inflowing groundwater. A border an inch or two above the ground helps prevent all these things.

A gravel-filled drain all around the pool will take care of water drainage along the surrounding surface. It's a good idea to also hook up an overflow pipe from the pool to the border drain.

When you come to edging materials, the choice is broad: a grass lawn; an adjoining bog garden or rock garden (often piled against a partially raised pool, or used at one end of a sloping site); native stones and boulders; flagstones laid in a mortar bed; a wide concrete lip (especially useful as a mowing strip if grass adjoins the area); brick laid in sand or mortar; redwood or other rot-resistant wood laid as rounds or upright in columns; terra cotta tiles; or railroad ties.

Everything in Its Place

A foreground spa, twin garden pools, and a swimming pool (not shown) all nest efficiently in this backyard scene. Wood decking ties all the elements together and provides a walkway for a leisurely stroll. Landscape architect: Michael Kobayashi/MHK Group. Additional design: American Landscape, Inc.

Ideas for Edgings

The world of these koi carp is circumscribed by four border materials: upright logs, a simple wooden bridge, flagstone paving, and native stones for accent.

The Inner Works: Pumps, Filters & Hardware

Small garden pools may maintain a relatively stable environment (see "Pool Ecology," at right) on their own after an initial start-up period, but large fish ponds, waterfalls, and fountain units require some basic hardware. Here's a discussion of the components you might need.

Pumps. A pump serves three basic purposes: (1) It recirculates water to a fountain or over a waterfall, conserving water and providing the pressure or "head" necessary to pull or push water through the plumbing system; (2) It allows you to drain the pool in the event of a leak or for routine cleaning and maintenance; and (3) It helps aerate water, adding oxygen and promoting clean water for fish. You'll need a pump to power most pool filters.

Pumps have two basic types: *submersible* and *recirculating*. The best submersible pumps are made from brass and stainless steel; housings coated with epoxy resin are also popular. These pumps are designed for low-volume, part-time use, such as driving a small fountain or waterfall.

Large volumes of water and a constant demand—such as a biological filter system (see below)—favor a recirculating pump housed outside the pool. Don't buy the swimming pool design; it's overly powerful and gobbles too much electricity. Instead, look for a *circulator* pump, which moves a higher volume of water at a lower pressure. Adding a strainer basket ahead of your pump's inlet helps keep leaves and other debris out of the pump itself.

For details on pump ratings and installation, see pages 80–81.

Filters. Filters for garden ponds run the gamut from simple strainer baskets to swimming pool filters to custom biological filters for large koi ponds. The three basic types are chemical, mechanical, and biological.

Chemical filtration simply means utilizing algicides and other water-clearing agents to attack particular impurities. This is often the method of choice for a small garden pool that has no plants or fish.

Mechanical filters use some type of straining mechanism to trap dirt particles in water passing through. One variety simply circulates water through a box or cylinder containing activated carbon, zeolite, brushes, or fiber padding. While these devices are economical, they tend to clog easily under heavy service (as in a fish pond), requiring frequent backwashing and/or replacement of the filter media. Most catalog models can be powered with a simple submersible pump.

POOL
ECOLOGY

"Why is the pool water pea-green, and what can I do about it?" The answer to this frequently asked question requires a short lesson in pool ecology.

When water gardeners speak of a "balanced" pool, they're referring to the ecological balance. *Algae* is the villain in green; a balanced pool is one in which the growth of algae is controlled naturally. Floating plants, oxygenating plants, and some assorted pool critters are the good guys.

Acting in direct competition for sunlight (on which algae thrive), floating plants such as water lilies keep water cool and clear. Small fish feed on algae and on insect larvae, keeping the mosquito problem around your pool to a minimum. Garden pool catalogs promote water snails as algae nibblers (though some pool experts feel they're more trouble than they're worth).

Owners of koi ponds have one additional concern: the build-up of toxic ammonia, which is excreted by fish. The key to grappling with ammonia lies in the *nitrogen cycle*. What this means is that successive stages of bacteria break down ammonia into *nitrites*, then into *nitrates*, which are much less toxic to fish and feed plants and algae—which in turn nourish fish. Biological filters are designed to promote the growth of helpful bacteria. Aeration via a waterfall, fountain, or some other means helps provide critical oxygen to both bacteria and their larger poolmates, the koi.

Clean water provides a happy home for a portly bullfrog. Floating plants, oxygenating plants, and critters work together to keep a pool free of algae and insects.

More efficient is the pressurized swimming pool filter; of the three major types—cartridge, diatomaceous earth (DE), and pressurized-sand—the sand filter gets the highest marks from experts. These filters do require regular backflushing, in addition to a change of sand (120 pounds or so) periodically.

A *biological* filter is a variation on the mechanical theme, relying on pumped water to circulate down or up through a filtering medium. The difference is that the filter bed supports a colony of live bacteria that consume ammonia, converting it into nitrates for use again by plants and fish. The system depends on constant aeration to keep the bacteria alive (without sufficient oxygen, they can die in as little as 6 to 8 hours); a recirculating pump—and perhaps an emergency air pump—is in order.

Other hardware. Need to keep a constant water level in your pool? Install a float valve, either a special pool model or the toilet-bowl type. When the water level sinks below a certain level, the valve opens and fresh water enters the pool. Another useful device for a large pool is a swimming pool skimmer, which is typically poured into place on the side of a concrete pool.

To run a pump or pool lighting (see below), you'll need a nearby outdoor 120-volt receptacle, protected by a ground-fault circuit interrupter (GFCI), which immediately shuts off power to the line in the case of an electrical short or power leakage. Also, don't forget an inside switch to run the pump for a waterfall or fountain, or to control light fixtures.

Installing a drain in your pool provides for easier maintenance. The lack of a drain means the pool has to be siphoned or pumped empty for cleaning, so the last water puddles will be hard to flush from the floor of the pool.

Lighting Your Pool

When it comes time to light up your garden, you have a choice of standard 120-volt or low voltage as well as a choice of surfaced or submerged pool fixtures.

Because they're safer, more energy efficient, and easier to install than standard 120-volt systems, low-voltage lights are often used outdoors. Such systems use a transformer to step down standard household current to 12 volts. Although low-voltage fixtures don't have the "punch" of line-current fixtures, a

State of the Art

Here's a koi pond, a waterfall, and a biological marvel all rolled into one. The twin pools (the upper one is shown at left) are concrete faced with fieldstone. Below the gravel bottom of each pond is a biological filter; below the filter system is what the owner calls the "submarine" or control center (see the photo below). A German recirculating pump keeps the entire show in motion. Landscape architect: George Girven & Associates. Landscape contractor: Anthony Bertotti Landscaping, Inc.

A Quiet Glow

By day, this pool commands attention with its exotic symmetry. By night, the focus shifts to the incandescence of the bubbler jets and spray, lit with four underwater uplights. Landscape architects: Tolley, Boughton & Tagaki.

little light goes a long way at night. But the standard 120-volt system still has some advantages outdoors: the buried cable and metallic fixtures give the installation a look of permanence, and light can be projected a great distance.

Outdoor surface fixtures range from well lights and other portable uplights, to spread lights that illuminate paths or bridges to downlights designed to be anchored to the house wall, eaves, and trees. Downlighting is tops for pinpointing special garden features; uplighting is good for accenting or silhouetting foliage. Low-voltage halogen MR-16 bulbs are popular for accenting; PAR spotlights, available in both low and standard voltage, are best for a wider light pattern, both in and out of water.

Most underwater lights are designed to be recessed in a concrete pool wall. You can also purchase portable lights with lead plates that keep them on the pool or stream bottom; move these about to accent a waterfall or plantings. Fountain units often come with their own integral lighting schemes, sometimes with optional filter kits for changing colors. For more on these, see pages 86–87.

What's best, submerged or surface lighting? It's a matter of taste. Surface lighting can be adjusted with more subtlety and precision; also, fish and plants tend to look best when illuminated from above. On the other hand, brash underwater lights produce dramatic effects, and they can be fine-tuned with a dimmer switch.

Rainpocket

A tiny reflecting pool mirrors an over-hanging tree fern; the "rainpocket" is freeform concrete, hand-shaped and "weathered" to resemble mountain granite. Design: Harland Hand.

A Bubbling Little Oasis

This small water feature was built where a pool existed long ago. Now a delightful addition to a backyard garden, it was easily constructed in a weekend using a 45-mil plastic liner over the old concrete pool bottom. Black dye formulated for pools and ponds is added periodically to give the water a more reflective quality.

One Step at a Time

Visitors cross this entry pool on poured concrete "islands." Water appears to flow continuously through the house, but there are really three adjacent systems, beginning with the entry pool. A self-contained stream section picks up inside and seems to exit through a back wall into the waterfall shown on page 37. Landscape designer: Michael Glassman/ Environmental Creations.

Life at the Beach

An existing stream provides the input for this backyard pool, the focal point of an extensive owner-built natural landscape. A small background dam helps form the pool, which is lined with 30-mil plastic; the fountain and waterfall are driven by a submersible pump. The plantings are about half "found" native species and half purchased. The owners added sand to make the foreground "beach." Design: Bill & Caroline Furnas.

Small Pool, Big Effect

This quarter-round pool, which doubles as a fountain, is the focal point of an urban courtyard too small for a traditional swimming pool. Landscape architects: Richard Dawson and Lawrence Estes.

Floating Deck, Japanese Style

A garden pool enclosed in an inner courtyard provides a tranquil, private space that delights from inside, too. An effective way to make a pool look larger is to cantilever a deck a foot or two over the edge, giving the impression that the water extends beyond.

A Garden Retreat

Two classic pools define an outdoor room and recall traditional European gardens. Set side-by-side, they invite inspection with a spacious walk and the sound of splashing water.

Desert Oasis

Defined by the brick edging and rear retaining wall, this semi-circular, sunken pool makes a subtle statement at one end of the wooden deck. The substructure has a poured concrete base and concrete block walls, and it is faced with tile, standard brick, and stabilized mud adobe bricks in the back. Landscape architect: Richard William/Oasis Gardens.

GARDEN
FOUNTAINS

Water in motion is nearly always dramatic, and a flowing fountain introduces water as a star performer in the garden scene. But in addition to merely entertaining with a colorful show, a fountain does more practical work. During the hot, dry days of summer, it fills the air with moisture, providing a cool garden retreat for you, your family, and guests. The musical sounds of a fountain also help wrap the area in privacy, screening off outside noise and distractions.

Contrary to popular notions, most contemporary fountains are *not* water guzzlers; in fact, many are not hooked up to water supply lines at all. A submersible or recirculating pump recycles the pool water and feeds it back to the fountain head or water inlet, where it's used again, again, and again.

Fountains that spray, fountains that spill, and fountains that splash are the three basic types. Versatile spray fountains have fountain heads that send water upward in shapes ranging from massive col-

A Sweet Idea

This rustic, bubbling basin—a focal point of a Louisiana plantation garden— was a sugar kettle in a former life. Where sugar cane once boiled into syrup, gold fish now swim and African lilies peep over the lip.

23

umns to sprays as delicate as lace. Spill fountains take two basic forms: either simple tiers of spill pans or more elaborate wall fountains. Splash fountains can contain either sprays or spills, but only in a splash fountain is water interrupted by a piece of sculpture.

Various fountain heads and spray or spill fountains can be purchased directly from the manufacturer or from garden supply, plumbing, and hardware stores, as well as some mail-order catalogs. Wall and splash fountains, on the other hand, are nearly always custom designed, either by the homeowner or by a landscape architect.

The Spray's the Thing

Basically, a spray fountain uses water in opposition to gravity, sometimes for picturesque water patterns, sometimes for interaction with sculpture, and, on occasion, simply for the sight and sound of falling water.

Choosing the spray pattern. With a little help from an array of available fountain heads, water can be sculpted into all kinds of fanciful shapes. Here are the basic options:

- A short, heavy, burbling column of water rising vertically from an open inlet pipe below the pool's surface.

- A burbling column of water from an open inlet pipe above the pool's surface. This column rises higher than one that begins below the surface.

- A fine, forceful spray coming from an inlet pipe with a spray jet smaller than the pipe's diameter. The spray rises vertically, describes a graceful arc, or rotates—depending upon the fountain head's design.

Popular spray heads include bell, mushroom, and calyx domes, cascade and aerating jets, many multi-tiered patterns, swivel jets, and spray rings with multiple, adjustable jets.

Design and location. The main rule in spray fountain design is this: Use a short, heavy column of water in windy spots. Go for height, distance, or drama only where the spray will not blow widely, drenching spectators and wasting water.

Professional designers try to position a spray fountain against a background that dramatizes the water's movement. Water in a heavy column tends to be translucent, so backgrounds ought to be dark. Fine sprays appear best when outlined against a flat surface. Heavy sprays dominate and stand out even against a lacy bower of leaves.

As water rises higher, the pool diameter must increase proportionately; otherwise, a steady loss occurs as the water falls, especially in a windy gar-

A Fountain Sampler...

Mollusk, bird, fish...no animal is safe from being immortalized in a fountain. The snail fountain at far left is a handsome variation on the spray fountain theme. The splash sculpture's cranes at center launch water skyward, only to get it right back. At right, a dolphin and riders wrestle through the years in a classic splash sculpture.

den. A general rule of thumb is that the basin should be a minimum of twice the diameter of the spray's height.

Unless you're building a bubbler fountain (see page 26), install the jet just above the water level. If your pool will include water plants or fish, plan the installation very carefully. Water lilies don't like heavy turbulence, though fish can benefit from the aeration a remote fountain provides. (For details, see Chapters 4 and 5.)

Hardware and accessories. Your spray fountain requires a submersible or recirculating pump (see page 15) to recycle water, plastic tubing to connect pump and fountain head, and, ideally, a separate drain connection. A control valve allows you to fine-tune fountain output from a soothing trickle to a thundering roar.

You'll also need a 120-volt, GFCI-protected receptacle for the pump, a switch to activate the fountain, and a separate switch for optional fountain lighting. Submerged, movable light fixtures positioned directly below the spray create the most drama; low-voltage halogen downlights are effective for pinpointing special features. Timers and color blenders that are programmed to automatic sequences can also be purchased for submerged light fixtures.

The simplest and most economical method of installing a fountain is to purchase a complete unit at a retail outlet or directly from the manufacturer. No plumbing is required. You simply put the kit together, fill the bowl with water, add an algicide, and connect the fountain unit to an electric power source. Other fountain assemblies include a pump, strainer, valve, and fountain head (and, in some cases, lights), all mounted in a single, compact, submersible base; you pick the pool.

Splash Sculpture

The wide range of designs for splash sculpture fountains suggests a long history. For centuries, pumping water up through a sculpture to splash over a series of surfaces into a pool has been a favored form for fountains. The water inlet was traditionally a Grecian urn or other art object, held by a cherubic nymph or symbolic figure. Nearly every city in Europe has a public square that displays some variation of the splash sculpture fountain style.

Remember, though, that a formal fountain requires lots of room. If you want to place a splash sculpture fountain in a limited space, you can scale down the design. A metal sculpture gives a strong contemporary appearance. Avoid using a traditional stone sculpture in a modern pool; artistic balance is a tricky accomplishment.

You will find both traditional and modern sculptures in stone and metal on sale at garden sup-

...Plus Three

A handcarved Mexican lion head and a tranquil Japanese bamboo spout are at opposite ends of the style spectrum, but they're both examples of spill fountains. The architectural fountain at right shows the effects of elegant lighting on moving water. Landscape architect for the lion fountain: Jeff Stone Associates. Bamboo fountain: landscape ceramist, Cevan Forristt.

DO-IT-YOURSELF

FOUNTAINS

Pleasing fountains and pools can be surprisingly simple. We show three designs here, but your own ingenuity will suggest more.

Installation is easier than ever before, with the ready availability of compact, inexpensive submersible pumps and tough pool liners. Water and energy costs need not add up: a small pump that circulates 140 gallons of water per hour over a 3-foot drop uses less electricity than a 70-watt light bulb, costing about 1/2 cent an hour.

You can convert a wooden planter box, a metal basin, or a large pot into a small fountain. Coat the inside of a wooden container with asphalt emulsion or epoxy paint, or use a flexible liner. If you're using an unglazed pan or clay pot, coat the interior with asphalt emulsion, epoxy, or polyester resin; a dark-colored sealant enhances the water's reflective quality. Then drop in a submersible pump with riser pipe (in shallow water, a few rocks can conceal the pump) and add water.

For larger holding pools, many designers prefer precast rigid fiberglass or reinforced concrete. PVC sheeting is an excellent, if less permanent, water holder; flexible liners can also go beneath concrete for extra water-holding insurance.

Any piece of hardware with a smaller aperture than that of the riser pipe can work as a homemade fountain jet: automotive grease fittings, drip irrigation components, and brass lamp conduit and caps are just three possibilities.

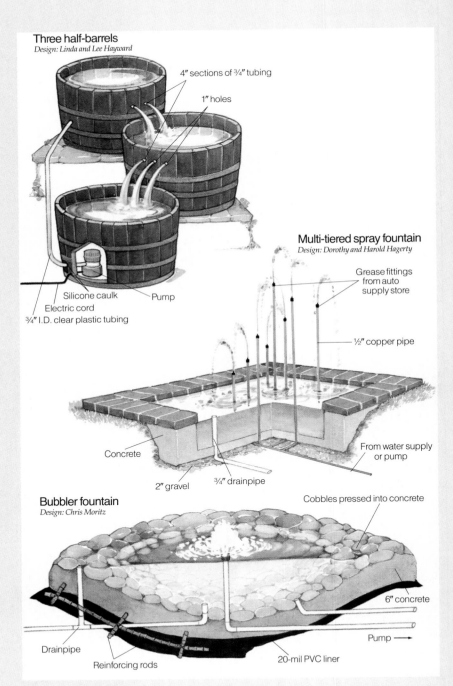

Three half-barrels
Design: Linda and Lee Hayward

4″ sections of ¾″ tubing

1″ holes

Silicone caulk

Electric cord

¾″ I.D. clear plastic tubing

Pump

Multi-tiered spray fountain
Design: Dorothy and Harold Hagerty

Grease fittings from auto supply store

½″ copper pipe

Concrete

From water supply or pump

2″ gravel

¾″ drainpipe

Bubbler fountain
Design: Chris Moritz

Cobbles pressed into concrete

6″ concrete

Pump →

Drainpipe

Reinforcing rods

20-mil PVC liner

ply centers, stone-cutting yards, and import stores. A few department stores also stock them. You can commission both stone and metal sculptures, usually at the artist's studio or at a gallery acting as the artist's agent.

Spill Fountains

Whether a spill fountain is an ordinary household pipe pouring water into a container, a series of spill pans attached to a wall, or a scaled-down version of the great Roman ornamental fountains, it is nearly always designed to capture a specific characteristic of falling water or create a particular tableau. For some people, the simple sound of falling water is adequate; others may want the fountain to carry a symbolic message in its design. Rarely is an attempt made to disguise the water source or to make the fountain appear to be a waterfall. No fountain head is used at the inlet for a fountain of falling water. Spill fountains, because of their customary design and sheltered location, do not usually present a wind problem.

The simplest spill fountain design, and the least expensive, is a single stream of water pouring into a pool or container. The pool can be large or small, depending on the space and budget allotted to it. The classic Japanese *tsukubai*—a hollowed-out bamboo rod trickling into a concave stone basin—is the model of simplicity. To save water, add a small sub-

The Dominant Theme

This garden provides a lavish example of a simple tenet: Use a strong central element to give order and focus to a design. Here, the star-shaped pool that frames the splash fountain dictates the shape of the lawn, flower beds, and paving. Landscape architect: Emmet L. Wemple & Associates.

Courtyard Retreat

Handmade raku wall tiles add the finishing touch to this brick wall fountain, which provides a musical refuge from neighborhood noise and views. The core structure is concrete block; spill shelves are supported by reinforcing rods. A submersible pump recycles the water; a 3-way valve regulates flow and allows drainage. Landscape designer: Michael Glassman/Environmental Creations.

Triple Header

Today's spas are increasingly serving as decorative pools and fountains in the off hours. In this case, three decorative water outlets fill the spa; PVC water supply pipe is directly behind each. Complementary tile colors link the fountain to the spa and surrounding paving. Landscape designer: Mark Gennaro/Landshape, Inc.

mersible pump in a concealed location; a tiny bit of overflow can feed a bog garden surrounding the pool.

Spill pans are available in two- and three-tiered plastic or metal sets that you can purchase at hardware or department stores and garden supply centers. If you have the necessary skills, you can make your own spill fountain from boiler ends or build a series of spill pans from your own materials and design.

More Ambitious: Wall Fountains

Wall fountains were practical public water sources long before the invention of indoor plumbing. The ancient form is seen frequently in Europe, most often along the Mediterranean coast. Water passing through a sculptured figure standing in a wall niche was usually employed to fill a servant's water jar.

Today, the fountain's principal role is ornamental. Water can pour directly into the pool from the pipe, overflow from a basin, or flow directly from a series of spill pans or trays. An increasingly popular variation adds a natural touch to today's swimming pools and spas. Water issues from lions' and gargoyles' mouths, wall niches, spill shelves, or gleaming high-tech nozzles into spa or pool—sometimes via a chain of streams or waterfall-joined holding pools. Indeed, it's hard to distinguish between this type of fountain and an architectural waterfall (see

Chapter 3). The distinction is unimportant; in either case, the effect is delightful.

Building a formal or classic wall fountain is relatively expensive. Not only is the formal fountain itself an extensive project but also the surrounding area must have complementary features if the fountain is to fit into its environment. Submersible pumps and water pipes can be combined to add a fountain to an existing wall. Construction is much simpler, though, if plumbing is incorporated into the wall during the building of the fountain. An electrical switch, perhaps located indoors, controls the pump-driven flow; a ball or 3-way valve allows alteration of the flow to match the mood. If you wish to replenish water evaporation automatically, hook up a float valve (page 16) to your water supply line.

The construction of the raised holding pool is critical: concrete or concrete block work well, covered with plaster or faced with brick, tile, or stone above the water level. Concrete fountains require several coats of waterproofing compound. To leakproof a pool, you can also sandwich a flexible liner (see page 12) between layers of brick or stone.

A wall fountain is typically lit from below each cascade or from the sides with submerged, low-voltage spotlights. Uplighting accentuates smooth sheets of water and projects dancing highlights onto the fountain, surrounding walls, and foliage. A dimmer switch (see page 87) helps set the mood.

Lion on the Loose

Brick, hand-painted Portuguese tile, and one very angry lion team up in this colorful wall fountain. The construction is concrete block coated with waterproofing compound, covered with tile on the inside and back walls and stucco elsewhere. A small exterior pump pulls water from the basin and drives it up to the concrete lion's head; a gate valve allows drainage to the street. Landscape architect: Jeff Stone Associates.

Old World Fountain

In a courtyard reminiscent of a Spanish Colonial plaza, this fanciful fountain commands attention. The water is a dark mirror now, but animates when water splashes down the tiers into the pool.

Heat and Light in the Night

This garden fountain plays a dual role as a heated spa: the underwater pool light can be dimmed for a relaxing soak. Low-voltage PAR-36 uplights accent the palm trees; other fixtures splash light on the birds of paradise. Landscape architects: Fry + Stone.

Not So Still Water

Though only 18 inches deep, this small rectangular reflecting pool gives an illusion of depth. Two fountains can be varied from gurgling jets to splashing columns of water to drown out unwanted noises and form a haven of peace and quiet. Landscape architect: René Fransen.

Classic Cherub

Cast iron maiden arches water from a lily pad, accenting this intimate natural pool. Subtle background plantings, Sonoma fieldstone, and flat border stones blending into slate patio paving all help this quiet corner merge with the surroundings. The figure is lit at night by a built-in pool light. Landscape designer: Kathryn Mathewson Associates.

Seen and Heard

In a spacious garden, water trickles from the fountain into a lead basin. The gentle splash does more than soothe. It also pinpoints the way for visitors seeking this tranquil spot. Garden designer: Charles Freeman.

Old is New Again

An old millstone found new purpose as a small fountain surrounded with river rocks. The water drains into buried plastic wading pools, while a 5-gallon bucket serves as the reservoir for the recirculating pump. Landscape architect: Patty Merson.

Oil and Water Do Mix

Water bubbling over the lip of an Italian oil urn is a prominent feature of this small brick courtyard. Perched on an underwater pedestal, the urn fountain gives the illusion of floating in its small pool. The hollow pedestal houses a submersible pump that keeps the water recirculating. Landscape architect: Terry Lewis.

WATERFALLS & STREAMS

Whether the sight is one of nature's monumental cascades at Yosemite National Park or a simple mountain stream falling over rustic terraces toward the sea, nearly everyone stops to watch a waterfall. The enchantment of flowing water is so pervasive that people often travel hundreds of miles to see it.

Inspired by such visits and wishing to bring a small piece of tranquility home, we can build naturalistic waterfalls and streams of varying sizes in our gardens, indoor-outdoor rooms, atriums—even in our living rooms.

"Natural" waterfalls and streams aren't the only option, either. Today's architectural waterfalls—much like wall fountains in design and effect—are becoming more popular in residential situations. Streams unify a waterfall with a nearby garden pool, tying the two together and lending a sense of continuity to the landscaping scheme. Today's swimming pool is also a scene for waterfalls; they soften the edges and create a new focus of interest, as well

Designed by Nature?

When planning a natural-looking cascade, take a cue from nature. This poolside waterfall has carefully placed native stones, varied channels and drop-offs, both shallow and deep holding pools, and a symphony of sounds. Landscape designer: Kathryn Mathewson Associates.

35

as a cooling curtain of water on scorching August afternoons. Streams can unite the spa with the pool, or a garden pool with the swimming pool—even serve as a water slide for adventurous swimmers. An existing stream is another option, even a dry streambed built into a native plant environment.

Remember that waterfalls and streams aren't necessarily a waste of water. What appears to be a never-ending, one-way flow is really a small amount of water circulated again and again by a small pump and connecting pipes.

Waterfall Basics

Architectural waterfalls are obviously man-made, tending to geometric shapes that reflect the urban environment. If you're thinking of building one, take a trip to nearby public squares, looking for designs to scale down, and study wall fountains you like. Or visit a landscape architect or designer and ask to see some formal waterfall designs.

Most do-it-yourself waterfall builders prefer to imitate nature, feeling that native waterfalls take the kind of tumble that looks proper in a home garden. Basically, the idea is to separate two or more pools at different heights so that they will appear to have been formed without man's help. (A torrential waterfall with its source mysteriously placed midway up a property line fence is not likely to appear credible.) The upper pool is usually the smallest of the two, just large enough to achieve a bustling flow of water. The inlet pipe enters below the surface or from a niche among border stones.

Wherever native stone plays a dominant part in a garden waterfall, ample space is a fundamental requirement. Boulders fill up space quickly. Some stones—mainly shales and other striable types—can be stacked in ways that look natural. Massive stones, such as the granites so common in western mountains, look far less at home when stacked.

By paying close attention to scale, it is possible to build a bustling small waterfall from a tiny volume of water. You can arrange fist-sized broken stones to appear much larger. Creative imagination can transform dwarf varieties of native plants into their standard-size counterparts.

Smooth as Glass
This striking waterfall was designed to be viewed from the dining room at the opposite end of the courtyard. At night, light glows from behind the glass-brick wall. Landscape architects: Richard Dawson and Lawrence Estes.

A Fall That Feeds Both Spa and Pool

This rock-bound fall—seemingly spilling right out of the house—tumbles down to a heated spa and swimming pool. A 30-mil plastic liner ensures a watertight base, with concrete on top; the cascades are further treated with a waterproofing compound. The framing boulders are secured in mortar, and others are simply stacked. Landscape designer: Michael Glassman/Environmental Creations.

Designing the Falls

How do you lay out a natural-looking waterfall? Carefully observe the way nature builds hers:

■ Stubborn flat rocks fortify the center of the stream, forming the edge of the falls.

■ Water rushes along lines of least resistance—between, around, and over the firmly entrenched stones—washing away dirt, gravel, and all other loose material.

■ Nature frames the falling water's path with stones cast aside or worn away by the rushing water and with appropriate plantings.

Water can take whatever course, direct or circuitous, you choose. You can opt for a more-or-less continuous waterfall—either a single "freefall" or interweaving channels—or for one that breaks into a series of holding pools or stairsteps. Step falls usu-

ally look best when the pump is shut down, as water remains in the small pools.

The placement of rocks is what really makes or breaks your fall's character. Irregular rocks in the center of the channel create a rapids effect. A big boulder at the base froths the water up even more. An overhang of several inches is best for a curtain effect; some designers add an acrylic lip to keep water from dribbling down the rock face (the acrylic is invisible unless viewed up close). Pinching in the sides of the fall compresses the water, forcing it into a thicker curtain. Gaps, grooves, and other irregularities in the lip create unique patterns.

There are no firm rules here. The key is experimentation—moving a rock here, a rock there—until the waterfall looks and sounds its best. What better excuse to kick off one's shoes, roll up one's pantlegs, and become a kid again for a few hours?

Tropical Paradise

Flat stones protrude from outlet slots to shape these clean, refreshing freefalls. The waterfalls are repeated all the way along the back wall of this extended swimming pool, creating the tropical look. The wall is concrete faced with Bouquet Canyon stone. Landscape designer: Mark Gennaro/Landshape, Inc.

Accent Falls

Your waterfall doesn't have to be an imitation of roaring Niagara Falls to be successful. This tiny version graces the hillside in perfect counterpoint to the elegant lamppost. A little concrete, some selected stones, and a small submersible pump are the basic ingredients. Design: Philip Neumann.

Waterfall Nuts & Bolts

The typical starting point for a waterfall project is either a natural incline or the mound of subsoil excavated for a garden pool. The entire face of the falls must be sealed to keep water from escaping and to prevent dirt from washing into the lower pool.

Your options are traditional concrete, premolded fiberglass watercourses and holding pools, and PVC, butyl-rubber, or other pool liners (see page 12). Hide the edges of the channels with natural stones and plantings. For construction details, see pages 78–79.

Water plants cling to remarkably precarious snatches of soil once established. The key is to form "pockets" of protected soil adjacent to or between waterfall channels, sealing the gaps between border stones with mortar. Try to place the mortar on the side away from view. Without mortaring, resign yourself to a certain amount of soil washing into the water with each rain.

You'll need a submersible or recirculating pump (see page 15) to move water from the bottom pool back up to the top, where gravity will send it on its way again.

Waterfalls for easy installation are sold by pump and fountain manufacturers. You can also buy simulated rock that appears almost realistic. Viewed from across a room, these waterfalls may appear very realistic, but such installations do not invite close scrutiny.

Would You Like to Build a Stream?

Streams are as varied as any of nature's creations. There are rushing streams amid granite mountains, lazy streams in upland meadows, and muddy streams through farm valleys, ranging in size from a tiny trickle to awesome rapids.

Before building a garden stream, a homeowner would be wise to settle on a single design drawn from his or her own experience. Streams designed only from imagination tend to encounter difficulties with nature's laws.

Water moving at a languid pace will wander through curves, always washing the outside bank of the curve. Streams, therefore, tend to grow wide at the midpoint of a curve. They become shallower along the inside because water moves more slowly and silt is deposited along the inside curve.

A fast stream rushes in a straight line, detouring only where rocks bar its path. The rushing water tends to keep such a streambed free of mud.

The choice between a slow- or fast-moving stream depends upon the topography of your land

Man-made Spring

This rock was cracked already and, with a little additional persuasion, was fitted with a water supply pipe and positioned as the perfect "natural source" at the head of this backyard stream. To produce a thicker flow, additional water issues from just below the rock. The handsome plantings reinforce the impression of a mountain spring. Landscape designer: Michael Glassman/Environmental Creations.

BRIDGES &

STEPPING STONES

The simplest way of crossing a small stream is over large stepping stones set in the water. This is not really a bridge but an extension of a path. Materials include poured concrete shapes, sliced log rounds, quarried flat stones, and natural boulders. For greater visual interest, lay stepping stones at an angle to the banks or stagger them. Close spacings are safer and induce visitors to linger awhile.

For wide streams and pools, you'll probably need a bridge instead. The design should plan for a bridge 2 to 3 feet wide to promote a sense of security for those who walk across it; a railing is recommended for long bridges or those over deep water.

Three basic bridge building materials are wood, cast concrete, and quarried stone. Wood is the commonest, most versatile, lightest, and least expensive. Three basic designs are shown below. Arched or flat, straight

designs are the norm, but a zig-zagging bridge (called *yatsuhashi* in Japan) encourages a leisurely stroll.

You can cast a slab bridge in reinforced concrete right on the spot. Pour the concrete into a pre-built form, and when it has set remove the sides of the form but leave the bottom—it'll never be seen.

Quarried stone is a frequently used bridge material in Japanese-style gardens, but it's tricky to work with for beginners. Some garden supply centers or specialty stone yards may have curved granite slabs that will give an arch to a stone bridge. Since these are imported from Japan, they are much more expensive than either a wooden plank bridge or one you cast yourself.

For spanning a distance of more than 4 or 5 feet, a bridge structure should be supported by a foundation, or by midspan piers or posts. A foun-

dation can be merely two blocks of concrete, one at each end, poured directly into holes dug in the ground. Set a couple of reinforcing rods vertically into each foundation before you pour, letting them extend far enough that you can secure the bridge structure to them. When the bridge is in place, conceal the foundation with soil, rocks, and plantings.

Piers can be made from pressure-treated poles or 6 by 6 posts sunk into the bottom of a pond or wide stream to give center support to a bridge. Simpler yet, support the center of a low bridge on a large rock.

Flat, unarched bridges should be 6 inches to a foot above the surface of the water; if the distance is much more than that, the feeling of intimacy may be lost. To further tie bridge and water together, arrange stones both on the banks and in the water beneath the end of a bridge.

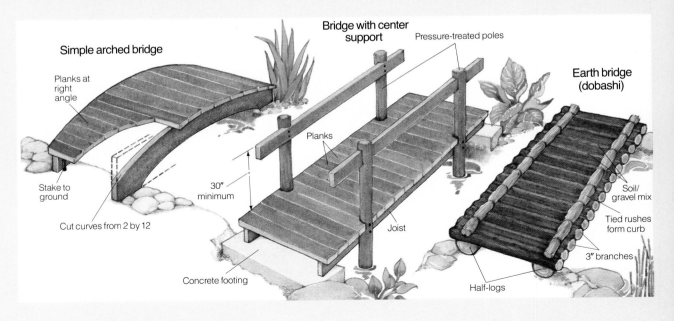

Simple arched bridge

Planks at right angle

Stake to ground

Cut curves from 2 by 12

Bridge with center support

Pressure-treated poles

Planks

30" minimum

Concrete footing

Joist

Earth bridge (dobashi)

Soil/gravel mix

Tied rushes form curb

3" branches

Half-logs

and may be entirely governed by the landscaping requirements of your site.

In a private garden, a "natural" stream ought to provide the kind of flow that your property can handle easily. Unless your stream burbles mysteriously out of the ground, the rushing water usually has a waterfall as its source. In this case, the water must be pumped from where the stream ends (perhaps where it flows into a pool) back to the waterfall, where it begins its journey again. An architectural stream typically issues from either a spray jet or a wall-mounted inlet.

Although a contemporary stream might be walled with angular brick, stone, stucco, or adobe, the typical natural stream is hand-packed concrete, overlaid with natural stones or pea gravel. Loose-aggregate concrete also creates a pebble-like effect. Streams may be fashioned from flexible liners (with or without concrete on top) or premolded fiberglass sections: camouflage edges with stones, turf, or border plantings.

Though we think of a natural stream as flowing noticeably downhill, most garden streams work best if laid out level or at a very gentle pitch. To negotiate a steeper slope, lower each level section as a unit, connecting sections with small cascades or falls. To create turbulence, decrease the depth of the channel slightly, narrow the banks, or add stones. Always build a deeper channel than you think you'll need: seasonal runoff can flood low banks. Alternately, plan an overflow course of perforated plastic drain pipe to a well-drained spot.

Working with an Existing Stream

If you are fortunate enough to have an existing stream running across your property, you've already saved construction time and expense. But if you want to change the stream in any way, be sure to contact the Department of Fish and Game in your state. Laws govern all stream changes, and the laws are very strictly enforced. In most areas, you will also need to contact your county and municipal planning officials.

In redesigning and changing the bed or course of a stream, take great care to keep each changed factor in scale with the rest of the stream bed. Oversights can be disastrous. Note where currents will work against soft banks and the extent of scouring action; in time the stream may chart a third course, to your great distress. Damming a stream to start a waterfall may bring the water level to a point at which it can exert force against a weak spot if left unguarded.

Touches of the Orient

What was once a plain grass yard is now a Japanese garden, complete with a small pond bordered with rock. A simple wood-plank bridge spans the water and joins a low boardwalk that leads to a pavilion. Landscape architect: J. Dabney Peebles.

Wettest Way Down

Whooooaaa! This stream doubles as a water slide; his slippery route to the pool curves through ferns and horsetails and between boulders. The slide is steel covered with plaster and troweled to a glass-slick surface. Landscape architect: Ned Bosworth.

Spa-to-Pool Creek

In this scene, a short, splashing accent stream links the spa and the nearby pool. Matching stonework on the spa steps, streambed, and pool lip ties the units together; border plantings emphasize the natural look. Landscape contractor: Grimes Natural Landscape, Inc.

Spaside Niche

A poolside spa provides a sheltered niche for this architectural waterfall. Handsome stonework, held together with mortar, sets the scene. The fall, designed like a wall fountain, has multiple outlets—above, below, right, and left—and a pair of rock-hewn spill shelves to create a variety of special effects. Landscape designer: Rogers Gardens.

Inspired by a Swimming Hole

Today's swimming pool increasingly does double duty as a natural water feature. Thanks to its recirculating rock waterfall and lush planting, this swimming pool resembles a spring-fed pond. The hollow beneath the spillway stone amplifies the sound of falling water. Landscape architect: Rosa Finley, Kings Creek Landscaping.

Cascading Tropical Stream

From its beginnings on the sheltered hillside, this stream makes its way through two upper pools, bends around a corner, and plunges between tight banks to a third holding pool. The basic structure is gunite shot over welded wire mesh; the large rocks were positioned before the pour, then smaller rocks and gravel were patted into the wet concrete to create the "riffle" effects. Landscape architect: Todd Fry.

Granite Falls

Water wells up into this koi pond over a granite-lipped waterfall; notches in the sloped lip funnel the water into graceful sheets. Pond consultant: Paul Cowley/ Potomac Waterworks.

A Cooler for Cats

A freeform concrete stream is one of the simplest types to make; a flexible liner makes it watertight. Border plantings, rocks, and a small footbridge soften the concrete edges.

High-country Cascade

Sonoma fieldstone boulders, dams and niches, colorful flowers, and ground covers team up to make this poolside waterfall a natural delight. The inspiration was a cascade in Yosemite's high country. When a waterfall is designed, only experimentation will show which configuration of rocks and channels creates just the right water volume, sights, and sounds. Landscape designer: Kathryn Mathewson Associates.

WATER GARDENS

Gardening possibilities multiply instantly when you add a pool to the landscape. In contrast to their long-accustomed, frequent problem of providing adequate drainage for plants, pool owners face an entirely different form of gardening in which plants often thrive in water alone.

From water lilies to floating, oxygenating, marginal, and bog plants, your choice of water plants is wide and varied. On pages 48–51, we take a look at the general characteristics and uses of each category, then offer planting suggestions for various garden situations—deep water, marginal shallows, and surrounding bog gardens. For illustrations and descriptions of specific water plants, see pages 52–55.

Which plants are sure-fire winners in your microclimate? It's a good idea to ask the local nursery personnel or another pool owner in the neighborhood; or call a mail-order supplier that sells a selection of plants nationwide (mail-order listings are on page 95).

Drifting Colors

The surface of your garden pool affords a shimmering "canvas" for Impressionist gardening arts. Shown here are tropical water lilies 'Blue Beauty', 'Dauben', 'Golden West', and 'Margaret Mary'. Lilypons Water Gardens, Lilypons, Maryland.

Floating Plants

Floating water plants break down into two basic types: (1) Those with their roots in the soil and their leaves floating on the surface—water lilies, for example; and (2) Floating plants such as water hyacinth or water lettuce, whose roots simply dangle in the water.

Rooted plants, sometimes called "semi-floaters," not only are beautiful, but help keep the pool healthy by providing shade and crowding out competing algae. They don't like heavy turbulence, so plant them away from the splash of a waterfall or fountain.

True floaters grow and multiply with great speed, gobbling up open water. Water hyacinth grew so rapidly when introduced in Florida streams that the plants became a menace to navigation. On the other hand, water hyacinth is considered an excellent purifier, soaking up ammonia and other potential toxins. Keep floaters away from koi, for the fish shred the roots, which in turn clog the pump.

Oxygenating Plants

These hard workers grow submerged beneath the pool's surface. Although they do not bloom and are rarely seen, they are, nevertheless, indispensable to a balanced water garden. Oxygenators such as Anacharis are frequently employed in indoor fish aquariums; they take up carbon dioxide and release oxygen to other plants and fish. In fact, you can often see tiny oxygen bubbles clinging to the surfaces of these plants. Oxygenators also provide a spawning area for fish and a handy hiding place for small-fry until they get big enough to fend for themselves.

Maintaining Margins

Colorful marginal plants help define your garden pool environment. Water irises, shown at left, are a natural with natural pools; so is the Japanese maple in the background. Above, umbrella palms soften the formal shapes. By planting in containers, you can move the plants as your moods—and the seasons—dictate. Filoli Gardens, Woodside, California.

Marginal Plants

Some water plants do best around the pool's margins, with their heads waving in the breeze and their feet in shallow water. Two classic examples are the Japanese iris and the umbrella plant. Most marginal plants prefer water 2 to 6 inches deep. These are the plants that benefit from a separate, adjoining shallow area in your pool or a series of shelves around the edges. Marginal plants help provide a smooth transition from pool to border in both formal and natural garden pools.

Bog Plants

Some plants grow best around the pool's borders where water splashes, keeping the ground wet. These bog plants camouflage the concrete or fiberglass edges of a pool, waterfall, or stream, lending a natural appearance. They can also extend the "water" environment, making the pool look larger or tying it to the surroundings. These plants often come from families seen in the garden at large—for example, primrose, lobelia, and calla lilies.

Two worthy mentions, not really bog plants but often associated with natural pool settings, are bamboo (many varieties are available) and Japanese maple (*Acer palmatum*).

Planting Techniques

Here's the number one rule for planning your water garden: Plant with restraint. Consider the mature growth of the plants when figuring layout and spacing; be sure to plant large marginal and bog plants well back from the edges of the pool. A garden sketch is a big help.

The Tall & Short of It

Above, horsetails form a tall, linear backdrop to this tranquil scene off the master bedroom. The adjacent floating plants are water four-leaf clover and parrot's feather. Design: Bill and Caroline Furnas. At right, thick layer of water lilies 'Marliac Carnea' and 'William Falconer' carpets the foreground; towering above is the pink lotus 'Roseum Plenum'.

ALL COLORS IN THE RAINBOW—

THE WATER LILIES

Water lilies (*Nymphaea*) will almost certainly be more widely planted when more gardeners begin to appreciate their beauty, their dependability, and the ease with which they can be grown. Lilies come in both hardy and tropical varieties. Hardy water lilies bloom during daylight, opening about 10 a.m. and closing after sunset, but tropicals include both day and night-blooming versions.

Hardy types are the easiest for a beginner to grow and can overwinter in the pool. Tropicals—larger, more prolific bloomers, available in a greater selection of varieties and colors—must be considered annuals in all but the balmiest climates. With some effort, however, they can be rescued and stored carefully in a greenhouse or other cozy spot.

Plant hardy water lilies from early spring through October in mild-winter areas. Although the tropicals can be grown in all areas, they shouldn't be planted until average daytime temperatures rise above 65 degrees—normally after the first of May. If set out at the recommended times, water lilies begin to flower in 1 to 4 weeks. Hardy lilies flower early in April and tropicals produce their first blooms in May.

The best tropicals will bear up to three times as many flowers as the hardy lilies. Most flowers live 4 days, once open; they last just as long if they're cut. (To keep cut flowers open, apply melted paraffin or candle wax with an eyedropper around the base of the stamens, petals, and sepals.)

You can grow all kinds of water lilies in a pool with vertical sides and a uniform depth of 18 to 24 inches. If the sides of the pool have a gradual slope, the water there is subject to extreme temperature variations that are unhealthy for your water plants. And, algae grows faster in the shallows.

Both hardy and tropical water lilies require full sun—4 to 6 hours each day is minimum—to open the flowers. If you have to build your pool in partial shade, choose a location that gets the morning sun.

Use a heavy garden soil for planting water lilies but don't add manure, peat moss, or ground bark to the soil. Manure encourages the growth of algae and fouls the water, and peat moss and bark will float to the surface and cloud the water.

Mix about a pound of slow-acting, granular-type fertilizer with the soil for each lily that you're planting. A complete fertilizer with a nitrogen content between 3 and 5 percent is considered almost ideal. Most water lily growers sell a specially formulated fertilizer.

Plant only one water lily in each container so that the leaf pattern of each plant will be displayed to best advantage. Cover the soil with about an inch or more of pebbles to prevent clouding the water. The top of each container should be 8 to 12 inches below the surface of the water.

Tropical lily 'Yellow Dazzler'

Tropical lily 'Attraction'

Bog/border plantings. Normally, these are used for borders or in a formal bog garden; however, many are quite at home in shallow water as well.

■ *Arrowhead (Sagittaria latifolia)*. From dark green, arrow-shaped leaves emerge spikelike clusters of 1-1/2-inch white flowers. Grows to 4 feet tall, in bog conditions or submerged up to 6 inches deep. Thin occasionally.

■ *Baby's tears (Soleirolia soleirolii)*. Creeping, moss-like, perennial herb with tiny white flowers makes cool, luxuriant ground cover near pools. Use it where it won't be stepped on, in shade.

■ *Bog arum (Calla palustris)*. Waterside plant, good for hiding edges of small pool. Grows 10–12 inches high, spreads laterally. Leaves 6 inches long, arrow shaped; flowers green outside, white inside. Red berries succeed flowers.

■ *Bog lily (Crinum americanum)*. White, droopy, 4–5-inch flowers grow on stalks up to 2 feet tall; very fragrant. Leaves are long and slender. Plant in up to 6 inches of water.

■ *Candelabra primrose (Primula japonica)*. Hardy Candelabra has stout stems to 2-1/2 feet with up to 5 whorls of purple flowers with yellow eyes. Blooms May to July. Likes semi-shade, lots of water.

■ *Cardinal flower (Lobelia cardinalis)*. Erect, single-stemmed, 2–4-foot-high plant with saw-edged leaves set directly on the stems. Spikes of flame red, inch-long flowers. Summer bloom. Sun or part shade. Border planting in moist soil or in water up to 2 inches.

■ *Elephant's ear/Taro (Colocasia esculenta)*. Tropical elephant's ear has mammoth, heart-shaped, gray-green leaves; stalks fast-growing to 6 feet. Thrives in warm filtered shade with protection from wind; plant in moist soil or in up to 12 inches of water. Hawaiian staple food poi is made from the starchy roots. Violet-stemmed taro is a smaller variety.

■ *Marsh marigold (Caltha palustris)*. Bog plant up to 2 feet tall, well adapted to edges of pools, streams. Sun or shade. Green leaves 2–7 inches across; vivid yellow flowers are 2 inches across, in clusters. Lush, glossy foliage gives an almost tropical effect.

■ *Plantain lily (Hosta plantaginea)*. Has scented white flowers, 4–5 inches long, on 2-foot stems. Leaves bright green, to 10 inches long. Many similar types of Hosta. A good poolside planting.

■ *Sweet flag (Acorus calamus)*. Fans of grasslike leaves resemble miniature iris; 1/4-inch-wide leaves, 1-1/2 feet tall. Variation *variegatus* has alternating green and cream-colored stripes. Plant at pool edge or in shallow water.

■ *Weeping sedge (Carex pendula)*. Subtle, grasslike clumps soften a pool's edge; long, narrow, evergreen leaves, drooping spikes. One of many species of sedges appropriate for water gardens.

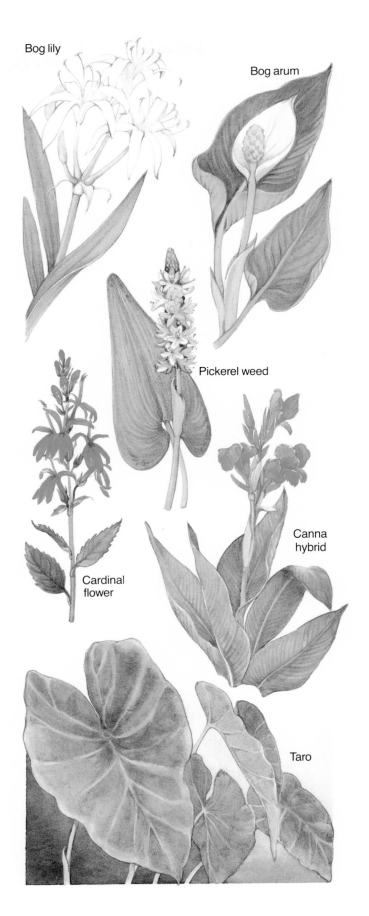

Bog lily

Bog arum

Pickerel weed

Cardinal flower

Canna hybrid

Taro

G O L D F I S H
& K O I

What's a garden pool without a lazily swimming school of goldfish or koi, softly gleaming in the sun? With some basic care, fish can be quite comfortable in your garden. On the following pages, we'll present the basics of fish-raising; for help in selecting your goldfish or koi, see the drawings and descriptions on pages 62–63.

For many of us, goldfish invoke memories of small, sloshing fishbowls lugged home as prizes from county fairs; contrary to our best intentions, the fish often died very soon. Why? As you'll learn, goldfish need plenty of oxygen and well-balanced water; the classic fishbowl is one of the worst possible designs in both of these regards.

Japanese koi become family pets, coming when called, following owners around the pool, taking food from outstretched fingers, even allowing themselves to be petted. These creatures outlive almost any other kind of pet, and they may even outlive their owners.

All Dressed Up

As shown at left, koi carp present a kaleidoscope of colors and patterns. These are just youngsters; in coming years they could grow as long as 2-1/2 feet. Golden State Fisheries, Sacramento, California.

Pond Fish: An Introduction

Goldfish, koi, and numerous other pond fish are available for stocking your garden pool. Here's a rundown of each basic type.

Goldfish. These perennial pets come to mind automatically at the mention of fish ponds in a garden. Goldfish have been bred for centuries as hobby fish; consequently there are countless types, and they are a good choice for a small pool. They're normally quite docile and can be mixed among themselves and with other types of fish; don't expect them to be as outgoing and friendly as koi.

Common varieties for outdoor ponds include Common, Comet, Calico, Fantail, Moor, Shubunkin, and Veiltail. More exotic species include the Lionhead, the Oranda, and the exceedingly strange Celestial. For details on these types, see page 62.

The Golden Orfe and Green Tench are two scavenger fish for hobbyists; both are European imports. Scavengers can help reduce algae and pond wastes. The Green Tench hides out at the pool bottom; its more gregarious cousin, the Golden Orfe, spends much more time at the surface.

Young goldfish haven't yet developed their distinctive colorings and are much less expensive than their larger kin. Just make sure they're 2 to 3 inches long when you purchase them; smaller fish have a great fatality rate. In an outdoor pond, some varieties of goldfish may reach lengths up to 10 or 12 inches. Under friendly conditions, you can expect your goldfish to live about 3 to 4 years; 6 to 12 years is considered a very long life.

Koi. Japanese koi, or *nishikigoi,* aren't goldfish; they're colorful carp. How can you tell the two apart? Koi have two pairs of whiskers, called *barbels,* on their upper mouths; goldfish do not. Breeders name them for their colors; they're bred to be viewed from the top. There are single-color, two-color, three-color, and multi-color varieties. A German variety of armored koi has been interbred with Japanese types to produce *Doitsu,* which are either armored or "scaleless" varieties. For details on koi types and nomenclature, see page 63.

A Wild Pond—Right Off the Deck

Pickerel weed, water lilies, and swirling fish make a wild statement here. The owners can observe the proceedings from the very civilized deck.

The Nitrogen Cycle

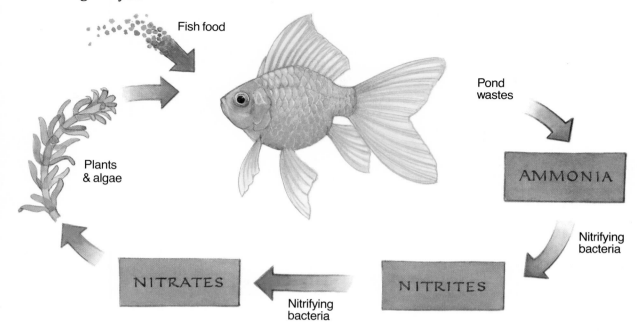

Fish food

Plants & algae

Pond wastes

AMMONIA

Nitrifying bacteria

NITRATES

NITRITES

Nitrifying bacteria

Nitrifying bacteria

Koi grow much bigger than goldfish: lengths of 27 inches or even 3 feet are not out of the question. With thoughtful care, a koi's potential life span is up to 60 years; one Japanese koi reputedly lived for over 200 years.

Prize koi specimens command great prices. It's best for the beginner to start with inexpensive fish (about 10 dollars), then move up as you become more involved. A koi club or helpful dealer can help you start off on the right track.

Other pond fish. Additional fish choices break down into small types, such as minnows, guppies, and tropical fish; and larger game fish, normally stocked in lakes and streams.

Generally, very small fish are unsuitable for ponds. They certainly can't compete if mixed with koi or goldfish (they may be gobbled up by their bigger poolmates). Tropical fish simply can't take the typical temperature fluctuations. A few minnows or other small-fry, however, help keep a tub garden free of insects and algae.

Game fish such as catfish, bluegills, and crappies are available for large ponds, but you'd best check with the Department of Fish and Game—they're banned in some areas. Many game fish have very specific temperature and aeration requirements, making them unsuitable for backyard pond life. These species may attack other fish.

Balancing the Water

Fish need oxygen just like land-based creatures; they absorb it from water passing through their

gills. To ensure that they'll get enough air, the pond's surface area must be as great as possible; in addition, some aeration—in the form of a fountain or waterfall—is beneficial. A small air pump, designed for the purpose, can provide extra aeration in still ponds and keep beneficial bacteria alive if the main pump fails.

A bigger problem is ammonia in the water. Fish respiration and other wastes produce ammonia; additional sources are uneaten food and plant debris on the pool bottom. The key to understanding ammonia build-up—and its eradication—lies in the nitrogen cycle (see drawing above). In the presence of beneficial bacteria, ammonia is reduced to nitrites, which in turn break down into nitrates, which can be taken up by plants and fish. Biological filtration is one way to deal with ammonia; mechanical filtration with zeolite as the medium is also touted by some experts. Natural filtration from plants such as the water hyacinth can be very effective, but you'll need to change the plants every 30 to 60 days. To monitor the ammonia situation in your pool, buy an ammonia test kit. Ponds with detectable levels should be treated with partial water changes or with a product intended for this purpose.

Other water problems include chlorine and chloramines. Chlorine, which is added to most municipal water supplies, is bad for fish in large amounts; fortunately, it will dissipate in a few days if left standing. Chloramines (combinations of chlorine and ammonia) are very toxic; and as more and more water suppliers are adding these to tap water, you'll have to take chemical steps to break them down.

POND

PROTECTION

Once you've established your fish pond, you may find that your friends and neighbors aren't the only ones interested in the progress of your goldfish or koi. Domestic explorers like the family cat or neighborhood basset hound, or wilder visitors such as herons, raccoons, and even skunks, may drop by looking for a little fun or the proverbial free lunch. Any one of these can devastate a prized fish collection in a very short time.

How do you ward them off? Sufficient pond depth, 24 inches or deeper, is a big help. Most mammals can't latch onto your fish while swimming; they must find solid footing in the pool. Overhanging pool borders and dense marginal plants provide fish with a temporary hiding place; so do hollowed-out "islands" made from wood or stones and covered with water plants. A pond running underneath a deck, with a solid wall above water and fish-sized openings below, is another option. Netting is the surest solution for marauding herons, though this is usually the least satisfactory option esthetically.

An electric fence wire, anchored to insulated posts and strung completely around the pond area, is very effective if carefully installed; these low-voltage units are available from hardware stores and some garden pool catalogs. At the high-tech end of the spectrum, you can install a motion-sensitive alarm, but be prepared for false alarms.

The pH (acidity) levels are also important. Whenever you're filling up a new pool, let it sit for a couple of weeks before introducing the fish. Concrete pools must be cured; check the pH of the water with a pH testing kit. The best pH for a fish pond is between 6.8 and 7.6.

Proprietary products for getting your pool water in shape are available from pet stores and mail-order sources. Don't make frequent water changes in your fish pond—not only is it a waste of water, but you'll need to treat it for chlorine, chloramines, and pH constantly. Instead, top up with a little bit of fresh water as necessary.

For more details on balancing and maintaining your pond water, see "Maintaining Your Pool" on pages 90–95.

Designing the Fish Pond

A fish pond can be any shape. However, adequate depth for koi is crucial. It must be no shallower than 18 inches and ideally between 24 and 36 inches, or deeper. The pond must also be large enough so the fish have room to swim. Figure on 1000 gallons as the minimum for a koi pond; that translates to a pool roughly 10 feet long by 8 feet wide by 20 inches deep. (To calculate pool volumes, see the feature box on page 91.) Goldfish can survive in smaller spaces.

If your pool is for fish only, place it where it gets some shade. This is good for the fish (colors tend to be richer and deeper in shade) and will keep down algae formation.

Surface exchange of oxygen and other gases is important, so don't cover more than 50 percent of the surface with floating plants. Protect new plants in cages until well established, and add rocks atop soil in plant containers to keep fish from rooting. A separate marginal area for plants, protected by a rock dam—or even better, a divided pool—is best for pool owners devoted to both plants and fish.

Goldfish live comfortably in water ranging from 50 to 80 degrees but prefer the narrower range from 60 to 70 degrees. Koi don't mind a change in water temperature if it's gradual. There's less temperature fluctuation in deeper pools.

If you really want to enjoy your colorful fish, pool water should be as clear as possible. Pool filters will keep the water clear; the best fish ponds often have a combination of biological and mechanical filter—typically, a pressurized-sand filter. The constantly operating biological filter is the workhorse; the pressure-sand unit simply serves as a "polishing" filter. But we've seen pools with no filters that are crystal clear. Water is simply well balanced or circulated so that fouled water is forced up a pipe from the bottom. For plumbing details, see Chapter 6, "Building Your Pool."

Introducing Fish to the Pond

One rule of thumb for stocking goldfish or koi in your pond is roughly 1 to 2 inches of fish for every square foot of surface area. But a better formula is *patience*. Simply start off with a few fish and work your way up. If your fish are healthy, your filtering system is in top shape, and the water is well aerated, you can add new fish to your collection.

Most fish arrive in a plastic bag containing a small amount of water and a blast of pure oxygen. When transferring your fish to the pool, float the bag on the surface for at least 15 minutes, which lets the water temperature in the bag gradually adjust to that in the pool. (If the day is warm and sunny, shade the bag with a towel.) Next, open the bag and let the pool water enter, then ease the fish into the pool. They'll probably take off and hide; gradually, over a period of days, they should begin to feed.

If you're introducing new fish into an established pond, many experts recommend that you place them in a quarantine pool, or separate tank, for up to 3 weeks. This will enable you to screen the fish for unusual actions or diseases; if a fish is sick, it can be treated before the entire pond is infected.

Feeding

The number one rule to remember is this: Don't overfeed your fish. They can only eat a small amount at a time and the rest sinks to the bottom where it quickly fouls the water. Feed them the amount they can eat in five minutes; no more. If they're hungry, fish nibble at insects in the pool and on algae or fast-growing oxygenating plants.

Goldfish and koi are omnivorous: they'll eat almost anything. Packaged fish foods, containing a balance of protein, carbohydrates, and vitamins, are recommended; some koi foods include spirulina (a high-protein algae) or carotene as "color enhancers." Floating foods won't foul the water; uneaten pellets can easily be netted and removed from the pond. Diversity is healthy for fish. Basic rations can be supplemented with table scraps and live foods; pet stores carry worms, daphnia, brine shrimp, and ant eggs for special treats.

As winter approaches and the water temperature dips, fish appetites decrease. At about 45 degrees, koi begin to effectively hibernate, living off body fat until spring and warmer water rouse them from dormancy.

Dinner on the Veranda

Koi are the prized tenants of this front-yard fish pond, which is complete with a state-of-the-art filter system. At top, koi dine from their built-in feeding shelf. A rock dam, shown at right, keeps the fish from munching the water plants for dessert. Landscape designer: Dennis Tromburg/Zierden Landscaping.

Veiltail

Chinese
Black
Moor

Japanese
Fantail

Shubunkin

Comet

Lionhead

A Guide to Goldfish

Goldfish have clearly discernible types, varied in color, fin size and shape, body shape, and even eyes. They also come with an assortment of scale patterns: matt (without luster), nacreous (mottled), and metallic. Here's a description for each type you're likely to run across.

■ *Common.* The "original model" from which the fancy varieties were developed. Has short fins all around, is an excellent swimmer, and is very hardy. Though color is normally orange gold, sometimes has other markings: silvery types are called *Pearl*; yellow types are called *Canaries*. Black patches often change to red with age.

■ *Comet.* Similar to the Common, but the body is a "stretch" version, with larger fins all around and a much longer and more deeply forked tail. The fastest of the fancy goldfish varieties, the Comet does very well in outdoor pools.

■ *Shubunkin.* Resembles the Common goldfish in shape, but *London* or *Calico* type has matt scales, beautiful colors—pale-blue background flecked with red, blue, black. The *Bristol* Shubunkin has larger fins.

■ *Fantail.* Double tail and fins, heavy egg-shaped body. Swims with deliberate, leisurely pace. Two popular types are the *Calico* (scaleless, colors like the Shubunkin) and *Japanese* (goldfish coloring). Fins and tail much longer than Common, drape down; body is rounded. Fins and tail should not be ragged.

■ *Veiltail.* Fins and tail are even longer than Fantail's, drape down; body is rounded. Fins and tail should not be ragged. Most popular type is *Calico*. The *Telescope* Veiltail has protruding eyes, poor eyesight.

■ *Chinese Black Moor.* Velvety black, body small and chunky, profile shape similar to Fantail, telescoping eyes. The only truly black goldfish.

■ *Lionhead.* Sought-after fish with short, chunky body; typically has gold or red-and-white coloring, but some are dark. Claim to fame is "raspberry-like" head growth, which increases with age. Has no dorsal fin, which makes it a poor swimmer.

■ *Oranda.* Similar to Lionhead but has a dorsal fin, which makes it a better swimmer. Not as much head growth. Good specimens shaped more like a Veiltail.

■ *Celestial.* A truly bizarre-looking fish; pupils are on top of the eyeballs, looking *heavenward*, hence the name. The Celestial and its close cousin, the *Bubble-eye*, are risky choices for a fish pond, as they can't see well enough to swim or feed competitively.

■ *Golden Orfe.* A European introduction new to the U. S.; technically a scavenger but comes to the surface to feed. Elongated body, up to 12 inches long, gold coloring. Fast swimmer, quite gregarious.

Japanese Koi Varieties

Japanese koi carp are differentiated by color, pattern, and scale type. Basically, fish can be divided into single-color, two-color, three-color, and multi-color categories. Scales may be *muji* (matt) or *ohgon* (metallic); in addition, *Doitsu,* German types, can be either heavily scaled or "armored," or scaleless ("leather skin"). Pattern distinctions include *Matsuba* (pinecone pattern), *Bekko* (tortoise shell), and even eye color.

If there is a koi club in your area, you might join it. More knowledgeable members will help you in your purchases and recommend the best dealers. Koi clubs also sponsor shows where you can learn which fish are considered the best in their class.

Some of the more popular koi varieties, listed in order from single to multi-colored, are as follows:

- *Shiromuji.* One-color, white with flat scales.
- *Kigoi.* One-color, yellow with flat scales.
- *Akamuji.* One-color, flat red.
- *Ohgon.* Metallic gold or orange gold in color; one of the most popular koi types in North America.
- *Shiro Ohgon.* Platinum metallic, popular variety. *Gin Matsuba* is metallic silver with pinecone pattern as well.
- *Kohaku.* Red on a white background. This group, with many sub-categories, is extremely popular; most champion koi are Kohaku type. The exact patterns determine type—Inazuma Kohaku, for example, has "lightning" pattern; Nidan Kohaku has two red patches.
- *Bekko.* Two-color koi with a tortoise shell pattern. *Shiro Bekko* is black-on-white, *Ki Bekko* black-on-yellow; *Aka Bekko* black-on-red.
- *Utsuri.* Two-color koi types: *Shiro Utsuri* is black-and-white, *Ki Utsuri* black-and-yellow, and *Hi Utsuri* black-and-red.
- *Asagi.* Light blue on top (dorsal) part of body, some red on head and below. May have pinecone pattern, have normal scales, or be armored (Doitsu) type.
- *Shusui.* Similar to the Asagi in color, but always has Doitsu scales. Head and back are light blue, with red below. Prominent dark blue scales run down the middle of the back.
- *Taisho Sanke.* Popular three-color koi variety. Taisho Sanke has red and black markings on a white background. A variation, the *Tancho Sanke,* is predominantly white with one red spot—or "rising sun"—on the head only, and small black patches behind.
- *Showa Sanke.* Similar to Taisho Sanke, but predominantly black with red-and-white markings.
- *Goshiki.* There are many multi-colored koi, but the goshiki is the most prized. It has five discernible colors: red, white, black, blue, and brown.

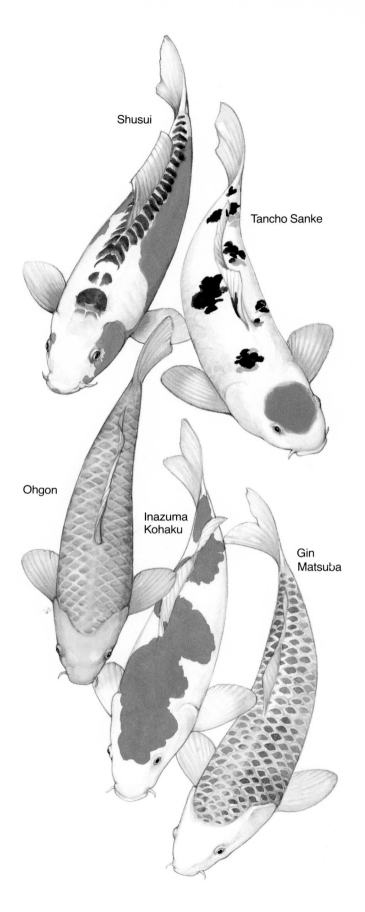

Shusui

Tancho Sanke

Ohgon

Inazuma Kohaku

Gin Matsuba

BUILDING

YOUR POOL

In the first five chapters, we focused on general pool planning guidelines, materials, and case studies in color photos and captions. Now it's time to show you how to build your garden pool, fountain, or waterfall.

This chapter covers construction methods for four basic pool types: flexible pool liners; rigid fiberglass shells; poured concrete pools; and concrete block pools veneered with stone, brick, or ceramic tile. Later sections tackle the ins and outs of pool plumbing, plus electrical wiring and outdoor lighting. In the final section, we present guidelines for maintaining your pool through the seasons.

Always check local ordinances and building codes before embarking on a pool-building project: restrictions may include pool site and surroundings, concrete construction and reinforcing, plumbing materials and installation, and electrical wiring. If you're in any doubt about design or your own abilities, a landscape architect, designer, or contractor can provide the help you need.

ol in Progress

flexible liner follows the contours of any e you dig; here, the pool is being filled wly to stretch the liner into shape. Ma- ry or another edging treatment will hide d protect liner edges. For more details, see ges 66–68.

INSTALLING A FLEXIBLE LINER

What's new in constructing garden pools? For do-it-yourselfers, it's flexible plastic or butyl-rubber pool liners. By applying a bit of elbow grease, even a beginner can fashion an average-size lined pool in a weekend's time. (Plantings and borders will take somewhat longer.) Here's a step-by-step account of the process.

Planning the size and shape. Before ordering the liner, create a design and figure the finished length, width, and depth of your pool. Remember, simple shapes usually look the best. Once you've come up with a design you like, add twice the pool's depth to its width, then tack on an extra two feet; repeat this procedure to find the correct length. In other words:

Liner size = *2d + w + 2 ft.* by *2d + l + 2 ft.*

For example, a pool roughly 5 feet wide by 8 feet long by 2 feet deep would require a liner 11 feet by 14 feet or the next larger size available.

What if you want an unusual shape? This is no problem, because the rectangular liner can handle a number of curves and undulations. Also, you can weld two pieces of liner together—or have the manufacturer or supplier do it for you.

Marking the layout. Take a garden hose or a length of rope and trace the intended outline of your pool, allowing about 2 inches extra all around for a layer of sand. Stand back and take a look from all sides—and from above if you have a second-story or veranda view. Once you have the perfect outline, pound in stakes to mark the corners or hold the hose in place while you're digging.

Making the excavation. Now it's calorie-burning time. Dig around the outline first, using a good sharp spade. If you're cutting into a lawn, peel back and remove the sod and keep it in a shady spot (you may need it for patching around the border).

Flexible Liner, Step-by-Step

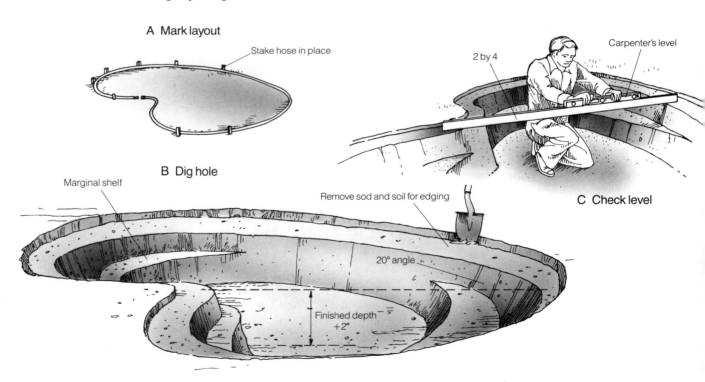

A Mark layout

Stake hose in place

B Dig hole

Marginal shelf

2 by 4

Carpenter's level

C Check level

Remove sod and soil for edging

20° angle

Finished depth + 2"

To lay a solid foundation for your liner, first mark its outline with a hose or a length of rope (A). Excavate the hole, adding 2 inches all around for a layer of sand (B). Check the level carefully with a carpenter's level, using a straight board to bridge the rim (C).

To prepare a brick or flagstone edging (see page 76), remove the sod from that area, too, and dig down just the thickness of the edging material. You may also wish to lay out a bog garden at this time.

The ideal angle for pool sides is about 20 degrees, which will prevent them from caving in and will help keep the liner snug. Do you want to add marginal shelves? The normal dimensions for plant shelves are about 10 inches deep and 10 inches wide, but varied shelves—for boulders and other landscaping—lend the pool a more naturalistic look. You won't need to figure extra liner for shelves.

When you begin to dig, add an extra 2 inches to the depth for a bed of sand. Keep measuring the depth as you go, or mark it on a stake and use that to chart your progress.

A large pool requires a lot of digging, especially if it's deep and the soil is hard-packed or rocky. A small backhoe, sometimes available with a driver, can make life easier.

Leveling the top. Water seeks its own level, so any discrepancy in the height of your pool's rim will be highly visible. Not only is it unattractive to see exposed liner, it's asking for trouble from abrasion and ultraviolet (UV) light degradation.

The simplest way to check the level is with a long, straight 2 by 4 and a carpenter's level. For a small pool, simply bridge the hole with the board; for a longer span, drive a center stake and use it as a pivot to measure out to all sides.

What if the pool is out of level? You'll need to rework the high side or build up the low side slightly. Shaving the high side is best, as loose, unsettled fill can't stand up to much water pressure.

This is the time to rough-in any plumbing or wiring, such as a drain line, a GFCI, or a lighting circuit. For details, see pages 80–89.

Adding sand. To protect the liner, remove all rough edges—roots, rocks, and debris—from the excava-

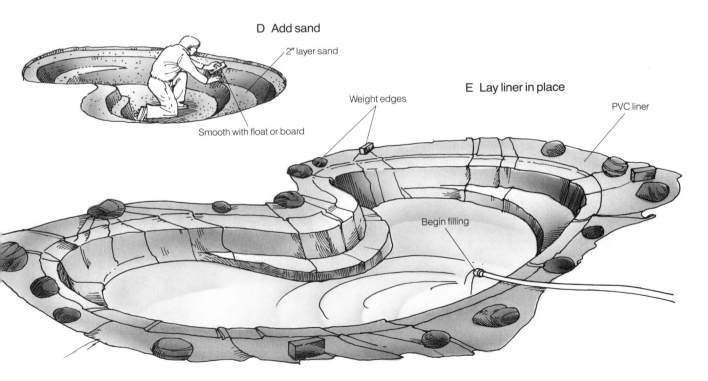

D Add sand

2" layer sand

Smooth with float or board

E Lay liner in place

Weight edges

PVC liner

Begin filling

Next, remove all protruding roots and rocks, fill the holes, and pack a 2-inch layer of clean, damp sand into the excavation (D). Smooth the sand, then drape the liner over the hole, evening up the overlap all around. Slowly begin filling the liner with water (E).

tion, fill any holes, and tamp down soft soil. Lay a 2-inch layer of fine, damp sand over all surfaces (your supplier can help you figure the amount). Spread the sand evenly, packing it into place, and smooth the surface with a board or a concrete float.

Positioning the liner. Warm up the liner by stretching it out in the sun. If you need to make a seam, now's the time. Use the solvent cement and method recommended by the maker of your liner.

Next, with a helper, center the liner over the excavation, draping the excess over the sides. Temporarily weight down the edges with bricks or stones; then slowly begin filling the pool. After adding 2 inches or so of water, start smoothing the liner into shape; sharp corners may require a folded pleat or two (you won't see the pleats once the pool is filled). One brave soul will probably need to roll up his or her pantlegs, wade in, and tuck the liner into place as necessary. The water's weight will make the liner fit the contour of the excavated hole. Continue working, adding a few inches of water at a time, until the pool is full.

Trimming the excess. Now make your way around the perimeter of the pool, adding a little soil here and there to level the top. Trim off the excess liner, leaving about 6 inches to tuck under the edging. For more security, push some long spikes through the edges into the subsoil below. Save the liner scraps for future repairs.

Finishing up. Your pool is ready for the border treatment. Flagstones or bricks laid in a thin bed of mortar are two popular choices—for instructions, see page 76. Native stones, a rock garden, and a bog garden are other options.

Drain the pool to rid it of any impurities from the building process. If you've installed a drain, this is easy; if not, either siphon the water off to lower ground with a hose or use a submersible pump or sump pump to push the water out.

Then fill the pool with fresh water and it's all set for the finishing touches. If you're adding a water garden or fish, first see the water-preparation tips on page 91.

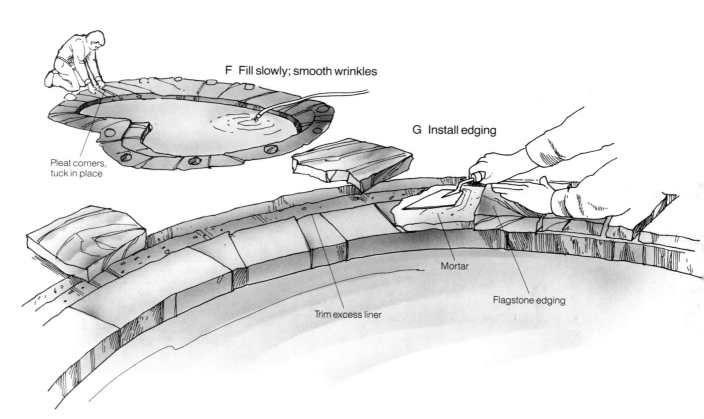

F Fill slowly; smooth wrinkles

Pleat corners, tuck in place

G Install edging

Mortar

Flagstone edging

Trim excess liner

Continue filling the liner, tucking in the wrinkles all around; as required, also fold pleats at hard corners (F), tucking them into place (the water will mask the folds). Finally, trim the excess liner all around and install the edging of your choice (G).

A POOL BUILDER'S

CHECKLIST

This chapter treats each part of the spectrum of pool-building operations—from installing a flexible liner to wiring outdoor light fixtures—as an individual subject. But below, we've devised a checklist to show you at a glance what's involved in building all four basic pool types: flexible liner, fiberglass shell, poured concrete, and concrete block with veneer. The lists will give you a feel for the interrelated tasks involved, as well as help you chart your progress. Before you start work, though, be sure to bone up on the specifics elsewhere in the chapter.

Flexible liner *(see pages 66–68)*

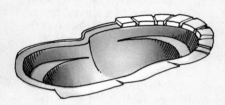

1 Choose site
2 Excavate for pool, marginal shelves, and edging
3 Dig trenches for drain and water supply lines (if any)
4 Dig trenches for wiring (if any)
5 Install GFCI receptacle for pump (if any)
6 Rough-in plumbing and wiring (if any)

7 Pack excavation with 2 inches of sand
8 Position liner; weight edges
9 Begin filling with water; tuck in folds
10 Trim excess liner
11 Apply edgings and borders as required
12 Drain and refill pool
13 Treat water as required

Fiberglass shell *(see pages 70–71)*

1 Choose site
2 Excavate hole
3 Dig trenches for drain and water supply lines (if any)
4 Dig trenches for wiring (if any)
5 Install GFCI receptacle for pump (if any)
6 Rough-in plumbing and wiring (if any)

7 Pack hole bottom with 2 inches of sand
8 Position shell
9 Backfill and add water in 4" increments
10 Add edgings and borders as required
11 Drain pool; refill
12 Treat water as required

Poured concrete *(see pages 72–73)*

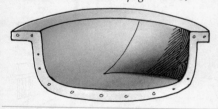

1 Choose site
2 Excavate hole
3 Dig trenches for drain and water supply lines (if any)
4 Dig trenches for wiring (if any)
5 Rough-in plumbing and wiring (if any)
6 Line excavation with gravel

7 Add steel reinforcement
8 Pour concrete
9 Waterproof or paint concrete
10 Finish plumbing and wiring
11 Add edgings and borders as desired
12 Cure concrete
13 Fill pool; treat water as required

Concrete block pool *(see page 74)*

1 Choose site
2 Excavate footings and pool floor
3 Dig trenches for drain and water supply lines (if any)
4 Dig trenches for wiring (if any)
5 Rough-in plumbing and wiring (if any)
6 Form and pour concrete footings
7 Build concrete block walls

8 Waterproof walls
9 Pour concrete floor
10 Add veneer and/or waterproofing to walls and floor
11 Finish plumbing and wiring
12 Add edgings and borders as desired
13 Cure concrete
14 Fill pool; treat water as required

INSTALLING A FIBERGLASS SHELL

Fiberglass shells are the easiest garden pools to install; and unlike those made with flexible liners, they can be used for semi-raised pools or on sloping sites. The only question mark is whether or not you'll find the shape you want or the right dimensions for plants or fish. The keys to success are maintaining level and providing solid support for the relatively weak fiberglass.

Do you have the perfect shell and location? If so, you're ready to begin the installation.

Marking the spot. First of all, bring the pool into the area and situate it in the correct position. Outline the pool's top edge on the ground with a hose or a length of rope, then add 2 inches all around. (The 2 inches are necessary for the sand you'll add, plus some room for "fudging.") It helps to drive stakes around the outline to keep it in place. Remove the shell and place it nearby.

Digging the hole. If you're working on grass, carefully peel back and remove the sod from the area

within the outline and set it aside in a shady place. Dig the outline of the pool with a sharp spade; if you plan a sunken flagstone, brick, or stone border, remove the sod and soil to this width and depth as well. A sizable excavation can be pretty heavy going in clay or rocky soil, so you may wish to hire some help and/or a small backhoe to rough out the area.

Make sure the excavation follows the same general taper as the shell walls, which will take some careful measuring and digging. If your pool includes a marginal shelf, shape this too, again leaving 2 inches extra all around. Take particular care with the depth and shape of the hole's bottom.

If your pool will be semi-raised or on a sloping site, you'll need to install fill and/or a masonry retaining wall in advance. Be sure the fill behind the wall is well-tamped and follows the basic shell shape as described above.

Checking for level. After the hole is roughed out, check the bottom with a carpenter's level. If it's level, you're ready to move on; if it's not, keep dig-

Fiberglass Shell, Step-by-Step

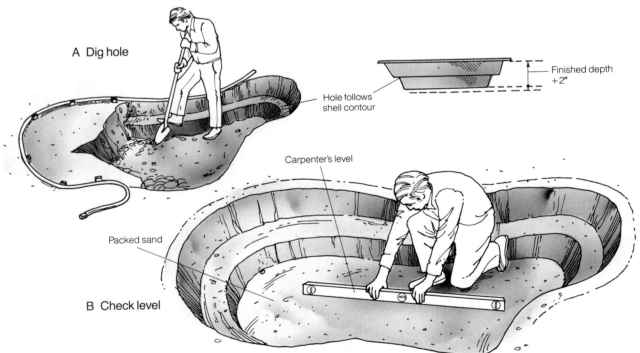

A properly shaped hole is the key to installing a fiberglass shell: add two inches all the way around, matching the taper and contours of your shell (A). Pack and smooth 2 inches of sand into the bottom, then check it carefully for level (B).

ging and filling until it is. Also remove any sharp objects such as rocks or roots, filling any gaps where these have been removed.

Planning on adding a drain or other plumbing? If so, now's the time for drilling the shell and roughing-in the pipes. See pages 80–85 for details. If electrical wiring is on your list, see pages 86–89.

Adding sand. A 2-inch layer of clean, damp sand comes next; the sand not only helps protect the fiberglass but also supports the shell snugly in its oversize hole. Spread sand evenly only along the bottom at this point, smoothing it carefully and checking again for level.

Positioning the shell. After recruiting some helpers, carefully lower the shell into the hole, and check the top edge for level. If it's off only slightly, you may be able to wiggle the shell into adjustment. If not, promptly remove the shell and level the bottom properly. (You don't want to have to do this after the shell is packed in place and filled with water!)

Backfilling with sand and soil. The secret to success here is patience. Slowly begin to fill the shell with water, and, at the same time, backfill along the sides with mixed sand and soil to support it at all points. Add 4 inches of sand and soil, then add 4 inches of water and check the shell for level. Add another 4 inches of mix, followed by another addition of water and check level. Keep it up until the water reaches the top.

Finishing the job. If you're planning a border around your fiberglass shell, now's the time to install it. Flagstones, fieldstones, and brick all make effective edge treatments. (Pages 76–77 will help with the fine points.) Most owners overhang edgings an inch or two over the water to hide the lip, but some feel the rolled lip looks fine as it is. Seal the joint between the edging and the shell with polyurethane or silicone caulk.

Now finish off any plumbing, treat the water as necessary (see page 91), and your fiberglass garden pool is ready for business.

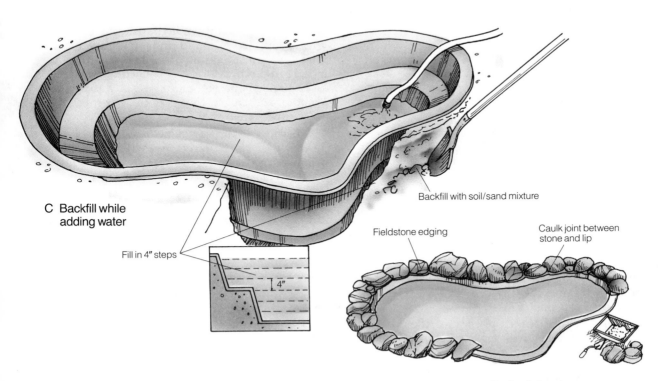

C Backfill while adding water

Fill in 4" steps

4"

Backfill with soil/sand mixture

Fieldstone edging

Caulk joint between stone and lip

D Apply border

Patience is the word now: lower the shell into position, then begin backfilling and adding water in 4-inch increments (C). Once the shell is full, check again for level and install the edging of your choice, overhanging it slightly over the shell edge (D).

THE MATTER OF MASONRY

The great majority of formal garden pools and fountains are still made of concrete, or concrete block in combination with brick, natural stone, or ceramic tile.

Below, we give an overview of the most popular uses of masonry for garden pool construction. Step-by-step instructions are beyond the scope of this book, however. If you need help with your project or you prefer to hire a professional to do the work for you, consult a landscape specialist who installs masonry pools.

Freeform Concrete Pools

A hand-packed concrete pool, such as the one shown on the facing page, is the simplest type of concrete pool for the do-it-yourselfer to build.

First, excavate and compact the pool site. In areas of severe freezing weather, allow an additional 3 to 4 inches for a layer of gravel under the concrete. Walls must be sloped: 45 degrees is about the limit. To prevent runoff from entering the pool in wet weather, allow for a 1- or 2-inch perimeter lip. Marginal shelves of varying widths and depths create a more natural look, and provide solid perches for boulders and other border treatments.

Add reinforcing either by bending 6- by 6-inch welded wire mesh to fit inside the pool or by using 1/4- or 3/8-inch reinforcing rods. Then drive stakes in every square foot, marked either 4 inches (warm climate) or 6 inches (colder areas) above the earth or gravel.

For anything larger than a tiny accent pool, it's a good idea to use premixed concrete—either carted home on a rental trailer or delivered to the site. Ask for "4- or 5-sack concrete with pea gravel," and request it a little on the dry side; the concrete supplier can help you pick the exact mix. For a large pour, you may also need a pump to reach the site from the street.

Using a shovel or trowel, pack the mix firmly around the reinforcing up to the marks on the stakes. Remove the stakes and fill the holes with concrete, then finish the surface with a trowel and cure the shell (see page 75).

To enhance the natural appearance, the walls may be covered with a rock mosaic, set in mortar.

More Advanced: Formwork

Although largely replaced by gunite where fluid shapes are required, and by concrete blocks where they're not, formed concrete is still useful for garden pools requiring crisp, sharp edges. Even a brick or block pool requires a poured floor and footings as a base.

The easiest route to a footing is simply to dig a trench and pour concrete in place in the earth. In cases where the earth is too soft or too damp to hold a vertical edge, you can build a simple form, as shown on the facing page. The footing must be flat on top if a block wall (see page 74) is to be built on top of it.

For the typical semi-raised pool, you can cast the walls at the same time you cast the footings. The combination form illlustrated is one example; you can also rent wall forms in some areas. If you're building a sunken pool, you may be able to dispense with wall forms if the soil is firm enough to stand without crumbling. Before pouring the concrete, you may need to add reinforcing rods to both footing and wall forms.

Once the footings and walls have set, lay down 6- by 6-inch welded wire mesh in the floor area and pour a 4-inch concrete slab.

The New Approach: Shotcrete or Gunite

Shotcrete is a mixture of hydrated cement and aggregate applied over and under a reinforcing grid directly against the soil. The mix is shot from a nozzle under pressure, allowing complete freedom of size and shape, since it follows any excavated contour. Shotcrete comes in both "wet-mix" and "dry-mix" versions: the drier mix is called *gunite*.

Because of the specialized equipment involved, however, this is a contractor-only job, but an industrious homeowner can do the excavation and prep work, then call in the contractor for the final application. As part of your prepwork, cover the surrounding area with plastic sheeting or other dropcloths to minimize the effects of overspray.

The basic setup for shotcrete or gunite, as shown on page 74, involves 3/8-inch reinforcing rods, wired together on a 12-inch grid and propped up off the gravel and soil by small rocks. Because the pressure-shot mix tends to "rebound," it's normal practice to add a layer of chicken wire over the gridwork to help secure the mixture. If your pool is on a slope, build up the outside of the shell with sandbags, form the inside, then pull down the sandbags and finish off the outside.

Once the pour is complete, use a trowel to smooth the surface to the desired shape; a rubber glove works well for final smoothing in tough-to-reach areas.

Freeform Concrete Pool

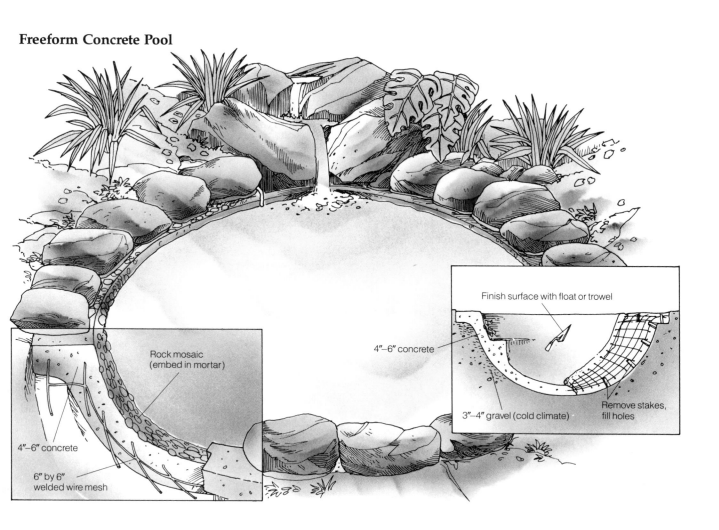

Finish surface with float or trowel

4″–6″ concrete

3″–4″ gravel (cold climate)

Remove stakes, fill holes

Rock mosaic (embed in mortar)

4″–6″ concrete

6″ by 6″ welded wire mesh

Concrete Formwork

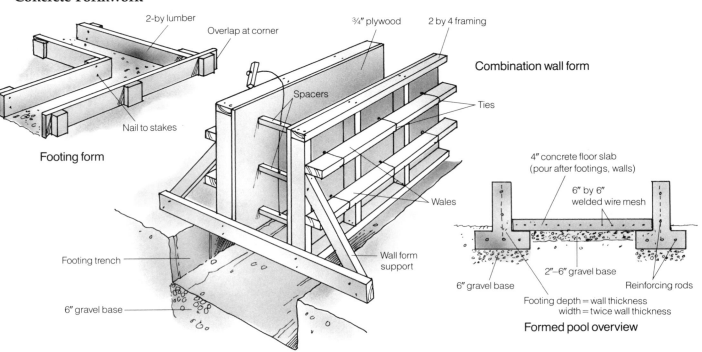

2-by lumber

Overlap at corner

¾″ plywood

2 by 4 framing

Combination wall form

Spacers

Ties

Nail to stakes

Footing form

Wales

Wall form support

4″ concrete floor slab (pour after footings, walls)

6″ by 6″ welded wire mesh

Footing trench

6″ gravel base

6″ gravel base

2″–6″ gravel base

Reinforcing rods

Footing depth = wall thickness
width = twice wall thickness

Formed pool overview

Concrete Block

For fast, inexpensive masonry wall construction, it's hard to beat concrete blocks. These rugged units make strong cores for formal pools or wall fountains; for a warmer appearance, veneer them with brick, stone, or tile.

The standard concrete block is a nominal 8 by 8 by 16 inches; actually, each dimension includes a standard 3/8-inch mortar joint. A whole series of fractional units is available to go with it. For veneering, builders often opt for thinner 4- or 6-inch blocks. It's easy to see that with a little planning and care in assembly, you'll never have to cut a block.

The drawing below shows a typical setup for a block-based wall fountain. Bond-beam blocks cap the walls, which, reinforced and grouted, substantially increase the strength. Note also how the corner units overlap for strength. A 4-inch-deep concrete floor completes the structure.

Brick, Stone & Tile Veneers

Veneers are among the most popular applications of masonry. A veneer saves expensive masonry materials by its use only on a project's visible surface, hiding a core of less attractive—and less costly—material.

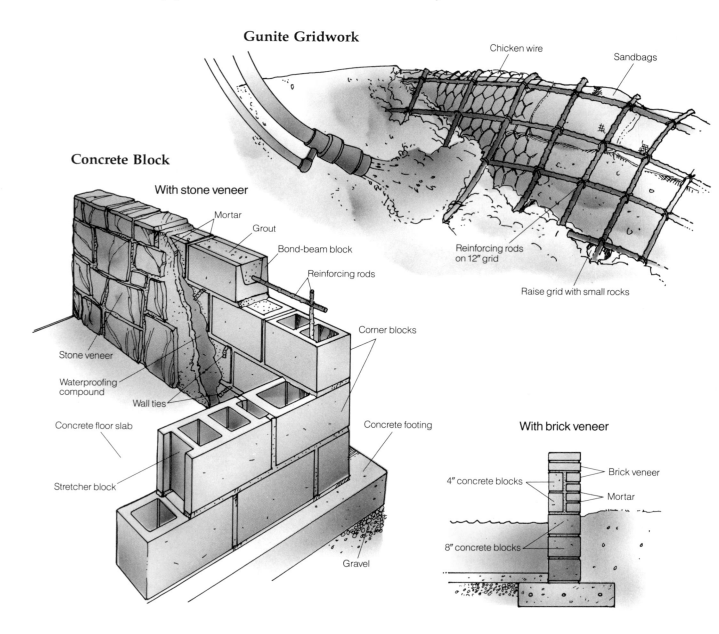

Gunite Gridwork

Chicken wire

Sandbags

Reinforcing rods on 12" grid

Raise grid with small rocks

Concrete Block

With stone veneer

Mortar

Grout

Bond-beam block

Reinforcing rods

Corner blocks

Stone veneer

Waterproofing compound

Wall ties

Concrete floor slab

Concrete footing

Stretcher block

Gravel

With brick veneer

Brick veneer

4" concrete blocks

Mortar

8" concrete blocks

Working with brick. One way to simplify the problems of brick masonry is to make a concrete shell and use it as the watertight interior face. A veneer of bricks on the outer face then produces the desired appearance without needing to be leakproof.

Only a few tools are needed for simple bricklaying: a 10-inch trowel with a pointed blade (for buttering mortar), a brickset (a cold chisel for cutting bricks), a hammer, a 2-foot carpenter's level, a carpenter's square, and a stretch of fishing line.

Brick mortar is a mixture of cement, fine sand, and water, with a small amount of lime or lime putty added for plasticity. Proportions are one part Portland cement, one-half part hydrated lime or lime putty, and four and one-half parts graded sand.

Common bricks should be damp but not wet when they are laid. It is best to build up the corners first and then work at the center section of a wall, using a plumb level to keep the bricks in vertical alignment. Stretch fishing line at each course to keep the horizontal level.

Stone on concrete block. Want to dress up plain concrete block wall? Veneer it with stone. The result appears to be a stone wall, but it can be achieved at much less labor and expense.

When installing a stone veneer wall, you'll need to attach wall ties to the block wall every 2 or 3 square feet. When building the concrete block core, simply insert the ties in the mortar joints between the blocks.

The veneer stones are attached to each other and to the concrete block wall with mortar, the wall ties providing a positive connection to the mortar. Bend as many of the ties as possible into the joints between stones. "Slush fill" the spaces between the wall and the stones completely with soupy—but not runny—mortar as you go.

Dressing up with tile. Poured concrete (especially if roughed-up), concrete block, and brick all make acceptable surfaces for ceramic tile. The tile itself should be a vitreous (nonabsorbent) type for any area in contact with water. In addition, thinset adhesive and grout are recommended, both mixed with latex additive.

Tiling a garden pool is much like tiling the shower inside the house. The basic procedure is this: (1) Prep the surface as necessary for level and plumb; (2) Determine tile spacing and cuts needed; (3) Mark layout lines on the backing; (4) Spread adhesive with a notched trowel; (5) Place the tiles. Once the adhesive is dry (a minimum of 24 hours), spread the grout and sponge it off immediately. Later, polish off the soft haze that sets up.

CONCRETE

TAKES THE CURE

The key to stable, leakproof masonry construction is proper curing, in addition to careful waterproofing or painting.

In concrete lingo, "moist-curing" is the process of keeping the surface wet while it slowly hardens, producing a stronger structure. It's also a good way to rid the new pool of its supply of free lime, which is toxic to plant and fish life. The traditional method is to fill the new pool with water and let it sit for 24 hours. Drain and refill, repeating the process three or four times. The last time, let the water stand for a week and then rinse the pool thoroughly.

In a hurry? Chemical solutions are on the market that get the curing job done more quickly.

Poured concrete pools that will retain their natural color should be given two coats of a commercial, cement-based waterproofing compound. It's best to finish shotcrete or gunite structures with plaster (a professional job), but 3 to 4 coats of waterproofing will also do the trick. Treat concrete block pools with waterproofing compound or another liquid membrane before veneering.

Two kinds of paint can be used on fresh concrete with success, provided the surface is prepared: rubber-base and epoxy. Rubber-base paint should be applied with a brush or roller to a clean surface. Epoxy should be brushed onto a spotless surface. The basic preparatory steps are the same for both types of paint. While the new concrete is still damp (but fully set), etch it with muriatic acid, mixing one part acid to two parts tap water in a nonmetallic bucket. A gallon of muriatic acid will cover from 300 to 500 square feet of surface.

Wearing galoshes, protective goggles (or glasses), and rubber gloves, use a long-handled brush to slosh the acid onto all surfaces. Scrub until the acid ceases to bubble and the concrete attains a uniform, open-grained texture similar to that of fine sandpaper. Wash the acid off and flush it thoroughly out of the pool. (Note: it can cause temporary burns to lawns and plant roots.)

Brush or roll on the paint, usually two or three coats, according to the manufacturer's instructions. Before filling the pool, let the paint dry for 14 days.

EDGINGS & BORDERS

Regardless of the shell material, a good edging (the material directly around the rim) and border (the adjacent landscape) will make or break your pool's appearance. The drawings on these two pages illustrate a number of your edging and border options. Below is additional information on how to work with these materials.

Masonry. In natural pools, masonry is the number one choice for making the transition between water and land.

To lay flagstone or other small stones, first arrange them in a pleasing pattern, cutting stones where necessary with a brickset. Then lay them in 1-inch-thick mortar (three parts sand to one part cement), checking continually for level. Clean the stones with a sponge and water as you work and remove any excess mortar from the perimeter after bedding the stones. Once the mortar has set for 24 hours, pack the joints with the same mix of mortar used for the bed, plus one-half part fire clay to improve workability, and smooth them with a trowel. Keep the grout damp for the first day by sprinkling it repeatedly or by covering it with plastic sheeting,

and keep off the paved area for 3 days to let the mortar harden.

Evenly-spaced bricks are simpler to work with than irregular flagstones. For pointers, see page 75.

Framing a garden pool with large boulders is not an easy way to do the job, but the results can be worth all the toil. Usually these stones look best if partially buried; otherwise, prop them up with smaller rocks, then pack the area with soil and plantings. Here's one trick for placing large rocks: break them with a sledge, move them piece by piece, and reassemble them with cement slurry. Some more back-saving tips: either slide a heavy rock on a large shovel, chain link fencing, or board; or roll it, using a steel bar or plank as a lever.

A mowing strip helps you mow the grass right up to the edge of a formal concrete pool. The strip can either be bricks, set in mortar or packed sand, or a poured concrete strip, screeded flush with simple forms, as shown below.

Wood. In addition to using rock around the edge of a pool, you can use wood posts or logs, in diameters ranging from 2 to 6 inches, to form a series of mini-

Edging Options

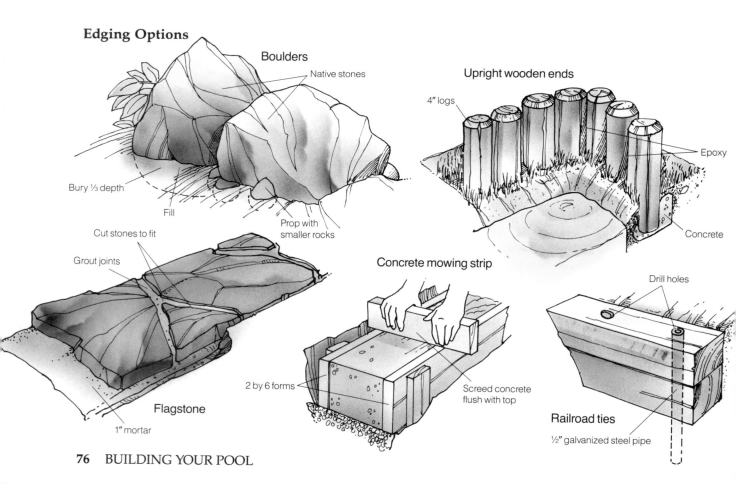

Boulders
Native stones
Bury ⅓ depth
Fill
Prop with smaller rocks

Upright wooden ends
4" logs
Epoxy
Concrete

Cut stones to fit
Grout joints
Flagstone
1" mortar

Concrete mowing strip
2 by 6 forms
Screed concrete flush with top

Drill holes
Railroad ties
½" galvanized steel pipe

ature pilings. Leave the bark on for a more natural appearance. Set the lengths vertically and butted tightly against one another; the bottom ends should rest in concrete, not in bare ground. Add additional concrete behind the pilings.

Railroad ties make effective retaining walls, especially when drilled and threaded with steel pipe, as shown below.

Benderboard forms a curved border for a gravel-edged pool, or serves as a transition between the pool and a surrounding lawn. Wet the boards down before trying to bend them to shape. (You may snap a few boards in the process!)

Running a deck or wooden walkway right up to and over the edge of a pool is another effective trick; make sure any submerged post that supports the deck is pressure treated and rests on a concrete footing and/or precast pier.

Bog gardens, rock gardens. A rock dam, as shown below, is one simple way to accommodate marginal plants. Fill the area with soil, add a short overflow pipe from the pool, and you have a bog garden.

A hillside pool that's shored up on one side presents a good opportunity to construct a rock garden, building up the downhill side with rocks and soil and adding plantings as you wish. If the slope is steep, terrace the rocks, forming crannies for soil where plantings can take a hold. To facilitate watering and to prevent dislodging, set out bank plants in "foxholes" formed by bottomless cans, by circles of aluminum lawn edging, or by buried boxes with the bottoms knocked out. By the time the surrounding material corrodes or rots, the plants will have plunged their roots to a self-supporting depth.

A mound or small berm requires a fair amount of soil, such as that excavated for your pool. Be sure water running off the berm won't enter the pool—a gravel drainage channel or perforated drain pipe (see page 84) is a good solution. Remove any sod and dig the ground up lightly to break the surface crust before you bring in any extra soil for the mound. Then spread out a layer of new soil and, using a shovel or tiller, mix it with the existing soil to ensure good drainage. Tamp it down lightly, smoothing the sides with the back of a rake, and plant the mound as you would any other hillside.

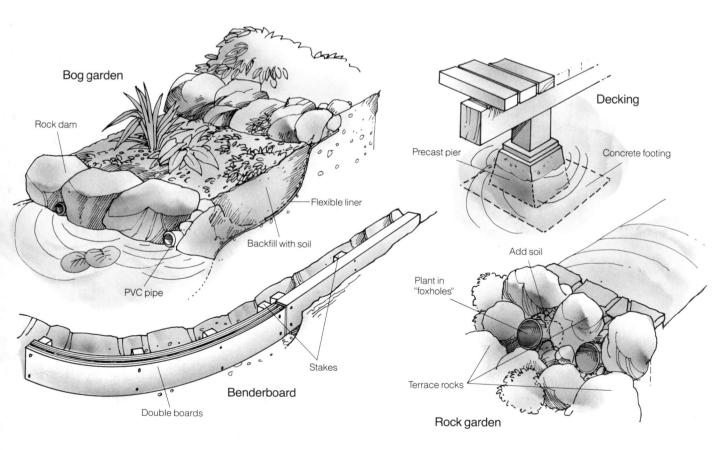

Bog garden

Rock dam

PVC pipe

Flexible liner

Backfill with soil

Double boards

Stakes

Benderboard

Decking

Precast pier

Concrete footing

Add soil

Plant in "foxholes"

Terrace rocks

Rock garden

WATERFALLS & STREAMS

Waterfalls and streams pose some unique technical and design considerations. In the technical department, the number one concern is *waterproofing*. When it comes to esthetics, only creative experimentation will reveal the most pleasing sights and sounds. Both waterfalls and streams benefit from tasteful border plantings.

Waterfalls

Water's continual scouring action plus constant wetting and drying—translated as swelling and contracting—can lead to leaky waterfalls. Therefore, you'll have to take careful steps to ensure a waterproof job. Before plunging into construction, determine the pump, pipes, and other plumbing hardware you'll need (see pages 80–85) to provide the desired flow. Your falls should look good when it's turned off, too.

Selecting waterfall materials. The drawing below shows an overview of one well-made waterfall. The foundation can often be the dirt excavated when you dug your pool, perhaps augmented by a retaining wall, sandbags, or other filler material. For a waterproof channel, use either a flexible liner, freeform concrete, a fiberglass shell or series of spill pans, or a combination of the above. The team of plastic liner and concrete is favored by many pros. If shotcrete or gunite (see page 72) is the choice, it can often be applied at the same time the adjacent pool is built.

You can apply concrete over chicken wire backing only, but a standard 12-inch grid of 3/8- or 1/2-inch reinforcing rod is better. Before pouring the falls, however, you'll need to place the primary rocks.

Building the channel. The toughest part of the whole project is getting any big boulders into place, and you may need help. If you're using a flexible liner, position these rocks carefully, making sure not to damage or displace the liner. If the rocks are outside the liner's path, dig out beds and settle them firmly in the soil. Working in manageable sections, pour 3 inches of concrete, working it up the sides of the channels and into all the nooks and crannies.

Once the concrete has set up, brush on two to three coats of cement-based waterproofing compound. You can also use hydraulic cement, designed for repair jobs, to waterproof and help shape as desired. This is the time to test for leaks.

Anatomy of a Waterfall

Flagstone lip

Grout gaps

Holding pool slopes back

Reinforcing rod, 12" grid

Bury boulders

Smaller rocks in mortar

Flexible liner

3" concrete

Adding rocks. Once the basic structure is complete, secure secondary stones, pebbles, and a flagstone or acrylic lip in a mortar bed, adding additional mix between seams to keep the water moving the way you want it to. When mortaring, concentrate on the "upstream" side, away from the main flow and main angle of view. Colored mortar—black or charcoal—blends in better than natural gray, appearing as "shadows" in the finished waterfall. Use a stiff, wet paintbrush for final troweling—it's easier to get into tight corners than a regular trowel.

Also add loose rocks or pebbles at this point to accent visually or form ripple patterns. To secure the border plantings, pack soil into the areas behind the boulders.

Streams

Streams share many construction details with both waterfalls and pools—in fact, they typically begin with a small falls and end in a holding pool.

To plan a stream, lay out a rope in the general course you want the stream to take. Be sure the proposed channel can handle the maximum flow from your pump (see page 80), plus some additional natural runoff. A finished depth of 3 to 7 inches works well: anything deeper than that requires a lot of water. The slope should be mild; a series of weirs, joined by small dammed cascades, keeps water from running off too quickly and retains some when the pump is switched off.

Stream materials include flexible liners, freeform concrete, and shotcrete or gunite. Plastic lining (see drawing at top right) may require some careful seamwork, but it's a fast way to create a waterproof membrane and is easy to camouflage.

Freeform concrete lends itself to simple "scooped out" stream designs, as the small channel serves as the form. Lay down 2 inches of 3/4-inch crushed rock, apply a layer of fine gravel, and cover with chicken wire. Pour 2 inches of concrete, working it into the base rocks or wire and troweling it up the sides. If you want to leave bare concrete for the bed, roughen the surface with a stiff broom after it has started to set up. Place any large boulders before the pour, adding smaller stones with mortar or leaving them loose.

The "dry streambed" is an effective option for a natural landscape, as well as for a drainage channel for seasonal runoff. You won't need a liner, just some perforated drain pipe to channel the water, mixed rocks and pebbles, and selected border plantings. A 2 percent grade is about right.

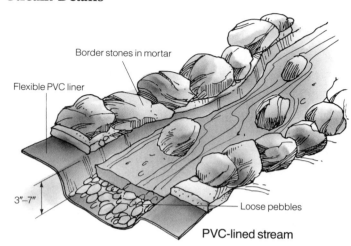

Border stones in mortar

Flexible PVC liner

3"–7"

Loose pebbles

PVC-lined stream

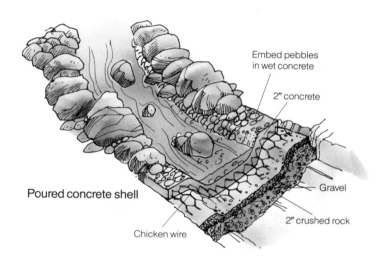

Embed pebbles in wet concrete

2" concrete

Poured concrete shell

Gravel

2" crushed rock

Chicken wire

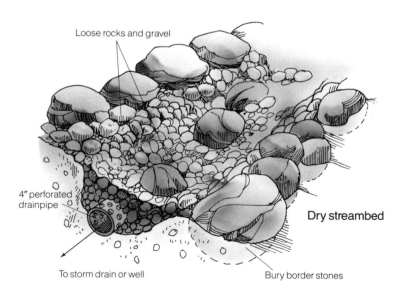

Loose rocks and gravel

4" perforated drainpipe

To storm drain or well

Dry streambed

Bury border stones

POOL PLUMBING

Pumps and plumbing for garden pools have been improved to the point where the weekend warrior can install them without much trouble. Some pools won't need plumbing at all—or at most a small submersible pump to drive a fountain jet. Larger structures, such as those including a waterfall or stream, require more elaborate plumbing systems. Accessories such as skimmers, float valves, or separate biological filters have requirements all their own. Here's a rundown on choosing a pump and using pipes, fittings, and accessories. For a look at six sample plumbing systems, see pages 84–85.

Choosing the Pump

The mechanical heart of a fountain or waterfall, the pump is merely a set of whirling blades through which the water passes and by which it is pressurized into further motion.

Submersible pumps simplify plumbing to the extreme. They sit on the floor of the pool, often hidden only by the water itself, and operate silently, one advantage over other pumps. Flexible tubing or rigid pipe (see facing page) carries water to the fountain or waterfall. Fill and drain piping, if any, are separate.

A recirculating pump is frequently the answer when the pump must be operated continuously or when water has a long distance to go from pump to outlet—often the case with waterfalls or streams. Some models are self-priming, but many are not and need to be installed in a flooded position (below water level) to retain their prime.

What size do you need? All manufacturers give electrical specifications—amps, watts, and horsepower—for their products, which are important because they measure how much electricity will be used to do the job. But the practical measure of a pump's performance is its head, the volume of water it will pump vertically, telling you how many gallons an hour a pump can deliver at a given height.

The performance specifications for a submersible pump may look like this:

Model	Gallons per hour					Amps	Watts	HP
	1 ft.	3 ft.	5 ft.	9 ft.	13 ft.			
0000	500	420	335	275	225	1.9	210	1/15

Fountain spray jets are usually designed for a specific pressure, but waterfalls and streams are more subjective. To choose a pump for a small water feature, measure the vertical distance from the water

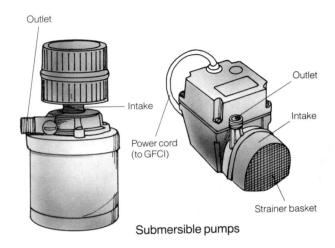
Submersible pumps

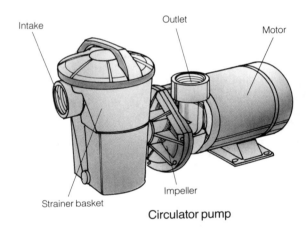
Circulator pump

level to the top of the stream or waterfall. Then, using a garden hose, start a flow of water from the top that approximates the volume of water you want. Collect this water in a 5-gallon bucket for a specified time (30 seconds or a minute), multiply the results to get gallons per hour, and compare that figure with the manufacturer's performance data.

When sizing a pump for a large system, it's best to hook up a temporary pump to a 1-1/2-inch hose or the finished plumbing. Your pump should be able to recycle an adequate flow to any filter system, so figure in this load as well.

Locating your pump. In most cases, install the pump to keep the distance it has to move the water as short as possible. For example, a waterfall pump is usually situated right at the base of the falls. The one exception is when the pump's primary function is to drive a filter: in this case, position the intake

Pipes & Fittings

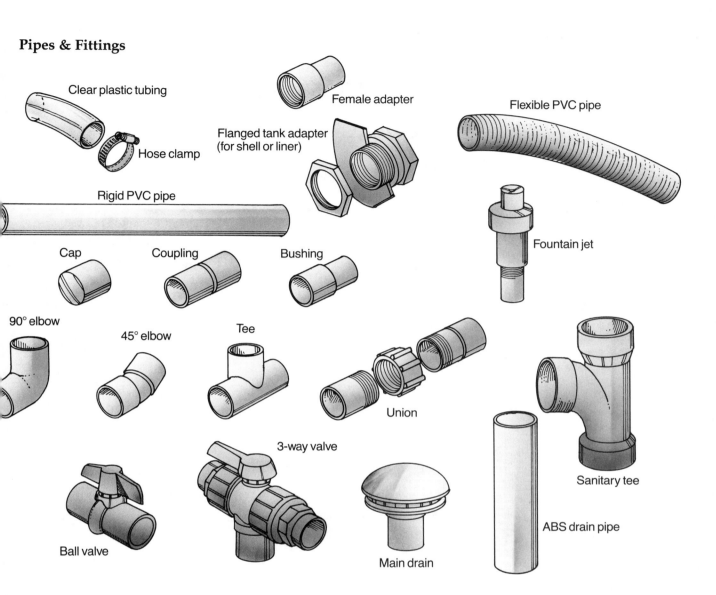

Clear plastic tubing

Hose clamp

Female adapter

Flanged tank adapter
(for shell or liner)

Flexible PVC pipe

Rigid PVC pipe

Fountain jet

Cap

Coupling

Bushing

90° elbow

45° elbow

Tee

Union

Sanitary tee

3-way valve

Ball valve

Main drain

ABS drain pipe

pipe—and the pump—at the opposite end of the pool to provide maximum circulation.

Elevate a submersible pump on bricks at the bottom of the pool to keep it free from silt and other pool debris. Alternatively, you may wish to form a small gravel-lined pump vault at the bottom of the pool, covering the opening with removable wire mesh. Always place some type of strainer in front of the pump to filter the worst dirt and leaves. (Many pumps include a built-in strainer.)

Ideally, a recirculating pump should be housed in a lidded 3 by 5 vault—cast in concrete or built from wood—to protect it and to eliminate clutter. You can camouflage the vault with plants or hide it behind a retaining wall.

Before placing your pump, consider how you'll supply electricity to power it. For options and details, see pages 86–89.

Pipefitting for Pools

Below you'll find a quick overview of pipes and pipefitting techniques; for help with materials, tools, and techniques, contact a plumbing equipment supplier or a professional plumber.

Pipes and fittings. The drawing above shows a sampling of popular pipes and fittings, allowing you to change direction, join pipe runs, change from plastic to copper or galvanized steel, go up or down in size, and change from a screw-on fitting to a push-in fitting. Pipes and fittings for garden pool pumps should be of plastic, copper, or galvanized steel, although on a very small pump, rubber or clear plastic tubing can be substituted for any pipe.

Whenever possible, opt for plastic pipe and fittings for both water supply and drain lines: plastic is easy to cut, is straightforward to assemble, and

A LOOK AT

BIOLOGICAL FILTERS

Biological filters use friendly bacteria to convert ammonia and nitrites in the pool water to nitrates and thus continue the purifying nitrogen cycle (see page 59). The key to designing a biological system is creating a sand, gravel, or synthetic media bed which the bacteria can call home, and pumping a steady flow of pool water through the filter media via a constantly operating pump.

Location. You can situate a biological filter at the bottom of the pool or in a remote location, connected by intake and outlet pipes. The remote tank is preferable (it's easier to maintain) but requires extra space and expense.

A concrete pool with built-in "false bottom" is ideal for an in-pool system; large, deep fiberglass shells are also relatively easy to retrofit. Fiberglass is the typical solution for a remote holding tank—it's easy to set up and drill for fittings. Even plastic industrial drums will work. The drawings on page 85 show both in-pool and remote setups.

Design. As shown below left, the biological filter is basically a 12- to 24-inch-deep media bed with an open space below, allowing the water to enter and exit at a leisurely pace. Water can travel up or down through the filter bed. Coarse aquarium sand is a traditional media choice, though fiber padding, ceramic beds, and other experimental materials are being used.

What's the best size for your biological filter? Ideally, it should be as large as the pool itself, but the filter can be much smaller—you'll just need to maintain it more intensely. The average size is 3 by 6 feet.

It takes up to 8 weeks for a bacterial colony to accumulate naturally, but you can speed up the process by "seeding" the filter with a shovelful of material from a friend's media bed.

Pump and hardware. Generally, garden pool designers figure that the pump should turn over 1 to 2 gallons per minute per square foot of filter bed surface. In practical terms, that means that the typical 3- by 6-foot biological filter will require 18 to 24 gallons per minute, or 1080 to 1440 gallons per hour. A recirculating pump is best, as the filter must operate 24 hours a day. As the filter media can die in as little as 6 to 8 hours without oxygen, you may wish to install a small air pump in case of emergencies.

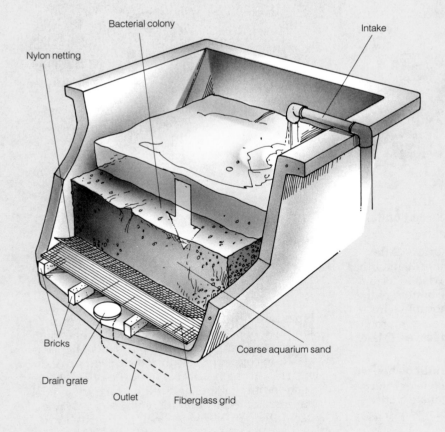

Bacterial colony

Intake

Nylon netting

Bricks

Drain grate

Outlet

Fiberglass grid

Coarse aquarium sand

...POOL PLUMBING

won't corrode like copper or galvanized. Rigid Schedule 40 PVC is the standby, though flexible PVC, available in many areas, fits around corners without fittings and helps you ease a fiberglass pool into place. ABS plastic can be substituted for PVC for larger drain lines. Consider 1-1/2 inch pipe and fittings the norm for garden pool systems; large volumes of water may require 2-inch lines.

Working with plastic pipe. Although you can cut PVC plastic pipe with a hacksaw, a pipe cutter or power miter saw make the cleanest, squarest cuts, which helps prevent leaks.

The techniques for connecting PVC pipe and fittings are shown at right. Before you cut the pipe, be sure that measurements are exact and that you've allowed for the distance the pipe will extend into the fitting. Are you sure you have the right solvent cement for the kind of plastic you're using? Some pipes also require a primer before cementing. After joining pipe and fitting, hold them together for a minute; wait at least 6 hours before allowing water to run through the pipe.

To make a watertight seal with screw-on fittings, first wrap nylon pipe tape around the threads of the pipe.

Valves. Valves allow you to control the flow to a fountain or waterfall, divert water to a nearby drain, or shut the entire system down for repairs or maintenance.

A gate valve is handy for simple on/off use, and for isolating a pump, filter, or drain line. Need to keep water flowing in one direction, or maintain a pump's prime? Install a check valve. To control flow, opt for a ball valve, as shown on page 81. A 3-way valve allows you to shut off the flow, send a controlled flow to a fountain head, or open up a line for draining the pool.

Drains. A small pool or fountain may not need a drain, especially if it has a submersible pump that can double as a sump pump. Larger pools, however, should have a main drain to allow the pool to be drained for maintenance or emergency repairs.

Drains come in a variety of shapes and sizes; swimming pool and spa suppliers are good bets for places to look for them. You won't need an anti-vortex attachment as on a swimming pool, but you will need some type of cap or screen to keep leaves, dirt, and even fish out of the drain. Special flanged fittings are made for liners and fiberglass shells to ensure a tight seal where the drain or pipe has penetrated the liner or shell material. An example is shown on page 81. Slope the pool floor slightly toward the drain.

PVC Pipefitting

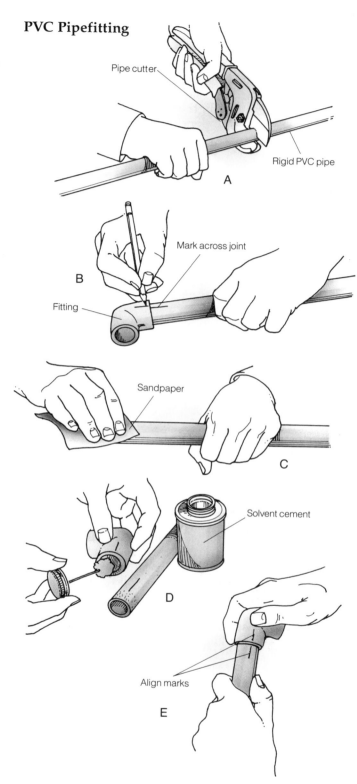

Leakproof pipefitting begins with a PVC pipe cutter (A); remove any burrs formed on the inside surface. Dry-fit pipe and fitting and mark the proper angle (B). The pipe may need light sanding or priming (C); then PVC solvent cement is brushed on both pipe and fitting (D). Join parts (E), quickly twist one-half turn, and align the marks.

...POOL PLUMBING

To install a border drain, use perforated drain pipe and run it to a low spot in the yard, a dry well, or simply to a nearby storm drain if allowed. Dig a 12-inch-deep ditch for the drain line and line it with gravel. A minimum slope of 1/4-inch per running foot is required. A simple PVC overflow pipe can maintain pool level.

Plumbing for Pool Accessories

Fountains, filters, skimmers, and float valves all require plumbing hookups. Here are installation guidelines; for a closer look, see the drawings at right.

Fountains. Though some spray fountains come as complete units, others include the spray jet only, requiring a riser pipe—or a series of nipples and adapters—to achieve the proper height. If required, fasten the riser tightly to a stake or support block, then screw the jet onto the riser's threads.

Typically, a spill or wall fountain has no jet, simply one or more pipe ends flush with the back wall. An example is shown at bottom right. Cover the pipe end with a decorative nozzle or figurine, or hide it between masonry units, leaving a narrow slot in mortar or grout. A ball or 3-way valve maintains the flow to any fountain.

Filters. Filters—whether cartridge, pressurized-sand, or biological—require intake and outlet plumbing; a biological filter may also require custom internal parts (see "Biological Filters" on page 82). Always position the filter on the outlet side of the pump, unless you're using a separate pump and plumbing route just for the filter, which is a good idea for large pools. A separate ball valve on this line is handy.

Skimmer. A surface skimmer connected to the pump intake pulls dirt, pollen, floating algae, and leaves into the filtration system. The typical skimmer is poured in place on the side of a concrete pool, though units that hang on the side of the pool are also available.

The skimmer is most effective when it is located on the down-wind side of the pool; the wind helps the pump by pushing debris toward the opening.

Float valve. To automatically top up water lost to evaporation and splash, a float valve can do the trick. You'll need access to a nearby cold water pipe, plus a fitting or two to make the hookup.

A float valve can be located in the holding pool of a wall fountain, a niche in a pool's rock edging, or a separate, lidded chamber near the main pool.

Sample Plumbing Designs

PVC liner with spray fountain

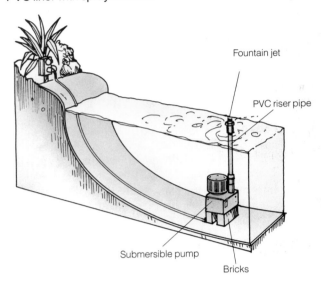

Fountain jet

PVC riser pipe

Submersible pump

Bricks

Fiberglass shell with waterfall

Waterfall inlet

Clear plastic tubing

Gravel border drain

Bricks

Submersible pump

Overflow pipe

4" perforated drain pipe

Wall fountain

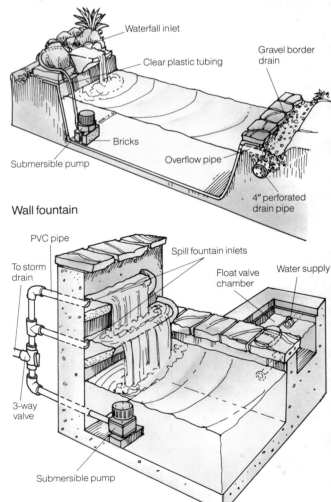

PVC pipe

Spill fountain inlets

To storm drain

Float valve chamber

Water supply

3-way valve

Submersible pump

Freeform concrete stream

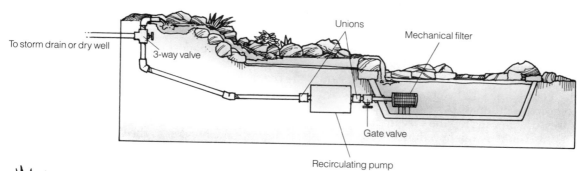

To storm drain or dry well

3-way valve

Unions

Mechanical filter

Gate valve

Recirculating pump

Split-level pools with biological filter

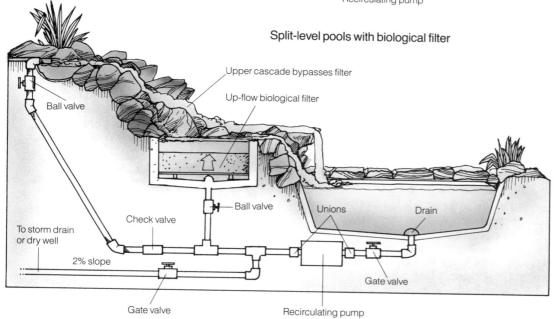

Upper cascade bypasses filter

Up-flow biological filter

Ball valve

Ball valve

Unions

Drain

Check valve

To storm drain
or dry well

2% slope

Gate valve

Recirculating pump

Gate valve

Koi pond with biological filter & pressurized-sand filter

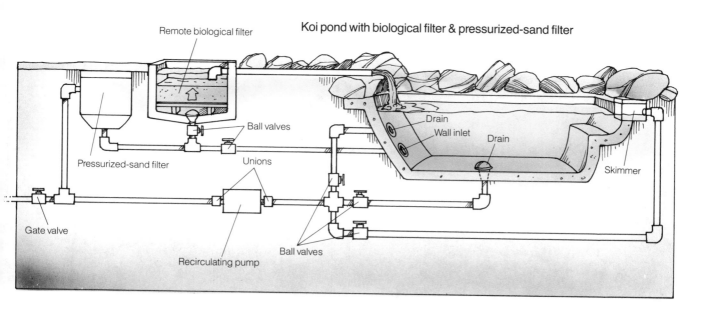

Remote biological filter

Ball valves

Drain

Wall inlet

Drain

Pressurized-sand filter

Unions

Skimmer

Gate valve

Recirculating pump

Ball valves

OUTDOOR WIRING & LIGHTING

For powering a submersible pump, accenting plants and fish, or illuminating paths, electricity is a welcome addition to any garden pool environment. You can extend your home's 120-volt system into the garden to power a pump or permanently placed light fixtures, or you can step the system down to 12 volts and use lighter-weight fixtures that can be easily moved.

A 12-volt installation is simple: cable can lie on top of the ground, perhaps hidden by foliage, or in a narrow trench, where there is much less danger that people or pets will suffer a harmful shock. In most areas, no electrical permit is required for installing a system that extends from a low-voltage plug-in transformer (the most common kind).

For brighter lighting, pumps, and other pool accessories, 120-volt wiring packs a bigger punch—and requires both buried cable and an electrical permit; code restrictions are particularly strict for installations near to and in the pool. (If you're planning a 220-volt installation for a heavy-duty recirculating pump, be sure to hire a professional.)

Before adding on to an existing circuit, add up the watts marked on the bulbs and appliances fed by that circuit. A 15-amp circuit can handle a continuous load of 1440 watts; a 20-amp circuit is rated for 1920 watts. The number of watts you can add is the difference between these figures and your total.

In purchasing light fixtures for above-water installation, be sure to get weather-resistant materials (aluminum, brass, copper, stainless steel, hard-finish plastics, ceramic clays). For underwater installation—whether fixtures are cast into the pool shell or portable—use only UL-approved types. Underwater is no place to have short circuits.

Here's the most important rule for all do-it-yourself electricians: *Never work on any "live" circuit, fixture, receptacle, or switch.* Your life may depend on it. If fuses protect your circuits, remove the appropriate fuse and take it with you. In a panel or subpanel equipped with circuit breakers, switch the appropriate breaker to the OFF position to disconnect the circuit, then tape over the switch for extra safety. If you need help to add a new circuit or you have any doubts about how to hook up to an existing one, consult an electrician.

Adding a 120-volt System

To install a 120-volt outdoor system, you may need housing boxes, a ground fault circuit interrupter (abbreviated GFCI or GFI), a set of light fixtures, and weatherproof 120-volt cable or conduit. You may also want to add an indoor switch and timer.

Choosing housing boxes. Outdoor boxes come in two types: so-called "driptight" boxes that seal vertically against falling water and "watertight" ones that seal against water coming from any direction. Unless you can ensure protection from rain, sprinklers, and even the garden hose, it's best to choose watertight boxes.

Wiring a GFCI. Even though you may plan to plug your pump or pool light into an existing outdoor receptacle, seriously consider replacing the outlet with one that has a built-in GFCI. This device works like a standard receptacle but cuts off power within 1/40 of a second if current begins leaking anywhere along the circuit.

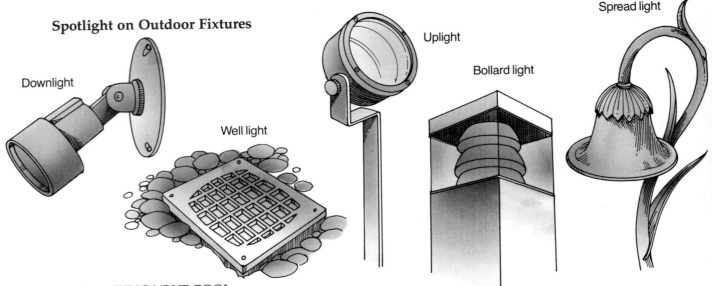

Spotlight on Outdoor Fixtures

Downlight

Well light

Uplight

Bollard light

Spread light

Wiring an Indoor Switch & Power Source to New GFCI

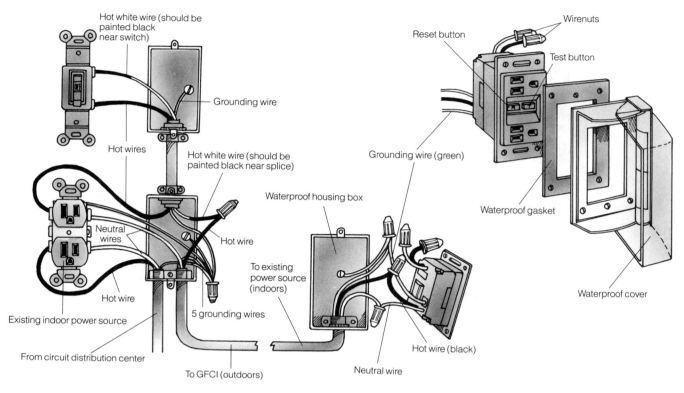

Hot white wire (should be painted black near switch)

Grounding wire

Hot wires

Hot white wire (should be painted black near splice)

Neutral wires

Hot wire

Hot wire

Existing indoor power source

5 grounding wires

From circuit distribution center

To GFCI (outdoors)

Waterproof housing box

To existing power source (indoors)

Hot wire (black)

Neutral wire

Wirenuts

Reset button

Test button

Grounding wire (green)

Waterproof gasket

Waterproof cover

The drawing above shows how to wire an outdoor GFCI. Make the connections with plastic wirenuts, following this sequence: (1) Strip 1 inch of insulation from the wire ends, and twist the ends clockwise 1-1/2 turns; (2) Snip 3/8 to 1/2 inch off the twisted wires; (3) Screw the wirenut clockwise onto the wires. Twist a short "jumper" wire from the box's grounding screw together with the other two grounding wires.

If this is the "end of the run," snip off the remaining outgoing wires from the GFCI and cover them with wirenuts as shown.

Dimmer switches allow you to set light fixtures at any level from a soft glow to full-throttle. Most dimmers can be wired in the same manner as the switch shown above. Use this setup for lights only—you won't want a dimmer-controlled pump!

Tapping a power source. Extending an inside power source to the outside is the same as extending wiring inside. You can tap into most switch, receptacle, fixture, or junction boxes as long as the box contains a neutral (white) wire and is not switch-controlled.

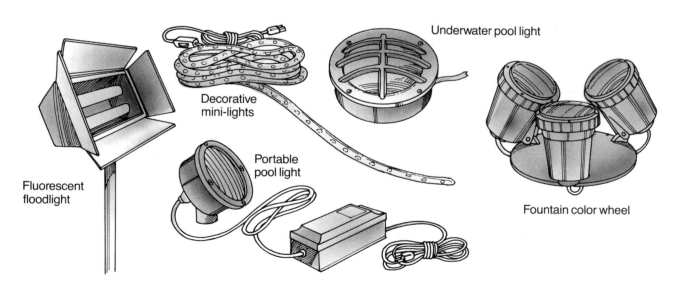

Fluorescent floodlight

Decorative mini-lights

Portable pool light

Underwater pool light

Fountain color wheel

Wiring an Indoor Switch & Timer

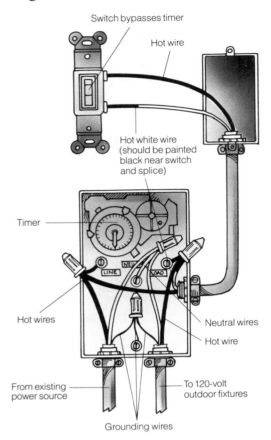

Switch bypasses timer

Hot wire

Hot white wire
(should be painted
black near switch
and splice)

Timer

Hot wires

From existing
power source

Neutral wires

Hot wire

To 120-volt
outdoor fixtures

Grounding wires

Wiring 120-volt Fixtures

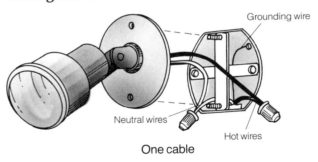

Grounding wire

Neutral wires

Hot wires

One cable

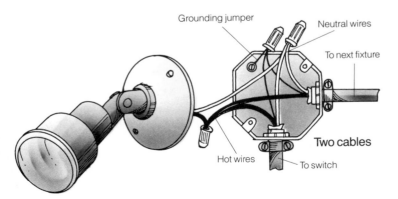

Grounding jumper

Neutral wires

To next fixture

Hot wires

To switch

Two cables

...OUTDOOR WIRING & LIGHTING

One simple method is to install an outdoor box back-to-back with an existing indoor box. Pull the indoor device from its box, remove a knockout, drill a hole through the house siding, and screw the new box in place. Then feed nonmetallic sheathed cable (NM) through the hole, leaving 8 inches of cable on each side. CAUTION: Be sure to shut off power to the circuit before beginning work.

It's also easy to add a watertight extender ring to an existing outdoor box—or even a porch light—and run new wire from there.

Installing an indoor switch and timer. By wiring in a switch and timer as shown in the drawing at left, you can turn the pump or lights on and off by hand or let the timer do it for you.

Choosing types of cable and conduit. The size wire that you must use depends on the total wattage ratings of the lighting fixtures you'll connnect to the system. Here are the maximum ratings for some typical wire sizes:

#14 wire—1440 watts at 120 volts

#12 wire—1920 watts at 120 volts

#10 wire—2880 watts at 120 volts

Many electrical codes require the use of rigid conduit for outdoor lighting. Plastic conduit, though lighter and less expensive than steel, must lie at least 18 inches underground. Steel conduit, on the other hand, can be as little as 6 inches underground. Run two thermoplastic-insulated wires (TW) through steel conduit, which is self-grounding; run three TW wires (including a ground wire) through plastic.

Some codes allow the use of flexible three-wire underground feeder cable (UF) instead of rigid conduit; the cable must be buried at least 18 inches deep. Work with UF cable in the same way you'd work with NM cable. Before covering the cable with dirt, lay a redwood board on top of it so you won't accidentally spade through it at a later time.

For details about working with conduit and cable, as well as more information on installing an outdoor electrical system, consult an electrical materials supplier or an electrician.

Hooking up the fixtures. Unless your new fixture includes a cover plate for wire connections, you'll need to furnish an accessible watertight box nearby. In most locales, metal conduit is required between the fixture and the ground.

Fixture installation varies according to type and style, so be sure to follow the manufacturer's instructions carefully. The drawing at left shows two typical arrangements.

Adding 12-volt Lighting

To install a 12-volt system, you'll need a transformer, some two-wire outdoor cable, and a set of 12-volt fixtures. To activate the system, you connect the transformer, and perhaps a separate switching device, to an existing power source.

Choosing wire thickness. Most low-voltage outdoor fixtures use stranded wire cable, the size of the wires in the cable depending on the aggregate wattage of the fixtures to be served. Here are the appropriate sizes for some typical wattages:

    #14 wire—up to 144 watts at 12 volts
    #12 wire—up to 192 watts at 12 volts
    #10 wire—up to 288 watts at 12 volts

Installing a transformer. Most transformers for outdoor lights are encased in watertight boxes, but to be safe, plan to install yours in a sheltered location at least a foot off the ground.

If you don't already have an outlet into which to plug the transformer, use an outlet equipped with a ground fault circuit interrupter (GFCI).

Though many transformers have built-in switches, some do not, in which case installing a separate switch indoors will probably prove more convenient than installing it outside.

Most transformers for home use are rated from 100 to 300 watts, which shows the total allowable wattage of the fixtures serviced. The higher the rating, the more lengths of 100-foot cable—up to a total of four—the transformer can supply power through; each length extends like a spoke from the transformer.

To connect one or more low-voltage cables to the transformer, simply wrap the bare wire ends of each cable clockwise around the screw terminals on the transformer and tighten the terminals.

Connecting fixtures to the cable. Once the transformer is in place and you've decided where to put the fixtures, you'll need to hook them into the cable or cables leading from the transformer.

With some fixtures, pierce the cable with a screw-down connector already attached to the back of the fixture. With others, you must screw an unattached connector to the main cable and to the end of a short cable leading from the fixture. Neither of these types of connector requires removing insulation from the cable.

A few fixture brands require splicing into the main cable with wirenuts. For these, use plastic housing boxes to insulate splices that can't be pushed back into the fixtures.

Wiring 12-volt Fixtures

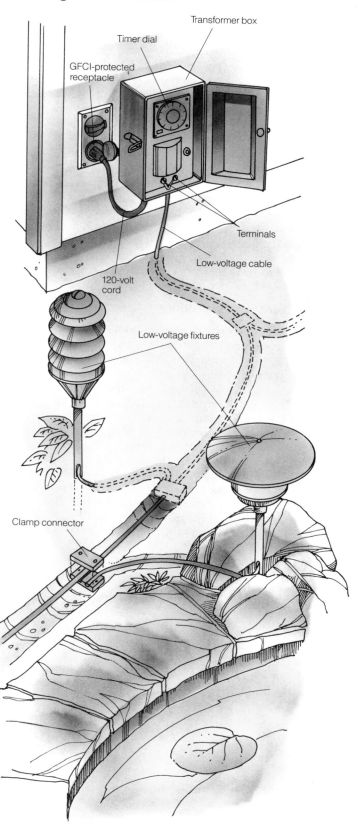

Transformer box
Timer dial
GFCI-protected receptacle
Terminals
Low-voltage cable
120-volt cord
Low-voltage fixtures
Clamp connector

MAINTAINING YOUR POOL

Once your garden pool is installed, you'll want to embark on a careful maintenance program to keep it in top shape. The following pages are intended as a quick reference guide to common procedures, problems, and their remedies. In addition, always read and follow the manufacturer's instructions in the owner's manuals for your pool hardware.

Maintaining a pool requires very few pieces of equipment. A hose-powered pool vacuum (see the drawing below), a leaf skimmer, and nylon-bristled brushes are the basic units. Aluminum handles that fit the vacuum cleaner, leaf skimmer, and brushes are available in lengths from 8 to 16 feet. You may choose from a wide variety of other accessories, but nothing more is really necessary.

Pool Cleaning Procedure

Although a properly balanced pool should keep itself in working condition for long periods at a stretch, an occasional draining and cleaning may be required.

Generally, fall and spring are the two best times for a pool-cleaning project. In fall, leaves have freshly fallen and you can extract them before they rot on the pool bottom, robbing plants and fish of oxygen. Also, it's the time to bring in tender water plants for the winter months (see page 94 for details) and to trim back dead stems and leaves. But spring is good too, just as the water warms up, plant life takes off, and fish are once again active and feeding. "Spring cleaning" is an especially apt term for fish ponds, as that's the time that fish diseases tend to swing into high gear.

If you've installed a main drain, it's easy to empty the pool; otherwise, drain it with a pump, or use a hose as a siphon to drain the water to a nearby low-lying area. Remove the bottom sediment and leaves, being careful not to damage a liner or shell.

If you have fish, remove them from the pool: drain the water part of the way down, then net the fish and move them to a shaded fiberglass holding tank, a large aquarium, or a large plastic garbage can filled with water. Shade the temporary container and, if possible, add some aeration in the form of a pool pump or at least a small aquarium aerator.

Carefully inspect the pool shell or liner, especially if you suspect leaks. Obviously, this is the time to correct any problems (see "Pool Repairs," pages 92–93).

To clean pool walls and bottom, simply spray them with a strong jet from your garden hose; then drain the pool once more before refilling it. Always use restraint when cleaning—strong scrubbing or scraping can remove all beneficial bacteria from the pool.

Refurbishing a concrete garden pool is a little more involved. First drain the pool. Scrub the sides (including tile) and bottom with a long-handled, stiff-bristled brush dipped in a solution of one part muriatic acid and one part water. Use this with caution, it's caustic; you'll need rubber gloves and eye protection. Rinse the pool with a strong jet from the garden hose and let it dry for 1 to 2 days; then wash it again with a solution of trisodium phosphate (dissolve according to label instructions). Rinse again with water and allow the pool to dry overnight.

Maintenance Tools & Accessories

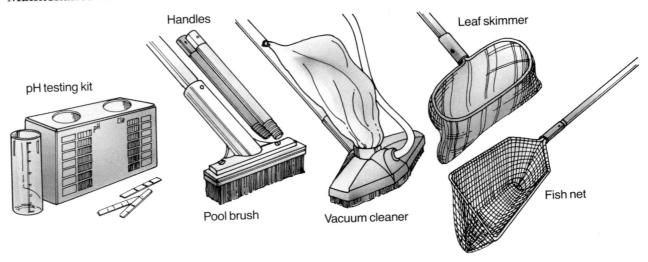

pH testing kit

Handles

Pool brush

Vacuum cleaner

Leaf skimmer

Fish net

To paint the pool surface, use a special epoxy or rubber-base paint (available in many colors). Brush or roll on the first coat, let it dry for 2 days, and apply a second coat. A gallon covers about 250 square feet. Before refilling the pool, let the paint dry for 14 days. Paint lasts 4 to 6 years if you keep the water clean.

Water Chemistry

Water chemistry in a garden pool refers to the balancing of several factors critical to water quality and the happiness of any water plants or fish. Measure the pH, or potential hydrogen, of your pool water before introducing plants or fish, and on a regular basis thereafter, which tells you where the water is on the acidity/alkalinity scale. On a logarithmic scale of 0 (total acidity) to 14 (total alkalinity), the ideal pH range for a garden pool is 6.8 to 7.6.

Soda ash or sodium bicarbonate raises the pH; phosphoric acid, sodium bisulfate, or vinegar will lower it. Most of these products are available under simpler proprietary names. A test kit that shows acid and alkali demand helps determine how much of either acid or alkali to add to the water. With some kits, you test the water by adding a reagent, in liquid or tablet form, to a precise amount of pool water contained in a device called a test block; comparing the resulting color variations with those shown on the test block tells what chemicals are needed. Other kits use paper strips that change color when dipped into the pool water. Again, the resulting hue is compared with a printed chart for interpretation. Test kit reagents must be fresh; throw them away once they're over 12 months old.

In addition to pH testing, you should test a fish pond for ammonia and nitrite levels. In light of the nitrogen cycle (see page 59), concentrations of both ammonia and nitrites should be as low as possible. You can buy separate test kits to monitor these factors, or a multi-test kit that measures pH, ammonia, and nitrites. To alter either ammonia or nitrites, small water changes are necessary until the levels come down to undetectable levels.

Both chlorine and chloramines are toxic to fish. Chlorine will dissipate out of standing water in a few days, but you'll need to take chemical steps if your water supply has chloramines added to it. Proprietary chemicals are available for dealing with both chlorine and chloramines; even small amounts of water for "topping up" must be treated in problem areas.

CALCULATING POOL VOLUME

Prescribing a pump, a filter, water treatment, or fish medication all hinge on a working knowledge of your pool's capacity in gallons. Generally, to find a pool's volume first calculate its area, which corresponds to the length times the width, then multiply the area by the average depth and a conversion factor (7.5). The trick is finding the "length and width" of an informal pool! If you can't find a shape below that approximates your pool, divide the outline up into units of simpler shapes, figure the volume of each chunk, and add them together for the total.

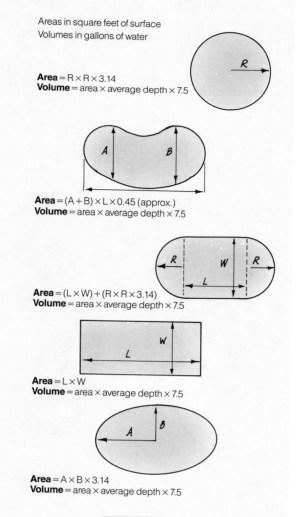

Areas in square feet of surface
Volumes in gallons of water

Area = R × R × 3.14
Volume = area × average depth × 7.5

Area = (A + B) × L × 0.45 (approx.)
Volume = area × average depth × 7.5

Area = (L × W) + (R × R × 3.14)
Volume = area × average depth × 7.5

Area = L × W
Volume = area × average depth × 7.5

Area = A × B × 3.14
Volume = area × average depth × 7.5

Maintaining Pool Hardware

The owner's manual for your pump outlines the maintenance the equipment requires. Usually, you'll only need to clean the debris from the strainer basket. To remove the basket, shut off the pump; if the pump is below water level, turn off any valves. Then take off the cover, lift out the basket, and either clean it or replace it with a spare. Though most pumps are self-priming, they may lose prime when the basket is removed. To prime the pump, take off the basket cover, start the pump, and within a few seconds it should be pumping water free of air bubbles. If not, try the priming procedure one more time. Running a pump dry or with air entering the system can overheat and do serious damage to both pump and motor. Inspect pump and filter once a month, or whenever you notice the water getting dirty.

If a submersible pump is causing problems, check the volute (intake pipe), which is held on by a few screws. Clean it, and the impeller, with a strong jet of water and reassemble the pieces.

To clean a cartridge filter, just remove the cartridge and hose it off, directing the water at an angle to the cartridge to remove the dirt. Return it to the housing, replace the cover and seal it, and restart the system.

A biological filter's media bed requires a light raking about once a month to remove accumulated debris. About twice a year, you'll need to either vacuum or backflush the system to get rid of excess sludge and sediments. A properly sized and maintained media bed should last several years.

A pressurized-sand filter needs more frequent backwashing. The filter has a valve, either slide or rotary, that controls the flow of water. If you must backwash your filter often and notice debris in the pool, open the filter and check the condition of the bed. If you find caked dirt in the sand, it's time to replace the sand.

Pool Repairs

Flexible liners, fiberglass shells, and concrete may develop cracks or leaks due to an accident or just

Cleaning Pump & Filter

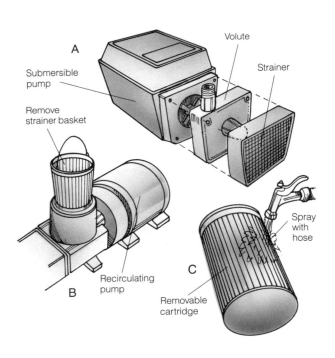

A submersible pump's intake may clog: to clean, remove the strainer and volute (A). Empty a recirculating pump's strainer basket regularly (B). Filters need attention, too: a cartridge filter requires a regular hosing down (C).

Repairing a PVC Liner

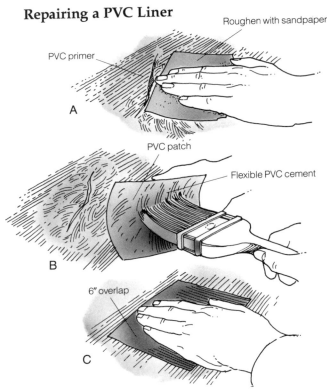

To repair the typical flexible liner, first prime and sand the damaged area (A), apply PVC solvent cement to both liner and patch (B), and smooth the patch firmly into place (C). If possible, weight the patch until it dries.

eventual wear and tear. Here's how to attack the problems.

Repairing a flexible liner. PVC and most other flexible liners can be repaired by patching with scraps of the original liner (see drawing on facing page); use the adhesive available from the manufacturer as recommended. Patch butyl-rubber liners with the 4-inch tape and adhesive made for joining seams.

Fiberglass repairs. Gelcoat deterioration detracts from the pool's appearance but rarely constitutes a serious problem. To repair a crack, use a standard fiberglass repair kit, containing sections of fiberglass and a two-part epoxy adhesive consisting of resin and hardener. If serious cracks are evident, you have an improperly supported shell; drain the pool and check its structural support.

A coat of epoxy paint improves the appearance of an older fiberglass pool. Be sure to follow the recommendation of the paint manufacturer; preparing the surface properly before painting is essential if the paint is to adhere.

Concrete repairs. Masonry sealers, primarily of Portland cement, chemical combinations, or both, will stop seepage through minor cracks and crazing. Most require a clean pool surface and two coats.

Portland cement—or hydraulic patching mixtures containing Portland cement—can be pressed into a crack after enlarging it with a cold chisel (see drawing below). Again, follow the instructions provided by the manufacturer. Several quick-drying compounds are formulated for making repairs underwater.

If your concrete pool has deteriorated to the point where it needs major repairs, you may want to consider installing a new shell inside the old one. Treating the old pool as a big hole in the ground, you or a contractor can add new concrete, slip a fiberglass shell inside the old pool, or drape a flexible liner over the inside. You can then add new edging and borders to the pool, as well as refurbish any mechanical systems. If you must run new pipes or conduit through old concrete, bore the holes with a core drill.

Refurbishing a Concrete Pool

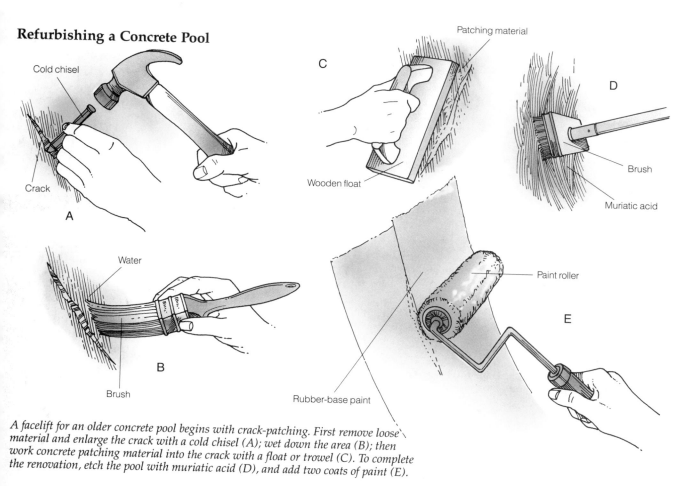

A facelift for an older concrete pool begins with crack-patching. First remove loose material and enlarge the crack with a cold chisel (A); wet down the area (B); then work concrete patching material into the crack with a float or trowel (C). To complete the renovation, etch the pool with muriatic acid (D), and add two coats of paint (E).

Fish Disease Reference Chart

Disease	Symptoms
Anchor worm Parasite	Tiny twiglike worms, up to ½ inch in length, attach themselves to skin; twin egg sacs may be visible at end.
Cloudy eye Nonspecific	As the name indicates, symptom is milky cloud over eyes; fish loses energy, appetite.
Columnarius **(mouth fungus)** Bacteria	As indicated at left, really a bacteria, not a fungus. Usually attacks head and mouth region. Contagious.
Dropsy **(pinecone** **disease)** Bacteria	Scales stand out from body as on a pinecone, hence the name. Swollen abdomen is common. Usually fatal.
Finrot/Tailrot Bacteria	Begins with light, foggy patches; progresses to bloody and rotted tail or fins. Indicative of unclean pond conditions.
Fish lice Parasite	Twin suckers attach to skin; lice are light green or brown, up to ½ inch in diameter, hard to see unaided; fish rub against pool sides and rocks in effort to "brush off" lice.
Flukes **(gill or skin)** Parasites	Fish swim with jerky motion, mouth at surface as if exhausted (if gill flukes). Fish skin appears whitish; fish attempt to rub against objects in pond (if skin flukes).
Fungus Fungus	Cotton- or wool-like appearance on body or fins. Attacks previously injured or stressed fish. May appear whitish or even greenish (mixed with algae).
Ich **(white spot)** Parasite	White spots may cover body; on close observation, "noodlelike" parasites may be visible. Fish rub against objects.
Leeches Parasite	Flattened worms, up to 1 inch long, brown or greyish in color.
Oxygen depletion Water condition	Fish mouth at surface, appear exhausted.
Ulcer **(hole-in-the-side** **disease)** Nonspecific	Ulcer appears on fish body; often fatal.

Plant Care

Remove yellowing leaves, faded flowers, and fruits periodically. Lopping shears or pole pruners are convenient tools if you have to reach far out over the water. Established plants need regular fertilizing during the growing season: feed them by burying slow-release 20-10-5 fertilizer tablets in their root zones, or by broadcasting dry pellets. (Use fertilizers with restraint in fish ponds, however.) Most water plants benefit from seasonal thinning and/or dividing.

Aphids, the commonest pest of water lilies, can usually be controlled by washing the plants with a garden hose, or if you have fish, they will soon consume the aphids. For heavier infestation, apply oil spray at growing-season strength; this will not adversely affect fish, snails, or plants. Spray on cloudy days or in the evening to prevent leaf scorch.

BT (Bacillus thuringiensis) is one insecticide safe for use near pools and is effective for combating caterpillars and other pests that feed on your marginal plants. A variety of BT is designed for eradicating mosquitos, but if you have fish, you should have no problem.

First frost marks the time to protect your hardy water plants: lower them to the bottom of the pool, cover them with plastic, or—best of all—bring the containers indoors for the winter, keeping the plants warm and moist in a snug greenhouse. Tropical water lilies and other warmth-loving plants are considered annuals in cold climates.

Caring for Fish

Fish don't ask for much, but a few basic procedures will keep them happy and healthy.

Spring cleaning. Spring is the time that water warms up and fish resume active feeding; it's also the time that fish diseases hit their stride. In this light, spring is the best time for a thorough inspection of your fish, shell or liner, and pump and filter system.

Overwintering. If your pond is 18 inches or deeper, you shouldn't have to worry about it freezing solid—especially if you keep a pump in operation. Lack of oxygen can be a problem, though; you may wish to run a small pool de-icer that keeps a small hole open to allow some air exchange. An improvised pool cover—netting and straw, canvas awning material, plastic grid and opaque sheeting—or more formal glazing can help maintain the water temperature, although a small pool heater is the premier choice.

Of course, if you have a pond or tub garden with just a few goldfish, simply move them to warmer quarters when winter winds howl.

Diseases. Most fish diseases are a result of stress, which weakens a fish's natural ability to fight off bacteria or parasites. Stressful conditions include overcrowding, rough handling and transport, insufficient oxygen, temperature swings, and toxins in the water. If pool conditions are up to par, you should have little trouble—especially after the fish have been in the pool for awhile—but make it a habit to observe your fish on a regular basis.

Fish diseases are either due to parasites, bacteria, or a fungus. To help you identify the problem, see the chart on the facing page.

Pet stores and mail-order sources sell many proprietary medications for treating fish diseases. Standard treatments for parasites include trichlorfon, and a mixture of malachite green and formalin. A variety of wide-spectrum antibiotics treat bacteria and fungus. A salt bath can help clear up many fish diseases. Mix in rock salt at the rate of 44 pounds per 1,000 gallons of pool water; or treat isolated fish for 1 hour at twice that concentration. A salt bath is a one-time proposition: salt concentrations build up in the water until flushed out.

Consult a veterinarian, koi expert, koi club, or textbook for help with any problem you don't understand. If you have a biological filter, be sure that whatever treatment you choose will not affect the bacteria in your filter media.

POOLS

BY MAIL

Flexible liners, fiberglass shells, submersible pumps, fountain jets, float valves, water lilies, oxygenating plants, fish food: here are places where you can access all the above and more. Some mail-order sources even send goldfish and koi (by express mail only, of course)! Be forewarned: these catalogs can be habit-forming.

This is only a partial listing, including a sampling of large, national mail-order sources; smaller, more regional companies, plus those specializing in water plants or koi, abound. Garden pool enthusiasts and builders can steer you to local favorites—or try a nearby koi club, a garden supplier, or the phone book.

Hermitage Garden Pools
P.O. Box 361
Canastota, NY 13032

Kingkoi International
5879 Avis Lane
Harrisburg, PA 17112

Lilypons Water Gardens
P. O. Box 10
Lilypons, MD 21717

McAllister Water Gardens
7420 St. Helena Highway
Yountville, CA 94599

Paradise Water Gardens
14 May St.
Whitman, MA 02382

Serenity Ponds & Streams
4488 Candleberry Ave.
Seal Beach, CA 90740

S. Scherer and Sons
104 Waterside Ave.
Northport, NY 11768

Slocum Water Gardens
1101 Cypress Gardens Blvd.
Winter Haven, FL 33880

Van Ness Water Gardens
2460 N. Euclid Ave.
Upland, CA 91786

Waterford Gardens
74 East Allendale Rd.
Saddle River, NJ 07458

Wicklein's Aquatic Farm & Nursery, Inc.
1820 Cromwell Bridge Rd.
Baltimore, MD 21234

INDEX

The DBM Career Continuation Program

Participant Workbook

DBM

DRAKE BEAM MORIN

TABLE OF CONTENTS

4. The Resume

5. Oral Communication

6. References

CHAPTER ONE
Adapting to Change

"Open a new window, open a new door, travel a new highway that's never been tried before..."

— Mame Dennis Burnside, *Auntie Mame*

POINTS OF INTEREST

In this chapter, you will learn to:

- ♦ Manage change so that it works on your behalf.
- ♦ Understand current trends that affect work opportunities.
- ♦ Positively Activate The Career Continuation Program.
- ♦ Implement ideas for an effective search for work.
- ♦ Create sound financial analysis and planning.
- ♦ Make the most of your Career Continuation opportunity.

Internal Psychological Process of Change

Every external change sets off an emotional chain of events called a "transition period." This transition period is a natural process that occurs within us. It allows us time to deal with current issues and concerns, while letting go of the past. Depending on your life experiences and how you have dealt with other transitions in the past, this process will vary in length and type of reaction.

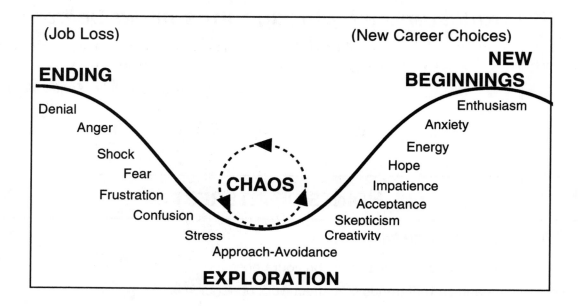

THE "NINE SQUARE" MODEL
DEGREES OF CHANGE

The choices in front of you vary in complexity in at least two dimensions: either the type of job or the type of industry. Those variables are combined into the model shown below. If you were basically content in your previous job with only a few things you wanted to modify, shift towards Squares two, three or four. Squares five and six require a re-organization of your skills to utilize a different array to facilitate a new career path. If most of what you were doing in your former job did not bring satisfaction, consider Squares seven, eight and nine. These are movements towards complete and drastic change. The farther away from Square #1, the longer and more difficult the transition will be.

Everyone perceives change with a different comfort level but regardless of your choice and the associated degree of change, *it is always necessary to put together a plan of action*.

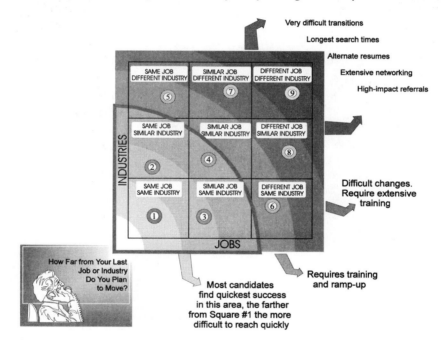

Regardless of the degree of change you take on, the process will be the same: Ending, Exploration, New Beginning.

MANAGING CHANGE

THE TRANSITION PROCESS

Directions:

1. Look at the illustration of the transition process. Assess the primary phase you are in (**Endings, Exploration, New Beginnings**) at this point in your personal transition process. Then, describe your reactions and mind-set.

Phase: _____

Reactions/Mind-Set:

Exercise #1-1, cont.

2. What things might/will you be *losing* as a result of this change & what coping skills and strategies can you apply?

WHAT I MIGHT/WILL LOSE	COPING STRATEGY

3. What things may you be *gaining* as a result of this change & what coping skills and strategies can you apply?

WHAT I MAY GAIN	COPING STRATEGY

Exercise #1-2

LEARNING FROM A SUCCESSFUL PAST CHANGE EVENT

Directions:

Think of a significant change in your personal or work life during your adult years. This should be a situation that was initially challenging or dramatic for you (or those around you), but *one that eventually worked out successfully.*

Examples might include: Changing careers, getting married, losing a job, relocating. Choose an event that you will feel comfortable sharing with others in the group.

1. Describe the change event and how you initially reacted to it.

_____

_____

2. How did you feel after a few weeks or months?

_____

_____

3. What resources did you draw upon to successfully manage the transition? What actions did you take?

_____

_____

4. What was the outcome of this change event?

_____

_____

5. What strategies and/or coping skills did you use to make your transition process a positive one?

_____

_____

TRENDS THAT WILL IMPACT YOUR SEARCH

Just as most businesses pay careful attention to new trends and adjust their strategies accordingly so must you. **You are now in business for yourself.** Not only must you figure out what you have of value to sell, you must also develop an understanding of the marketplace in which you will sell your wares.

The following is a list of current and emerging business trends that are affecting the way organizations conduct business.

1. **Globalization.** The availability of modern technology means that we are now dealing with a more accessible world economy, in which many workers are playing.

2. **Outsourcing/virtual organizations** The need to cut overhead and operating costs is driving organizations to outsource functions that historically were handled by internal departments. Many companies are moving towards the virtual organization whereby only the major functions are in-house while all the non-proprietary functions are outsourced.

3. **Commitment to Customer Focus.** Customers worldwide are demanding and receiving what they want, when they want it, and at a price they consider to be acceptable. Companies that are not up to the challenge are quickly being eliminated.

4. **Diversity.** While our formally insular business world thrived without it, today's world demands an understanding of the value of diversity and how to use it to create a competitive edge.

5. **Organizational Structure Redesign.** Companies that are truly customer focused find that flatter organizations drive down costs, improve customer response time and are more adaptable to change.

6. **The Demands of Stockholders.** Enhancing stockholder value is an ongoing trend that is experiencing greater emphasis, often resulting in cost-cutting strategies and a focus on short-term profitability.

7. **Rapidly Evolving Technology.** The availability of information and the evolution of technology has eliminated positions by automating many labor-intensive functions. It has also changed how business people communicate and manage, enabling small companies to compete in large-company markets.

8. **Stockholder emphasis.** Some organizations have a broader perspective than simply stockholder emphasis. They realize the anyone who has a vested interest in the company is an important consideration. This could be the employees, the stockholders, the community and the customer.

9. **Entrepreneurship.** The focus of organizations is on individual innovation and creativity.

THE DBM CAREER CONTINUATION PROGRAM

A career change is traumatic regardless of whether it is personally initiated or thrust upon you. You are going from a familiar situation where you "know the rules" to an unfamiliar one with many unknowns. The unknowns will trigger a range of emotions from resentment, anger or fear to relief or excitement. The task that faces you will be made easier or more difficult by how you harness and control these emotions. Your emotions, no matter how deep, sincere, or justified, will not make the task go away. **Emotions, however, are comprised of energy. Decide now....Will you use those emotions to power positive constructive actions or to sustain destructive, non-productive actions that will drain you?** A major step in gaining control is productive activity.

The DBM Career Continuation Program is based on extensive research using the most up-to-date strategies, techniques and practices. Its purpose is to quickly help you locate the position most appropriate to your background, skills and interests.

DBM CAREER CONTINUATION PROGRAM

Preparation: What do I have to sell a prospective employer?

Target Marketing: To whom shall I sell my skills, abilities & motivation?

Qualifying the prospective employer: Do I want to work here?

Closing the deal.

DISCOVERY	DIRECTION	DISCUSSION	DECISION

Pre-planning	Self Assessment	Resume	Networking Research, Targeting, & Campaigning	Interviewing & Follow-Up	Negotiating	Transition
Home Office Set-Up	Skills/Knowledge	Resume Type vs. Search	Strategy	Interview Types	Strategy	Accepting The Job
Select Mentor	Satisfiers/ Dissatisfiers	Approach	Research	Active Listening	Evaluation	Announcing New Job To Your Network
Schedule Of Milestones	Accomplishments (PARS)	Resume Components	Sifting	Letters	Contracts	Creating Good Working Relations With New Manager
Define: Record Keeping Procedures	Communication Style	Electronic Media Considerations	Targeting	Preparation Questions		
Financial Resources	Work Preferences	Career Shifting	Campaigning			Planning For The Future
	Employee Selection Criteria		Weekly Action Plan			
			Campaign Stalls...			
			Resume Revisions To Fit Market			
			90-Second Introduction			

DISCOVERY, DIRECTION, DISCUSSION, DECISION

As you can see, there is an evolving process for getting control beginning with **Discovery** and ending with the **Decision**. These macro's are broken down into their component parts:

Discovery: Prepare -- You need to be ready to present yourself with opportunities.

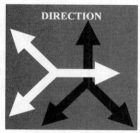

Direction: Target Market -- You need to determine what kinds of organizations would have an interest in your skills.

Discussion: Qualify the prospective employer -- You want to make sure that you are interested in them.

Decision: Close the deal -- and like any good sales person, you want to close the deal to everyone's mutual satisfaction.

MANAGING YOUR TASK

GET CONTROL

- **Set a transition timeline.** Ask yourself two questions. "When must I be working?" "When do I want to be working?" Then plan accordingly.

- **Create a Plan.** Plan, organize, and implement your career transition/work search in a formal, written format just as you would any large, complicated work project.

- **Set specific goals with action steps and dates for their completion.** Goals need to be realistic and attainable. Many small ones, add up to successful large ones.

- **Prioritize and schedule your time.** Build and maintain a daily and weekly schedule.

MAINTAIN YOUR MENTAL AND PHYSICAL HEALTH

- **Commit to balance.** Find ways to maintain a balance in your life so you don't burn out. Although we stress that a career search is a full-time job in itself, downtime can help renew creativity, energy and self-esteem.

- **Select a Mentor.** Find a person to whom you can report progress at a regularly scheduled time either in person or by telephone (once a week for an hour is good). This person should be someone you respect who is a good listener. A mentor need not be an expert in your field or in job hunting; he/she is not an "advisor". The purpose of meeting regularly with a mentor is to provide you with a flesh and blood focal point. At this time you will present your progress of the past week and your specific action items for the next week. This is not a social event.

- **Build a support system.** Take advantage of the motivation and help others can provide. Keep your family and friends involved.

- **Use outside resources.** Use federal, state and local resources designed to assist transitioning workers. Religious organizations and other service groups offer both assistance and support. Check the business calendar section of your newspaper.

TAKE CARE OF DETAILS

- **Commit your time.** Your current full time job is to find your next opportunity. This means 40-50 hours per week.

- **Create a Home Office.** You need to set up a dedicated space for an office and equip it with the appropriate supplies and tools.

- **Implement Record Keeping Forms/Procedures.** As you progress through your search, you will amass a great deal of information, correspondence, materials, etc. You will need to keep it organized and instantly accessible. At the least, you will need forms and a system for:

    ◊ Tracking on-going Action Items of desired accomplishments and due dates.
    ◊ Keeping track of people with whom to network.
    ◊ Keeping a correspondence/contacts log organized by company so you know when, what and to whom you've communicated and when, what and by whom the next action is required.

Exercise #1-3

BUDGETING FOR TRANSITION

"When must I be working?" "When do I want to be working?" These two questions make financial issues a primary consideration during career transition. By analyzing your past income and current expenses, you can be more realistic in estimating future cash flow needs. The results of your analysis and planning will tell you how long you can afford to be out of work without implementing a contingency plan to provide interim financing. Also, while you are calculating...don't forget:

1. **Unemployment compensation:** When you have been involuntarily separated from your employer, you may be eligible for unemployment compensation. (Note: rules vary from state to state and country to country.) Be aware that it may take a few weeks to process the paperwork. Make an appointment with the state Labor Department/Unemployment Compensation Division to determine the extent of your benefits and filing requirements. (If you are in another country, check the local rules.)

2. **Company benefits:** Investigate any company benefits or conversion rights to which you are entitled. See your company human resources representative for information on this and other tax-related matters. Don't overlook your need to decide how these benefits will be paid out. Some companies have a deadline for your decisions (e.g., 30 days from termination to extend or convert life insurance, health insurance or exercise stock options).

3. **Tax matters:** Many of your search expenses may be tax deductible or reimbursable, so maintain good records. If you have accrued benefits payable to you at termination (e.g., thrift plans, vested pension), seek tax advice on how and when to receive any payouts. For example, pension payouts can often be tax sheltered by "rolling them over" into other investments.

    Obtain professional advice, especially if your termination prompts major financial decisions, such as investing lump sum payments or selling assets.

On the pages that follow, please fill in the appropriate information for your circumstances and make the calculations that are indicated.

Exercise #1-3

Monthly Income	Month 1	Month 2	Month 3	Month 4	Month 5	Month 6
Unemployment Compensation						
Severance pay						
Other Wages						
Other Sources						
TOTAL MONTHLY INCOME						

Monthly Expenses	Month 1	Month 2	Month 3	Month	Month 5	Month 6
Housing:						
Rent or Mortgage						
Maintenance						
Home insurance						
Taxes (Real Estate)						
Utilities:						
Electricity						
Heat						
Telephone						
Water						
Food/Drink						
Transportation:						
Gasoline/Oil						
Car repairs & maintenance						
Insurance, car payments						
Commuter expenses						
Education:						
Tuition, books						
Professional dues						
Newspapers, subscriptions						
Health/Personal:						
Health club						
Life insurance						
Doctors, dentists						
Pharmacy						
Hair/beauty						
Recreation/Entertainment:						
Meals out						
Vacation, trips						
Parties, presents, shows						
Hobbies, cable TV						
Household Purchases:						
Furniture						
Appliances						
Gadgets, supplies						
Clothing Purchases:						
Adults						
Children						
Taxes:						
Income (federal, state)						
Other						
Misc. Expenses						
TOTAL MONTHLY OUTGO						
DIFFERENCE:(Income-Outgo)						

Exercise #1-3, cont.

If your bottom line was a deficit, you must develop a contingency plan now. First go through your expenses and see which ones can be reduced or put off into the future. After re-totaling your budget numbers, if you're still projecting a deficit you must look for other sources of cash.

SOURCE	$ AMOUNT	TRANSACTION TYPE /TERMS /AVAILABILITY
Assets in Savings Account #1		
Assets in Savings Account #2		
Assets in Checking Account #1		
Assets in Checking Account #2		
Cash Available via Equity Loans		
Liquid Possessions:		
car		
boat		
jewelry		
other		
Lines of Credit:		
banks		
credit cards		
Liquid Investment Assets:		
Other Sources:		
family		
friends		

After you complete the above, select the cash generating options that are least painful but will get you through the short term. You can revisit this list if your search outlasts your budget.

Now that you have completed your budget review, what conclusions can you draw?

What is your financial time frame?

Are there tax consequences that need attention?

Summarize your findings on next page. Use extra paper if necessary.

Summarize your budgetary findings on this page. Use extra paper if necessary.

THIS OPPORTUNITY AND YOUR CAREER

This is the beginning of a new chapter in your career. It is an opportunity to take a fresh look at what you value, the environment in which you are the most productive, and the kind of work that brings you the most satisfaction. Consider the Career Continuation Program to be one portion of your total career/life management plan.

People who are successful at making work transitions today have:

- A plan in progress as part of ongoing career management

- Technical competence

- Transferable skills that reflect what the marketplace values

- Search and presentation skills

- Initiative and implementation strategies

- Resilience

PERSONAL DEVELOPMENT PLAN

While you prepare for work you may want to engage in a Personal Development Plan.

This time is also an opportunity to be proactive -- to take back the control in your life and make your own choices. You can augment your transition activities and design a long-range personal career development plan. Here are some ideas to consider:

- ◆ Take appropriate courses at a local college or university to learn new skills or update your current skills. Think, "I am re-energizing my mental battery."

- ◆ Browse through a bookstore with a good business section and select a few books for continuing your business education. Think, "Is there anything I've missed lately?"

- ◆ If you have been meaning to take off weight, get serious about a new diet regimen and begin an exercise program. Package your whole self!

- ◆ Join an organization such as Toastmasters or Dale Carnegie to upgrade your presentation and communication skills. Enjoy the experience...there could be lots of laughs to perk up your spirits. And, who knows who might be there....

- ◆ Join local business organizations or professional groups that are committed to developing the skills of their members. Here's an opportunity to learn and, at the same time, network.

- ◆ Become computer literate by enrolling in seminars or joining a local computer club. Or, ask your kids for some lessons...sometimes it's nice for them to feel valued and sharing this time is a good stress-reducer.

SUMMARY

The purpose of the DBM materials is to support your skills, search effort and self-confidence during this period of transition. Here are some important points to keep in mind:

- Recognize that the *work environment has undergone dramatic changes* in just a few years. It will undoubtedly continue to change rapidly.

- Realize that *any work or career change involves disruption and uncertainty.* To get through the difficult moments successfully requires knowledge of the process, patience with yourself and the marketplace, perspective and hard work.

- *Acknowledge* what you're leaving behind and the opportunities ahead of you.

- *Be open to learning a variety of techniques* that will help you assess your work-related skills, interests and characteristics. This will help you reach the marketplace and negotiate work offers.

- *Make a commitment of time, energy and attitude.* Steady progress can be made through strategic time management in order to achieve your goals as quickly as possible.

- *Find yourself a mentor.* "No Man Stands Alone" said John Doone. Human beings need support and an occasional helping hand. A mentor is perfect for this role. He or she is objective, yet committed to supporting your endeavors with a good ear and substantive feedback.

CHAPTER TWO
Self-Assessment
Determining What I Have To Sell

"It is better to light a candle than to curse in the darkness."

Chinese Proverb

POINTS OF INTEREST

In Chapter Two, you will:

- ♦ Participate in the self-assessment process.
- ♦ Identify your accomplishments and specific skills.
- ♦ Explore what you want from your career.
- ♦ Discover your Ideal Work Preferences.
- ♦ Align your self-assessment results with work opportunities.

Exercise #2-1

"ARE YOU READY?" CHECKLIST

Place a check beside those statements with which you agree:

❑ My career field is changing rapidly.

❑ My career field is not growing, or is shrinking.

❑ My industry is shrinking or changing rapidly.

❑ I have not been particularly happy in my work in recent years.

❑ My career interests have changed in recent years.

❑ I am close to retiring and do not have the same work needs that I had a few years ago.

❑ I am not sure what skills I have that could be transferred to a new career situation.

❑ I am not completely clear about the specific factors that bring satisfaction and fulfillment to my work.

❑ There have been recent personal changes in my life that might impact my work choices.

❑ My work has negatively impacted my health.

❑ I am not confident that I can clearly summarize my skills and qualifications on my resume.

Scoring: If you checked more than three boxes, you will want to make the commitment to complete the thorough self-assessment that follows in this chapter. It will prepare you to be successful in your search for work.

THE ASSESSMENT PROCESS

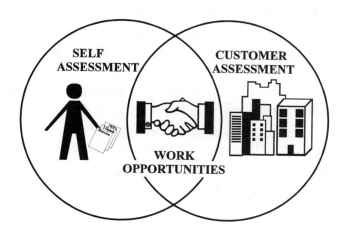

"Employers Ask..."

These are the key questions any interviewer or resume screener has in mind in evaluating a candidate for a potential assignment.

- ♦ *Can* He or She Do the Work? What competencies and specific skills does this candidate have and how do they match the requirements for success in this assignment or position? What kinds of work assignments motivate and satisfy this candidate?

- ♦ *How* Will He or She "Fit" into our Culture? How does her/his pattern of motivation fit with the work we need to have done? Overall, does the picture I get of this candidate's motivation and style fit with the culture of our organization?

SPECIFYING ACCOMPLISHMENTS USING PARS

The **PARS** formula will help you to describe and clarify your accomplishments.

P The *PERFORMANCE OBJECTIVE* for which you were accountable or for which you took responsibility. This presented you with an opportunity to exhibit your initiative or solve a problem.

A The *ACTION* you took in seizing the opportunity or solving the problem; usually begins with an *action verb* (see examples on Page 2-8).

R The *RESULTS* you obtained, expressed in quantifiable or numerical terms (dollars, percentages, time saved, money saved, sales volumes, revenues/profits, etc.) where relevant.

S The *ACCOMPLISHMENT STATEMENT* you compose from the above information, beginning with the Action and ending with the Result.

SAMPLE ACCOMPLISHMENT STATEMENTS

The following examples have been extracted from resumes. Some accomplishment statements illustrate the clarity and conciseness you want to achieve in your accomplishment statements. Others are not so well written. Please sort through these statements and

- Identify the result and the action portion of each statement;

- Distinguish between well-written and poorly written statements.

All Accomplishment Statements have an *Action and a Result*, **usually in that order.**

1. Reduced the annual security operating budget 22% by developing and implementing several cost savings projects while increasing the level of security.

2. Reorganized and consolidated accounting, analysis and forecasting activities, achieving a $50,000 annual cost saving.

3. Systematized a manual system for order intake, saving 8 processing days per month.

4. Created and conducted a selection interview training program for managers and supervisors, reducing candidate selection ratio from 1:15 to 1:5.

5. Reduced internal product rejections from 14% of sales to 2% and customer quality returns from 3% to 0.1%.

6. Initiated an Employee Opinion Survey that resulted in the implementation of new policies and procedures and significantly increased morale.

7. Reduced receivables from 45 days to 30 days.

8. Increased sales activities with new prospects and static accounts, expanding sales by 35%.

9. Designed equipment and techniques for a new chemical process that raised product market potential from $1 million to over $12 million per year.

10. Devised E-mail registry that saved my boss 12% of his discretionary time.

Notice........ Good Accomplishment Statements use action verbs - *Designed, Developed, Reduced, Systematized...* You will want to do the same with your own accomplishment statements.

ACTION VERBS FOR ACCOMPLISHMENT STATEMENTS

Action Verbs tell a prospective employer what you do. They imply energy, motivation, purpose and end results. When you write your accomplishments, make sure to use an action verb to describe your activity.3

Accelerated	Established	Persuaded	Stressed
Accomplished	Evaluated	Planned	Stretched
Achieved	Expanded	Presented	Structured
Administered	Financed	Processed	Succeeded
Analyzed	Forecast	Produced	Summarized
Approved	Formulated	Programmed	Superseded
Budgeted	Founded	Promoted	Supervised
Built	Generated	Proposed	Systematized
Completed	Headed	Provided	Terminated
Conceived	Implemented	Purchased	Traced
Conducted	Improved	Recommended	Tracked
Consolidated	Improvised	Recruited	Traded
Controlled	Increased	Redesigned	Trained
Converted	Influenced	Reduced	Transferred
Convinced	Innovated	Reorganized	Transformed
Coordinated	Installed	Researched	Translated
Created	Instituted	Revised	Trimmed
Cut	Introduced	Scheduled	Tripled
Delegated	Invented	Serviced	Uncovered
Delivered	Launched	Set up	Unified
Demonstrated	Led	Simplified	Unraveled
Designed	Maintained	Sold	Utilized
Developed	Managed	Solved	Vacated
Devised	Motivated	Sparked	Verified
Directed	Negotiated	Spearheaded	Widened
Doubled	Operated	Staffed	Withdrew
Earned	Organized	Started	Won
Edited	Originated	Streamlined	Worked
Eliminated	Performed	Strengthened	Wrote

Exercise #2-3

WRITING YOUR OWN PARS

Performance **O**bjective➔ **A**ction➔ **R**esult = Accomplishment Statement

Directions: In the space below, capture your career accomplishments using the PARS format. This will help you later both in the construction of your resume and as well as in networking and during interviews. Use as much space as you need to identify the P, A and R, then write your Accomplishment Statement. Skills and Key Words will be added to this later.

Employer/Job title:	Skills - KeyWords
P1	
A	
R	
S	
P2	
A	
R	
S	

Exercise #2-3, cont.

WRITING YOUR OWN PARS

Performance Objective➔ Action➔ Result = Accomplishment Statement

Directions:. In the space below, capture your career accomplishments using the PARS format. This will help you later both in the construction of your resume and as well as in networking and during interviews. Use as much space as you need to identify the P, A and R, then write your Accomplishment Statement. Skills and Key Words will be added to this later.

Employer/Job title:	Skills - KeyWords
P3	
A	
R	
S	
P4	
A	
R	
S	

WRITING YOUR OWN PARS

Performance **O**bjective➜ **A**ction➜ **R**esult = **Accomplishment Statement**

Directions:. In the space below, capture your career accomplishments using the PARS format. This will help you later both in the construction of your resume and as well as in networking and during interviews. Use as much space as you need to identify the P, A and R, then write your Accomplishment Statement. Skills and Key Words will be added to this later.

Employer/Job title:	Skills - KeyWords
P5	
A	
R	
S	
P6	
A	
R	
S	

WRITING YOUR OWN PARS

Performance **O**bjective➔ **A**ction➔ **R**esult = **Accomplishment Statement**

Directions:. In the space below, capture your career accomplishments using the PARS format. This will help you later both in the construction of your resume and as well as in networking and during interviews. Use as much space as you need to identify the P, A and R, then write your Accomplishment Statement. Skills and Key Words will be added to this later.

Employer/Job title:	Skills - KeyWords
P7	
A	
R	
S	
P8	
A	
R	
S	

Exercise #2-4

SAMPLE SKILLS AND KNOWLEDGE

The following list of Skills and Knowledge are listed by functional area. Check the skills for which you have background and expertise, jotting down your specific application in the margin. These are not all inclusive, so if you think of something else, add it to the list.

GENERAL MANAGEMENT & ADMINISTRATION

- Administration
- Strategic Planning
- Organizational Planning
- Project Management
- Contract/Union Negotiations
- Time Management
- Purchasing
- Directing Others
- Motivating Others

- Problem Solving
- Scheduling
- Supervision
- Communication: Verbal/Written
- Coaching/Counseling
- Decision Making
- Goal Setting
- Leadership
- Performance Appraisal

RESEARCH & ENGINEERING

- Research & Development
- Licensing/Patents
- Field Applied Research
- Process Engineering
- Synthesizing

- Process Development
- New Product Development
- Plant Design & Construction
- Diagnostics
- Scientific Methodology

SALES/MARKETING/CUSTOMER SERVICE

- Marketing
- Sales Development
- Retailing
- Fund Raising
- Promotional Writing
- New Business Development
- Cost Analysis

- Selling/Influencing/Persuading
- Advertising
- Purchasing
- Comparative/Competitive Analysis
- Strategic Planning
- New Business Development
- Communication

INFORMATION TECHNOLOGY

- Systems Development
- Hardware/Software Technology
- Information Management
- Business Systems Planning
- System Design & Programming
- Database Technology
- Human Resources Systems

- Data Center Operation
- Distributed Processing
- Distributed Systems
- Voice/Data Communication
- Performance Monitoring
- Financial Systems
- Networking

OPERATIONS

- Production
- Process Engineering
- Administration
- Quality Assurance
- Materials Management
- Management
- Systems Development
- Budget Planning
- Warehousing
- Project Direction

- Research & Development
- Construction
- Financial
- Distribution
- Inventory & Production
- Customer Service
- Procurement
- Expense Control
- Engineering
- Total Quality Management

FINANCE & ACCOUNTING

- Audit
- Strategic Financial Planning
- Treasury
- Internal Controls
- Capital Budgeting
- New Business Development
- Information Systems
- Foreign Exchange
- Actuarial/Rating Analysis
- Inventory Control Analysis

- Planning & Analysis
- General and Cost Accounting
- Credit
- Management Reporting
- General Tax Planning
- Cash Management
- Debt Negotiations
- Risk Management
- Pricing/Forecast Modeling
- Financial Data Processing

Exercise #2-4, cont.

HUMAN RESOURCES	
◆ Staff Planning & Management	◆ Labor Relations
◆ Union Avoidance	◆ Compensation/Benefits
◆ Community Relations	◆ Health & Safety
◆ Career Development	◆ Performance Evaluation & Measurement
◆ Career Counseling	◆ Wage & Salary Administration
◆ Policy & Procedures Planning	◆ Employee Relations
◆ Affirmative Action	◆ Training & Development
◆ Change Management	◆ Employee Communications
◆ Training Administration	◆ Staffing/Recruiting

IDENTIFYING YOUR SPECIFIC SKILLS

Directions:

1. If the skills you identified in Exercise #2-4 triggered ideas for accomplishments you overlooked, add them to those you created in Exercise #2-3.

2. Now you will complete Exercise #2-3. Review your **PARS** in Exercise #2-3. For each **Accomplishment Statement**, identify the specific **Skills** you used to achieve it.

3. Then capture those **Key Words** that you believe a recruiter would use to find a specialist in your field.

Example:

Accomplishment Statement: Identified redundant inventory by consolidating and centralizing inventory records resulting in a 20% reduction in excess inventory.

Skills:
  Database Setup
  Inventory Control
  Materials Management

Key Words:

      1. Database Setup   _____

      2. Inventory Control   _____

      3. Materials Management   _____

THE SUMMARY STATEMENT

A summary statement captures the essence of your experience, skills and accomplishments. It's a good place to use some of those key words, just in case the company uses electronic scanning.

Example: Dedicated, results-oriented supervisor with 10 years of increasing responsibilities in Client-Server, LAN, WAN environment. Effective problem-solver with strong goal orientation. Proven ability to set up new organizational framework as well as to make under-performing operations efficient. Skilled in JIT and JCL.

Directions:

In a few lines, write your summary statement.

Remember: It may be useful to create more than one summary, since you have the option to customize your resume.

Write your resume summary here.

_____

_____

_____

_____

_____

_____

_____

_____

_____

_____

_____

_____

WORK OBJECTIVE

You have just completed a very significant piece of work. You identified your accomplishments and the skills it took to achieve those accomplishments. This information needs to be channeled into getting your next job. As you look at the model below showing the various degrees of change, ask yourself, "Where do I want to go?".

Your Work Objective is the MISSION STATEMENT for your ideal career. Just as a company has a mission statement so must you and for the same reasons. You need a focal point for all your efforts and activities; one that embraces what you are or wish to be. When you know where you want to go, it is manifested with enthusiasm and confidence when presenting yourself. You need this same point of focus to engage the attention of potential employers so they will pursue a dialog with you. *You can have more than one Work Objective -- but if you do, treat each one separately as it will correspond to a different job needing a different resume or cover letter.*

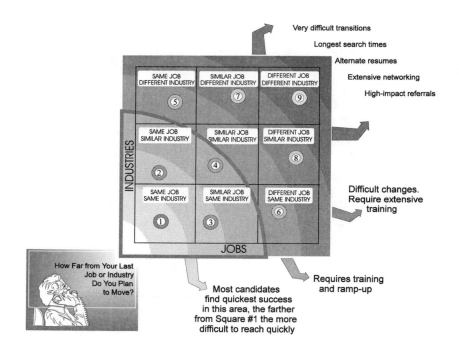

Regardless of the degree of change you take on, the process will be the same. You need an objective on which to focus your accomplishments, skills and abilities.

Exercise #2-7

WORK OBJECTIVE

A work objective tells the resume reader what you want to do. It focuses the attention of the reader in a specific direction.

Examples: - To obtain a full-time position in marketing. (1)

- To use my marketing expertise to introduce new products. (2)

- A marketing related executive function, with emphasis on the planning aspects of marketing management. (3)

All of the examples are good. Notice how each statement gets more specific. They get more specific because each writer had a clear idea of what s/he wanted to accomplish. One (1) wanted to work in the marketing department. The next person (2) wanted to work in the new product development department doing marketing. The last person (3) wanted to be an executive who, at the least, wanted to manage the planning aspects of the marketing function.

In the space below, start work on writing your work objective. The more specific you are the more you narrow your options . That isn't all bad -- you can't be everything to everyone! Perhaps you really want to be a marketing person in a new product area. Then say so. If all you want to do is work in marketing, then be less specific. It is totally up to you. Think about what you have discovered in the self-assessment and *write down what you want* in the form of a work objective.

Exercise #2-8

YOUR SATISFIERS AND DISSATISFIERS

Below are some common career issues that can be <u>classified as either</u> Satisfiers or Dissatisfiers. These are only examples. As you reflect on your career history, work to uncover the issues that are important to you.

Examples of Satisfiers	**Examples of Dissatisfiers**
Travel	Commuting
Managing employees	Direct sales
Managing change	Working in teams
Dealing directly with customers	Long hours (including nights and weekends)
Flexible hours	
	Pay for performance
Working on commission	Status
Working with little direction	Unrealistic deadlines
Moral/ethical standards	Routine
Dealing with budgets/numbers	Job security
Workaholic culture	Conflict
Structured environment	Managers

Directions:

In your mind, carefully review your work history and identify both the pleasant and the unpleasant parts. Then on the next page:

- In the left column, record "**Satisfiers**," the specific tasks and situations that brought you joy and satisfaction.

- In the right column, record the tasks and situations that you found unpleasant or unsatisfying, "**Dissatisfiers.**"

Exercise #2-8, cont.

SATISFIERS	DISSATISFIERS
– Perform scientific Research	– Commute
– Presentations	– routine tasks
– Attend Conferences	
– Journal Publishing	
– Project Leader	
–	

Satisfiers and Dissatisfiers are negotiables and will be discussion points with potential employers.

DEFINING YOUR IDEAL WORK PREFERENCES

In this exercise you will identify your Ideal Work Preferences (IWPs) and determine which are most important to you.

Directions:

Step 1. **Transfer your work objective from Exercise #2-7 so you will be focusing on it as you do the rest of the sheet.**

Step 2. List Your Ideal Work Preferences (IWPs). Based on your assessment data and practical issues you have already considered regarding your personal situation, lifestyle and finances, define your IWPs in the left-hand columns of the worksheets on the following pages. Your "Satisfiers" from Exercise #2-8 will give you a good start on this exercise. Add additional factors where necessary to the worksheets. For now, ignore the column on the right-hand side of the worksheets.

In thinking about your IWPs, be sure to take into account both *tangible* and *intangible* work factors:

♦ **Tangible aspects** can be observed and may even be quantified. Examples include responsibilities of the position, reporting relationships, organization size, industry, work location, salary and benefits.

♦ **Intangible aspects**, not directly observable, are related to the working climate. Examples include professionalism of the people who would be your colleagues, the managerial style of the organization, corporate culture and values.

In completing this step, *your objective is to compile the most complete and accurate description of your ideal work situation without regard to priorities or current possibilities.* As you progress through your work search, you will find that defining your IWPs is valuable (1) in assessing whether or not to change careers; (2) during interviews, when evaluating if a company is a good match for you; and (3) in negotiating offers with prospective employers.

You may want to begin by brainstorming ideas on another sheet of paper and then summarizing your thoughts on the worksheet.

Step 3. Weighting Your Ideal Work Preferences (IWPs)

Reality is what matters. *Assign a weight to each of your IWPs in terms of importance to you (M = Must have; 1 = lowest importance; 10 = highest importance). Assigning these weights now will help you to be objective in evaluating different career options and employment offers during your search.*

DEFINING YOUR IDEAL WORK PREFERENCES

Work Objective: _____

_____

_____

_____

TANGIBLE CRITERIA

Major Considerations	*Ideal Work Preferences*	Weight "M" = Must "10" = Highest "1" = Lowest
Industry: (Same, Related Or Different?)	National lab / university	
Geographic Location: (Location Base, Travel Requirements, Commuting Requirements, etc.)	US anywhere, live within 45 min	
Compensation Package: (Base & Bonus/ Profit Sharing, etc.)	$50 – $100 K	
Benefits: (Disability, Medical, Life Insurance, Vacation, etc.)	Medical – Vacation	
Company Profile: (Size of Company, Growth, Profitability, etc.)	100 ~ 1000 employees. R&D based	
Position / Goals: (Type of Work , Use of Talents, Promotion Potential, etc.)	Research Scientist (R&D)	
Basis of Promotion: (Merit, Tenure, etc.)	Tenure	

Exercise #2-9, cont.

INTANGIBLE CRITERIA

Major Considerations	*Ideal Work Preferences*	<u>Weight</u> "M" = Must "10" = Highest "1" = Lowest
Company Culture: *(Management Style, Work Diversity of People, etc.)*	Academic environment	
Lifestyle / Workstyle: *(White Collar, Open Collar, Flex-time, Telecommute, etc.)*		
Type of Boss:, *(Acts as Teacher or Mentor, Allows Freedom, Gives Feedback, Tolerates Trial-and-error Learning)*	Acts as teacher or mentor	
Other: *(Additional Personal Considerations)*		

Exercise #2-10

Using the Best Fit Analysis

Copy your IWPs to the left column, followed by the weight you assigned each one. Note: you do not have to use every category. You may find it useful to **make copies of this worksheet**. List options/offers you are considering across the top of your worksheet, and evaluate them using the following evaluation system:

- ♦ Yes/No   For each of the **Must Have** criteria

- ♦ 1 - 10   Degree to which the option/offer fits each of the other criteria

- ♦ 0   Cannot judge; get more information

Any option getting a "No" against a Must criterion is out of the running. Derive "best fit" totals for the remaining options by multiplying each criterion's weight (1-10) by the rating (1-10) you gave it.

The option that has met all the Must criteria and has highest "best fit" points is the position you should seriously consider. You should not be surprised at the results of these calculations if you have accurately reflected the priority of your needs.

On the next page, a sample sheet has been filled out to illustrate this part of the process. Under each major heading (e.g., Company, Position, etc.) you fill in your IWPs and their respective weights. Then you evaluate each of your options using columns 1 - 3.

The evaluation:

If you look at the options you will see that option 3 was dropped because it did not meet a Must criterion. Between options 1 and 2, option 2 was the clear winner because it fulfilled the criteria better than 1 and consequently got the higher "best fit" score. This is exactly what you will do to evaluate your options.

SAMPLE "BEST FIT" ANALYSIS

SAMPLE IDEAL WORK PREFERENCES	CAREER OPTIONS/OFFERS					
	Weighting	1: XYZ Corp.		2: ABC Corp.		3: TelpCon	
	(1-10)	Rating	Total[1]	Rating	Total	Rating	Total
Company							
Profitable/growing	M	Y	Y	Y	Y	N	N
Service/Utilities	M	Y	Y	Y	Y		
Stable performance	4	9	36	10	40		
Medium size (250-500)	6	10	60	10	60		
Position: Management							
Set policy; head operations	M	Y	Y	Y	Y		
Responsible for training	7	2	14	8	56		
Increase customer satisfaction	7	10	70	5	35		
Management/Style							
Service-oriented	8	10	80	10	80		
Team-oriented	6	9	54	8	48		
Empowering/autonomous	9	9	81	7	63		
Geographic Location							
Metropolitan Area (SE/SW)	9	2	18	10	90		
Compensation/Benefits							
$65-75K, 401K	8	6	48	10	80		
Excellent medical/hospitalization	8	7	56	9	72		
Relocation policy	6	0	0	5	30		
Lifestyle/Culture							
Moderate travel	5	3	15	5	25		
Progressive environment	6	5	30	6	36		
Family-oriented culture	M	Y	Y	Y	Y		
POINTS FOR "BEST FIT"			All Y's & 562		All Y's & 715		No

[1] Formula Total = Weight x Rating (except for the Must criteria)

Exercise #2-10, cont.

"BEST FIT" ANALYSIS

YOUR IDEAL WORK PREFERENCES - PAGE 1	CAREER OPTIONS/OFFERS						
Company	Weighting	1: _____		2: _____		3: _____	
	(1-10)	Rating	Total	Rating	Total	Rating	Total
Industry							
Geographic Location							
Compensation Package							
Benefits							
Company Profile							
Position/Goals							

Exercise #2-10, cont.

YOUR IDEAL WORK PREFERENCES - PAGE 2	CAREER OPTIONS/OFFERS					
Company	Weighting	1: _____		2: _____		3: _____	
	(1-10)	Rating	Total	Rating	Total	Rating	Total
Basis of Promotion							
Company Culture							
Lifestyle/Workstyle							
Type of Boss							
Other Personal Considerations							
TOTAL POINTS FOR "BEST FIT"							

SCORING YOUR I-SPEAK® SURVEY

I-SPEAK Your Language®, developed from research conducted by Dr. Carl Jung, reveals your individual communication style. Although everyone has four styles of communication available, one style tends to be dominant.

Familiarity with the four styles allows you to recognize your own and that of others, and will give you a quick sense of your best work fit and how to communicate most effectively.

At the end of the I-SPEAK® Survey (paper version) you will find instructions for tallying numbers to arrive at scores for I, T, F and S under both Favorable and Stress conditions.

❑ Tally these numbers as instructed.

- The letter with the highest score in the row labeled "Favorable" is the code **for your preferred communication style under favorable (i.e., low stress) conditions.**

- The letter with the next highest score in the row of scores labeled "Favorable" is your back-up score under favorable conditions.

- At the bottom of the score sheet is a row labeled "Stress Conditions."

- Your highest score there indicates **your preferred communication style under stress conditions**; and your second highest score is your back-up style under stress conditions.

❑ Circle the letters indicating your preferred and back-up communication styles under stress conditions.

- Think about these scores as you read on to interpret your results. Here is what your scores (the circled letters) represent.

I-SPEAK Your Language® Style Descriptions

Letter = Communication Style	Focus
I = Intuitor style	Conceiving, projecting, inducing

- ◆ Places emphasis on ideas, innovation, long-range thinking.
- ◆ Imaginative, "hard to pin down."
- ◆ May be perceived as long on vision, short on action.
- ◆ Orientation towards the future, not what has gone before.
- ◆ Values communication that is ground-breaking, "out of the box" creative.

T = Thinker style	Analyzing, organizing thoughts and activities in a logical fashion

- ◆ Responds to logic, reason and systematic inquiry.
- ◆ Functions in a steady, tenacious manner.
- ◆ Prefers to correctly and consistently relate facts from the present to the past and future.
- ◆ Emphasizes facts, well-documented conclusions and specifics.
- ◆ Values communication that is organized, systematic, fact-based and logical.

F = Feeler style	Understanding experience through emotions, values and response to feelings

- ◆ Focuses on human interaction and values.
- ◆ Seeks and enjoys stimulation of contact with others.
- ◆ Expresses concern for and an understanding of people.
- ◆ Relates human experiences to the context of the past.
- ◆ Values communication that sounds personal; relies on "real people" illustrations.

S = Senser style	Taking action mainly on the basis of sensory perceptions

- ◆ Focuses on action and activities that provide tangible, immediate feedback.
- ◆ May be viewed as the driving force within an organization.
- ◆ Sought out for energy and ability to translate ideas into products, sales and profits.
- ◆ Wants to know what others intend to do, what is expected of them and for what purpose.
- ◆ Values communication that is specific, pragmatic and bottom-line oriented.

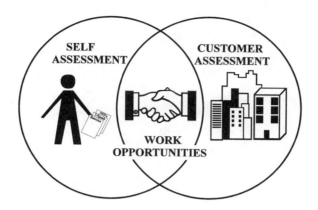

SUMMARY

Connecting Self-Assessment to your Search

A thorough self-assessment is a critical aspect of successful career transition.

- ◆ The assessment process will help you to:

  - Analyze what you have to offer before you begin your search

  - Articulate what you want during your search.

  - Help you to manage your career after your search is concluded

- ◆ Potential employers look for work competencies related directly to performance:

  - Skills

  - Knowledge Base

  - Experience

  - Accomplishments

Now it is time to target specific work goals and put your Discoveries to work at moving in a specific Direction.

CHAPTER THREE
Changing Careers

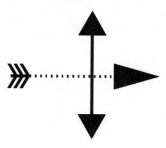

"Two roads diverged in a wood,
and I took the one less traveled by,
And that has made all the difference."

Robert Frost, *The Road Not Taken*

POINTS OF INTEREST

In Chapter Three you will investigate:

♦ Options for career changers

♦ How to identify your transferable skills

♦ The steps necessary to implement a career change plan

♦ Resources for retooling if you change careers

NINE-SQUARE MODEL OF DEGREES OF CHANGE

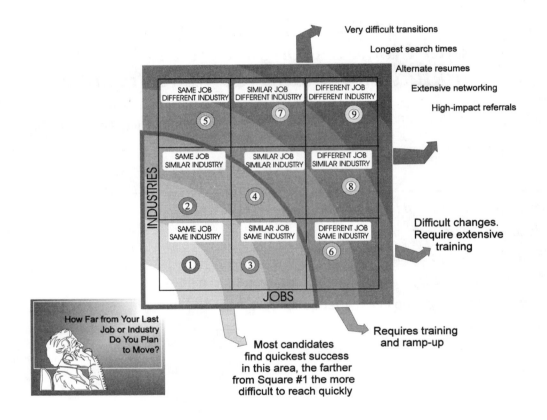

Very difficult transitions

Longest search times

Alternate resumes

Extensive networking

High-impact referrals

Difficult changes.
Require extensive
training

Requires training
and ramp-up

Most candidates
find quickest success
in this area, the farther
from Square #1 the more
difficult to reach quickly

How Far from Your Last
Job or Industry
Do You Plan
to Move?

INDUSTRIES

JOBS

SAME JOB DIFFERENT INDUSTRY ⑤	SIMILAR JOB DIFFERENT INDUSTRY ⑦	DIFFERENT JOB DIFFERENT INDUSTRY ⑨
SAME JOB SIMILAR INDUSTRY ②	SIMILAR JOB SIMILAR INDUSTRY ④	DIFFERENT JOB SIMILAR INDUSTRY ⑧
SAME JOB SAME INDUSTRY ①	SIMILAR JOB SAME INDUSTRY ③	DIFFERENT JOB SAME INDUSTRY ⑥

Notes for Brainstorming Exercise #3-1

Directions: Each of you has a wealth of experience and different perspectives on the business world. This is a great time to brainstorm the potential applications of each class member's previous knowledge, experience and skills.

Spend the next 20 minutes brainstorming opportunities for your team members spending about 2 minutes per person. Do so without judgmental comments at this point. Include all ideas as long as someone sees a skill fit, that's all that matters.

One at a time, each class member will stand in front of the group, give a brief career recap, emphasizing the skills and keywords s/he defined in the previous chapter (exercise #2-5) and then capture the brainstorming ideas on a flip chart. The individual at the flip chart does not discuss these ideas with the group s/he merely writes them down. If the "writer" has an idea s/he can add it to the chart as well. The group is to generate different applications for those skills, how they could be used in different jobs, different companies or different industries. Ideas and job titles are the desired end result. The individual at the flip chart takes his/her own page at the conclusion of his/her turn.

TRANSFERABLE SKILLS

Transferable skills are the tools that enable you to move seamlessly from industry to industry, from career to career. Transferable skills can clearly illustrate to a prospective employer that:

♦ You've done this before and you can do it again.

♦ You've done something similar and you can adapt.

Simply put, *they are skills you possess that can be used in an array of work situations*. The skill sets required will vary considerably from industry to industry, and by work responsibilities. They can be derived from a variety of sources: your accomplishments, both personal and professional; your diverse work experiences; at-work training and educational background.

TRANSFERABLE SKILLS ASSESSMENT

Directions: Check the experience/skill descriptor that indicates your competency level.

	Entry Level	Mid-Level	Expert
1. Managing People/Projects/Budgets	☐	☐	☐
2. Leading or Participating in Teams	☐	☐	☐
3. Improving Work Processes	☐	☐	☐
4. Project Management	☐	☐	☐
5. Communicating: Verbal/Written	☐	☐	☐
6. Using Computers/Technology	☐	☐	☐
7. Selling/Influencing	☐	☐	☐
8. Analyzing/Planning/Organizing	☐	☐	☐
9. Staffing/Recruiting	☐	☐	☐
10. Speaking/Presenting	☐	☐	☐
11. Training/Coaching	☐	☐	☐

Although this is not a complete list of essential skills, it does highlight some of those considered to be most important. The degree to which you are able to link your transferable skills to your chosen career work objective will be a guidepost to your success in changing careers. You may also wish to look at the more extensive skill list you created in Chapter 2. Create a similar matrix and check which of those are highly transferable.

ASSESSING PREPAREDNESS FOR A CAREER CHANGE

Directions:

Match up the skills required in your target career/industry/ functional area to your current skill set and competency levels. **To help you complete this Exercise, refer to Chapter 2, Assessment Exercise #2-5, "Identifying your Specific Skills," and the "Transferable Skills Assessment," Exercise #3-2 in this Chapter.**

CAREER/INDUSTRY/ FUNCTIONAL AREA	SKILLS REQUIRED[1]	YOUR SKILLS	COMPETENCY LEVEL

The more skills you possess for the position to which you aspire and the higher your competency level, the greater the likelihood that you will be able to transfer your skills and make the change rapidly and successfully.

CAREER/INDUSTRY/ FUNCTIONAL AREA	SKILLS REQUIRED[2]	YOUR SKILLS	COMPETENCY LEVEL

[1] This information is researched before being written into this column
[2] This information is researched before being written into this column

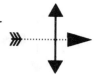

Exercise #3-4

CAREER CHANGE DECISION CRITERIA

Directions: Check "**yes**" or "**no**" for each statement.

	Yes	No	
1.	☐	☐	I am willing and able to relocate.
2.	☐	☐	I can afford to take a sizable cut in pay if necessary.
3.	☐	☐	I can afford to be out of work for some time if that is what it takes to change fields.
4.	☐	☐	My skills are highly transferable to the new industry.
5.	☐	☐	I am willing to spend money and long hours off the job on retraining or learning new skills.
6.	☐	☐	I am flexible and willing to accept a variety of roles and responsibilities even if it means taking a step backward in my career.
7.	☐	☐	My current field is depressed and competition for positions is high.
8.	☐	☐	I have wanted to be something else for a long time.

Questions 1-4 examine your personal situation. Can you afford it? Are you able to go where the work is? Do you have skills that are needed in the new industry? **Questions 5 and 6** examine your willingness and commitment to make the required changes. **Question 7** is about the necessity of changing direction. **The last question** is about your own driving need for change...fulfilling your personal vision.

If you said yes to most of these questions, then changing careers or starting your own business is a good idea. While changing careers, even if it is the right choice, is difficult, people with a vision can achieve whatever they desire. It will require tenacity and a great deal of research and networking. A person with a vision will focus on the goal, how to get there, how to get around every obstacle. That person seeks to find reasons for success, not excuses for failure or not trying. The person with a vision puts up with rejection, non-believers, and long hours because s/he can see the realistic probability of achieving the dream.

PLAN FOR CHANGING CAREER

If you determine that a career change is more appropriate for you than simply transferring your skills, the following career-change guidelines will help you move more easily through the process.

Step 1:
Conduct a thorough self-appraisal, including strengths and weaknesses.

Self-appraisal enables you to identify your strongest interests and your strongest working abilities. It also permits you to assess your educational and work experience in terms of qualifications for a second career of your choosing.

Step 2:
If you don't know what you want, make an initial choice of a second-career field.

Once you have completed your self-appraisal, you will be able to search more systematically for suitable careers and begin to narrow your focus.

Step 3:
Begin moving toward your second-career goal.

After setting short-term objectives and long-term goals, you will need to start learning about your second-career field by meeting with people connected with it.

Step 4:
Plan for and obtain needed education and training/retraining.

Next, you will need to obtain the best qualifications for your second career; (a) acquire the necessary education and training; (b) obtain hands-on experience. Since this may require a major investment of time, money and energy, think about your long-term goals. Will this training or education move you in the right direction? What will be the return on your investment?

Step 5:
Begin to network while still in training.

While you are getting your second-career education and training, begin to develop networks of acquaintances in your second-career field. Learn about and cultivate other possible sources of leads, such as professional and trade associations in the field.

Step 6:
Choose a position and start work in your second career.

You will need solid training, effective search techniques, persistence and determination to be able to choose from among a number of positions in your second-career field. Accepting the one that seems best for you is the first step toward success.

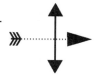

OPTIONS FOR ALL DEGREES OF CAREER CHANGERS

The following career options warrant further consideration for career changers regardless of the degree of change involved:

♦ *Investigate former Competitors*

For maximum credibility, consider moving to the same type of work with a competitive company, where you are knowledgeable about the industry.

♦ *Contact former Customers*

Former company customers with whom you have had a solid relationship already know of your expertise and that you understand their issues and concerns.

♦ *Consider Vendors*

They will see you as having credibility and in-depth industry knowledge, even though you are not technically in their industry.

♦ *Be an Independent Contractor*

If you have highly regarded technical capability or skills, you could become an independent contractor to your former company and its competitors.

♦ *Simplify and Shift Down*

Combine a career change with a downscaling in lifestyle. Could you sell your current home and move to a less expensive one? Many (older) professionals consider a career change that may pay less, yet give them exactly what they need at this point in their life.

♦ *Combine Two Jobs*

Combining two diverse work situations to make a living is now making a comeback. Here are a few real-life examples: teacher and restorer of antique furniture; part-time salesperson and caterer; office repair technician and corporate chauffeur; free-lance editor and administrator of a counseling center.

♦ *Take on Temporary/Contract Positions*

Many companies now recruit temporary executives and professionals, and search firms are also growing that segment of their business. Think about combining temping with starting your own business. The flexibility is enormous, and benefits include time for family, hobbies, longer vacations, and for studying, writing or traveling. (Realize that the downside of interim assignments is often lower income, lack of benefits and a more solitary existence.)

♦ *Run a Business from Home*

Twenty-five million Americans run full-time or part-time businesses at home. Many people attempt to eliminate the commute, politics and their managers and live by their own schedule and initiative. All types of consulting, selling and information-based businesses can be run from home.

♦ *Be an Entrepreneur*

Starting a business, buying a small business, starting a consulting or contracting business, or buying a franchise are all viable options for career changers. Do your research before making a commitment.

YOUR ROAD TO CREDIBILITY

What do you need to know about your new field to be taken seriously? Here are questions to get you started.

1. What are major problems in your target career/industry/functional area? How are they being solved?

2. What has happened in this area in the last five years?

3. What is going to happen over the next five years?

4. What kinds of people work in this field? What are their backgrounds?

5. How does one make money in this career/industry/field?

6. What are the key concerns from the *customers'* point of view?

7. What kinds of skills and education are required to work in this field at your level?

8. Do your interests fit the industry?

9. Do your skills fit?

10. Overall, do your interests and skills fit well enough to be taken seriously as a candidate?

11. What specific kinds of work could you realistically compete for?

12. What will hiring managers see as your strengths?

13. What will they see as your weaknesses?

IMPORTANT CONSIDERATIONS FOR THOSE WHO GO DEEPER INTO THE DEGREES OF CHANGE

1. **Plan for the search.** For every level deeper you move on the degree of change scale, the longer it takes to find a position. It is recommended that you examine your financial requirements carefully and make some realistic decisions. You may want to consider an interim position or part-time work to bridge to your new career.

2. **Network, network, network.** The odds are that a successful career change will happen because of a referral or contact. Meet everyone you can, any way you can, in your chosen field. An excellent way to meet people is to attend an industry convention or trade show. You may also want to join a professional group in your target field or industry. Start by checking out their local meetings.

3. **Learn the language.** Every field has its own culture and language. Inventory what you have to sell, align it with the industry needs and translate it into the industry lingo. Learn about the cultural norms and adjust your image and behavior so that you will be perceived as "fitting in".

4. **Optimism versus realism.** Keep a healthy balance between these two elements. Many people are searching for their "dream work" — many even find it — yet it must be weighed in a realistic context. It may take time to get to the compensation level you desire, so be flexible when looking to change careers. It is often best approached in incremental steps.

5. **Search firms and ads are not reliable resources.** Except for entry level positions, companies usually run ads to recruit prospects who have specific experience. Career changers need not apply. This is also true of search firms, who are paid to find highly experienced people.

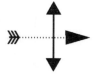

SUMMARY

At this point in your career, you have the opportunity to take a fresh look at what you value and enjoy doing to determine the kind of position and work environment that would give you pleasure and satisfaction in the future. When considering the option of a career change, keep the following points in mind:

♦ **Successful career changing can be achieved when approached with tenacity and determination** combined with thoughtful self-appraisal, skill identification, research, necessary retraining and networking.

♦ **Changing careers requires in-depth knowledge of your target industry** and enhanced work-search skills.

♦ **Transferable skills can pave the way to a smoother transition** between industries and functions.

♦ **Transferring skills is simpler** when you already possess a number of the skills required for the change.

♦ **The narrower the gap** between your former career and your prospective new one, **the easier it is to make a successful transition.**

♦ **There are several career-change options available to you:**

- Working for former competitors

- Working for former Customers or Vendors

- Contracting

- Running a business from home

- Entrepreneurship

- Temporary professional positions

- Holding multiple part-time jobs

CHAPTER FOUR

The Resume

*"The next thing most like living one's life
over again seems to be a recollection of
that life, and to make that recollection
as durable as possible by putting it
down in writing."*

Benjamin Franklin, *Autobiography (Everyman's Edition)*

POINTS OF INTEREST

In Chapter Four you will learn how your resume:

♦ Serves as your "ad copy," highlighting pertinent information about your skills, experience and achievements

♦ Should be formatted (chronological or functional) to:

    • Accurately reflect you and the work you are seeking

    • Document your qualifications

    • Be customized for the reader and the position of interest

    • Convey information that emphasizes your "fit"

THE RESUME

The resume continues to be the fundamental marketing tool for work seekers. However, today's changing work market is driving significant changes in how resumes are designed and used.

WHAT ARE RESUME READERS LOOKING FOR?

STYLE	CONTENT
◆ Clarity	◆ Focused on critical skills that impact business bottom line
◆ Succinctness	◆ Summary of work-related experience
◆ Attractive Format	◆ Documentation of achieved results
◆ Professional Appearance	◆ Synopsis of work-related accomplishments
◆ High Impact	◆ Link between your skills and experience and their business needs
	◆ Keywords

YOUR RESUME

The resume is a skillfully designed summary that provides information about your education, work experience and other qualifications that are pertinent to prospective employers. Your resume should not be an all inclusive biography, but should select and highlight your background and achievements in such a way *that it will generate job interviews*. Although a quality resume will not guarantee the work of your dreams, it will dramatically increase the odds that you will be considered.

The resume is your:

- Calling card
- Door opener
- Statement of competencies

In business terms, the resume is a marketing brochure featuring *you as the product*. Just like any other marketing literature, it must clarify to the buyer the "features and functions" you are offering and the benefits you provide.

What Kind of Resume Do I Need?

The two primary styles of resume are the **chronological** and **functional**. In addition, we will be looking at customizing your resume under certain circumstances.

The chart below illustrates the differences between the two styles of resume. Examples of each type are included in the Index of Resources.

CHRONOLOGICAL	FUNCTIONAL
◆ Most widely used and accepted	◆ Emphasizes skills and knowledge, current or past, in or out of your career
◆ Emphasizes employment history	
◆ Lists positions in reverse chronological order with no gaps in time	◆ De-emphasizes chronology, minimizes gaps in time
◆ Highlights position titles, company, skills, responsibilities, accomplishments	◆ Focuses on business functions, range of accomplishments
◆ Effective when seeking position or skill use in same or similar field	◆ Effective when changing careers or for those with a diverse work history
◆ Demonstrates stability and track record of accomplishments	◆ Demonstrates skills relevant to your work objective

KEY RESUME COMPONENTS

All resumes are composed of several key components, regardless of the style you select to present them. They are listed in the general order in which they are most likely to appear.

HEADING

The heading includes identifying information, such as name, address, home and/or office telephone numbers with area codes and an e-mail address if applicable.

OBJECTIVE

Targeted to a specific industry or work function, the objective informs the reader in a concise, definitive way about what you are truly interested in doing. See your personal example in exercise #2-7. **Note**: If you do not have a specific objective, you can customize information in your cover letter regarding an objective as it relates to a specific company.

> **Example 1**: A position in the development and implementation of skill training for technology-related projects.

> **Example 2**: A sales management position in the pharmaceutical or consumer products industry.

> **Example 3**: A supervisory position with a manufacturer of electronic products.

SUMMARY

This section is your summary of qualifications. Its purpose is to create a positive snapshot in the mind of the reader, similar to the blurb on the back of a book or the coming attractions for a movie. In a few lines, it captures the essence of your experience, skills, traits and sometimes even your accomplishments. It is also a good place to insert "keywords" for electronic scanning. (See exercise #2-6 for your personal summary).

Key Point: The summary should *support your objective*, i.e., why you are able to do what your objective states that you want to do, as the following examples illustrate.

> **Example 1**: Ten years experience in the design and delivery of PC training programs, with a focus on customized software applications and solutions. Ability to translate internal customer needs into technology solutions and communicate the implementation through state-of-the-art training.

> **Example 2**: A Sales Manager with 12 years experience in expanding territories and profits to exceptional levels. A hands-on team player skilled at developing staff and increasing morale while enhancing the bottom line.

> **Example 3**: Eight years experience in the electronics industry managing new product development and introduction. Introduced new implementation strategy shortening time to market by 15%.

PROFESSIONAL EXPERIENCE /ACCOMPLISHMENTS

The purpose of this section is to present your achievements, with results, that give further support to the objective and summary. It is, in fact, a more expanded set of credentials as delineated in the summary.

In a **Chronological Resume**, this section contains a listing of your employers with city and state, the positions you held and the dates of employment, arranged in *reverse chronological order*. Describe each position incorporating your most important achievements. You may want to begin with those performance objectives (e.g., job duties) requiring the highest level of skill, responsibility and judgment. Begin each phrase with action verbs. Quantify and qualify your accomplishments. (See Exercise #2-3 for your personal examples.)

In a **Functional Resume**, group your work accomplishments, responsibilities and duties according to functional skill such as "Project Planning Skills", "Managerial Skills" or "Sales". Choose skill headings relating to your job objective and briefly describe your accomplishments in each of the broad categories, using action statements. For example, if you did financial analysis and planning in previous positions, describe these responsibilities under the heading "Financial Planning" and treat your experience in this area as one complete unit. Work experience can be briefly listed in reverse chronological order. (This can also be found in Exercise #2-3 where you added your skills to your accomplishments.)

EDUCATION

Your educational background is listed beginning with the highest degree first (e.g., Ph.D., Master's, Bachelor's, Associates, some college), followed by major concentration, name of school, location and, optionally, the year of graduation. High school diploma should be shown only if you have not had college-level education, and only if it is relevant to your Work Objective.

Example: M.B.A., Finance, University of Chicago
B.S., Education, Penn State University

PROFESSIONAL DEVELOPMENT

This section contains any non-academic training you completed, such as courses in management, communication, presentation skills, computer-related training, etc. **Note:** extensive technical competencies can be listed separately.

ASSOCIATIONS

Use this section to list professional organizations in which you are *currently a member*. You might also list former organizational memberships in which you held office, as long as they are relevant to your Work Objective.

OTHER RELEVANT DATA

This last section is optional, and is used to pique additional enthusiasm in the resume reader. It can include professional certificates or licenses, special skills or abilities such as a foreign language, publications, military experience, availability, volunteer or community work, or any information that would support your Objective or further entice the reader to ask you in for an interview.

RESUME GUIDELINES

The following guidelines will help you in the resume-writing process:

Your new resume will not be like your first resume: Experienced people must demonstrate a proven track record of accomplishments that are relevant to potential employers. You need to research the needs of an organization and tailor your resume to show how your past accomplishments meet those needs.

Emphasize accomplishments not just responsibilities. Include relevant activities that relate directly to your self-improvement efforts, not hobbies.

Open with a Summary statement highlighting three or four skills that match the employer's needs. Include a specific Objective in the resume or put it in a cover letter. If you have more than one Objective, create another resume/cover letter for it.

Select the resume type (chronological, functional) that will best market your capabilities.

Make your resume visually appealing, with sufficient white space and margins.

Do not exceed two pages in length.

If the resume will not be scanned or put through the Internet -- Use bullets, and write in direct, succinct phrases supported by powerful action verbs.

Omit the personal pronouns "I" and "they". Use "we" where it appropriately demonstrates your "teamsmanship."

Proofread carefully.

Ask for feedback on your resume before sending it out.

Remember, **every company believes it is unique, and, in many ways it is. Hence, your marketing (e.g., resume) must respond to that belief. With the availability of computer technology, it is valuable to customize your resume to meet the *specific requirements* of a potential employer. This means *changing*, when necessary, your work objective, *selecting* certain accomplishment statements over others, or changing *keywords* in your summary statement. In addition to having a customized cover letter, the resume can now reflect the specific skills and experience for which a potential employer is looking.**

WRITING A RESUME ACTIVITY

Directions: We have just discussed the key ingredients to resume writing. During your self-assessment in Chapter 2 you actually created the major ingredients of a resume. How you go about laying out your resume is a matter of strategic marketing, however, the components in every resume are the same.

For the next 60 minutes, construct your resume. Choose either Exercise #4-1 or #4-2, whichever is most appropriate for your personal qualifications. As you go along, if you have any questions, feel free to ask the instructor or one of your classmates for an opinion for assistance. You can also look in your Index of Resources.

WORKSHEET #1
Chronological Resume Format

_____
(Name)

_____
(Street Address)

_____
(City, State, ZIP)

_____
(Telephone)

Summary

_____

_____

Experience

(Most recent company)	(City, State)	(Overall dates employed)
(Position Title)		(Dates)

(Scope of responsibilities)

• (Accomplishment statement)

• (Accomplishment statement)

• (Accomplishment statement)

• (Accomplishment statement)

• (Accomplishment statement)

Chronological Resume Format, cont'd.

_____
(Name)

_____   _____   _____
(Previous company)   (City, State)   (Overall dates employed)

_____   _____
(Position Title)   (Dates)

_____
(Scope of responsibilities)

- _____
(Accomplishment statement)

- _____
(Accomplishment statement)

- _____
(Accomplishment statement)

Education

_____
(Degree awarded and major field)

(School, City, State)

Professional Development

_____
(Course title, provider)

Other (optional)

_____
(Special Awards/Professional Memberships/Community Leadership)

Personal (optional, only if it adds value)

_____

WORKSHEET #2
Functional Resume Format

_____
(Name)

_____
(Street Address)

(City, State, ZIP)

_____
(Telephone)

Summary

_____
_____
_____
_____

Major Accomplishments

(Function)

• _____
• _____
• _____

(Function)

• _____
• _____
• _____

(Function)

• _____
• _____
• _____
•

Functional Resume Format, cont'd.

Professional Experience

_____
(Name)

(Most recent company)	(City, State)	(Overall dates employed)
(Position Title)		(Dates)
(Position Title)		(Dates)
(Previous company)	(City, State)	(Overall dates employed)
(Position Title)		(Dates)
(Position Title)		(Dates)

Education

_____
(Degree awarded and major field)

(School, City, State)

Professional Development

_____
(Course title, provider)

Other (optional)

_____
(Special Awards/Professional Memberships/Community Leadership)

Personal (optional, only if it adds value)

_____

ELECTRONIC SCANNING

A growing number of organizations and search firms are taking advantage of computer technology to store resumes received from employment seekers. Think of this technology as a giant resume inventory system. The computer program allows an employer to rapidly scan the resume and to "match" open position specifications. Associations, companies and on-line services have compiled extensive resume databases that can be scanned electronically for specific work profiles.

These automated resume management systems search for *keywords*. Keywords tend to be more of the noun or noun phrase type (Total Quality Management, UNIX, Bio-Chemist) as opposed to power action verbs often found in traditional resumes (Developed, Coordinated, Empowered, Organized). Keywords are single words or phrases that describe education, experience, skills and accomplishments. Jargon is perfectly OK, as long as you spell out abbreviations. Examples of keywords and phrases are:

Business Skills

Strategic planning	Operations management	Staffing
Total quality management	Sales trainer	Customer service
New business development	Administration	Start-up specialist

Interpersonal Skills

Presentation skills	Team leader	Verbal communication
Negotiating	Coaching	Change management

Knowledge

Windows 3.1	Microsoft Access	Activity-based accounting
Microsoft Excel	Microsoft Word	Project management

Once a work or position profile has been defined, a keyword list is compiled to reflect the business skills, knowledge, work experience and interpersonal skills that support the profile. The computer then scans the database, recording the number of "matches". The more matches that are found in your resume, the greater the odds that you will be selected for consideration.

Resumes can be written using a keyword summary. This will increase the probability that a computer, as well as a human reader, will catch the qualifications of the person described.

GUIDELINES FOR CONSTRUCTING RESUMES THAT EXPEDITE ELECTRONIC SCANNING:

Do not use staples. Scanners may misinterpret them.

Eliminate tabs and hard returns wherever possible.

Avoid bolding, italics, underlining, shading, vertical and horizontal lines.

Use white or cream colored 8 ½" x 11" paper, printed on one side only.

Use a common font such as Helvetica, Optima, Times New Roman with a font size between 11 and 14.

RESUMES ON-LINE

The E-mail Resume

Many companies and recruiters are soliciting resumes via e-mail, and indicating precise specifications for the reader. In general, this version is designed with bulleted lists, bold and italicized text, underlining, shading and other highlights for sending to potential contacts.

Here are points to keep in mind if you are sending your resume via e-mail:

Inquire whether the individuals receiving the resume would also like a printed hard copy for their records.

Unless otherwise instructed, include a cover letter, and be sure to note why you are contacting this person.

Send the resume and cover letter in a single e-mail message.

If responding to an ad or position posting, be sure to use the position title and/or noted reference number as the **Subject** of your message.

Know the software environment of the receiver (e.g., Lotus Notes).

Some positions advertise on-line, but do not accept resumes via e-mail. Be sure to read and follow the instructions given.

Preparing Your Resume for the Internet

There are millions of people and thousands of companies exchanging information over computer networks such as the Internet. Within this complex network different word processing applications exist (e.g., Microsoft Word, WriteNow, ClarisWorks, etc.) which operate on various computer platforms (for example a MacIntosh computer versus a PC). This can make it difficult to know how to send information because you may be unsure which specific program or platform the receiver uses to view documents. Fortunately there is a standard, common text language that allows different word processing applications to read and display the same text information. That common text language is known as ASCII text. Because of its simplicity, ASCII text enables anyone to construct an on-line resume. ASCII allows prospective employers to retrieve your resume via the Internet or e-mail and to view it no matter what kind of computer you are using. This is good news for Internet users. Now you can write or paste a text document, specifically your ASCII resume, into an Employer's Online Response Form, CareerMosaic's ResumeCM, or the message field of an e-mail document. Using the ASCII format means your resume will be easily viewed regardless of the type of computer platform you and the receiver use to transfer the information.

How to write a resume in ASCII

To create an ASCII resume, first type your resume using your favorite wordprocessing application. Then save it as a text only document (sometimes called Rich Text Format or RTF). This should be an option under your "save" or "save as" command. You can also use a simple text program to compose your resume.

When your resume is written in ASCII text, special formatting commands specific to your wordprocessing program will not be recognized. Therefore, you must watch for these common mistakes:

Avoid using special characters (such as "smart quotes," or mathematical symbols) -- these do not get accurately transferred in the text save.

Omit the use of bullets, lines, bold, italicized or underlined text.

Substitute symbols such as asterisks (*) for bullets, dashes for lines, capital letters for bold or underlined text.

Do not use Tabs -- use your spacebar instead.

Alignment - The default for ASCII is to make everything left justified (which is the preferred format for scanning resumes and on-line viewing). If you want to indent a sentence or center a heading, use the spacebar.

Do not use word wrap when composing your resume, instead use hard carriage returns to insert line breaks.

Fonts will become whatever a computer uses as its default face and size so boldface, italics, and various sizes will NOT appear in the ASCII version.

Spell check your document before you save it as a text file.

Proofread your entire resume after you paste it in the message field and before you hit the submit button.

Examine other text resumes to compare what others have done to present their resume information. Examples included on:

- *"Career Magazine"* (http://www.careermag.com)

- "Career Mosaic" (http://www.careermosaic.com)

OTHER RESUME VARIATIONS

Curriculum Vitae

In the academic world, a resume is referred to as a *curriculum vitae*, which emphasizes educational background and published papers. The format is usually chronological, and it is acceptable for this version to exceed two pages because it includes publications and presentations.

Biography

Written in a narrative form of about one page, the biography is used extensively by individuals who become consultants or independent contractors. The biography documents qualifications and credentials for the work they are proposing.

(Samples of the chronological and functional resume and biography can be found in your Index of Resources.)

SUMMARY

A resume is a marketing tool featuring **_you as the product_** which:

> **Grabs the attention** of the person or company with a current business need.

> **Highlights pertinent information** about your skills, experience and achievements in a manner that responds to the business need.

It should have content that:

> **Accurately markets you**, the individual -- the skills/ability you have to sell, and the work you are seeking.

> **Responds** to the needs of the company and/or a specific individual.

> **Documents your qualifications** by citing accomplishments.

> **Conveys information that will "rule you in"**, not "screen you out".

It should have a format and appearance that is:

> **Compatible** with the way in which resumes are managed (scanned, read by humans, etc.).

> **Visually** easy to read -- good font size, white space, bullets, etc., where appropriate.

CHAPTER FIVE
Oral Communication:
Networking that Gets Results

"*His word burned like a lamp.*"

—Douay Bible, *The Apocrypha, XLVIII, 1*

POINTS OF INTEREST

Chapter Five will provide you with valuable tools, such as:
 ♦ The major components of communication:
     • I-SPEAK® Your Language
     • Your 90-Second Introduction
     • Active Listening
 ♦ A five-step process to increase networking success
 ♦ Networking telephone scripts
 ♦ Five steps to conducting a networking meeting
 ♦ Effective telephone techniques and the use of voice-mail

INTRODUCTION TO COMMUNICATION

Networking: A process of building relationships. It is communication for the purpose of:

- Getting coaching

- Gathering contacts

- Gaining feedback

- Brainstorming ideas

- Assembling additional knowledge about a field, an occupation, an individual, etc. through Informational Interviews and other means

Interviewing: The interaction between the person with the skills for sale and the person with a need for those skills. A mutual dialogue about the meeting of individual and organizational needs.

Negotiating: The activity of reaching agreement or to settle on the terms and conditions upon which both parties will make a commitment. Some negotiable terms include benefits, wages, flexible time, severance packages, performance reviews, pay increases, job requirements, human or technical support, future career considerations, additional education, etc. This *Negotiable Moment* happens at the point at which both parties agree that the skills the individual has for sale match the needs of the organization.

Your ability to ***articulate*** your career goals, ***demonstrate*** competencies through past accomplishments and training, and ***illustrate*** the benefits of hiring you will go a long way to secure the position of your choice. Doing this well is the Art of Communication.

FACILITATING THE COMMUNICATION PROCESS
INTRODUCING YOURSELF

Creating Your 90-Second Introduction

Ask yourself what you would say if someone said, "Tell me about yourself?" Responding without preparation could be a fatal mistake on a job interview. "Dah" makes a bad impression.

The 90-Second Introduction is your answer and an introductory marketing pitch in one package. It is an important part of any networking meeting or interview, since it can provide an overview of what you have done and what you are looking for. Use a 90-second introduction:

- To respond to the question, "Tell me about yourself"
- During an informational interview
- At a pre-screening interview
- At a job interview
- In social situations
- Wherever there is an occasion to market yourself

These are opportunities to clearly articulate your career goals and, at the same time, create a positive, lasting impression with the listener.

90-SECOND INTRODUCTIONS

YOUR QUICK "COMMERCIAL"
TYPICAL CONTENT-225 WORDS

Purposes:

- Alerts listener to your employment background and aspirations
- Stimulates their interest in learning more about you
- Confines your introduction to an average adult's attention span
- Identifies your position by title or specialty
- Identifies career high-spots
- Provides some background sprinkled with quantified accomplishments
- It announces your current situation - what you are looking for (ie. the purpose of the conversation.)

Here is a suggested format for the 90-Second Introduction.

The 90-Second Introduction

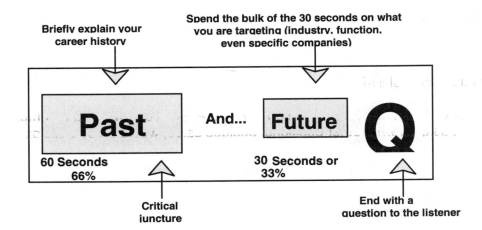

Past: Career Summary (60 seconds). Present the "big picture" and allow your listener to ask you to elaborate on anything that is of interest. During this time, you can include (1) your *most recent* career history; (2) a snapshot of the type of work you have been performing; and (3) the type of organization, industry or functional area where you performed it.

Example: "For the past 10 years my career has focused on sales management and sales training, primarily in the pharmaceutical industry. Most recently, I was Supervisor of Sales at Johnson Medical Supplies."

Critical Juncture (10 seconds - if asked). At this point, *if asked*, explain why you are looking for work. It is important to talk about this in a brief, matter-of-fact way.

Example: "As you may be aware, Johnson Medical is moving its corporate facility to North Carolina, and I have chosen not to relocate."

Future: Your Target Career (30 seconds). This is where you talk about your target industry, target position, function or role. Mentioning the names of organizations you are targeting or meeting with is also important here. It is easier for people to make connections and offer support when they have specific information.

Example: "I'd like to continue my career in this field, so I am targeting pharmaceutical as well as biomedical companies."

At this point, your networking contact might mention that he or she has a friend/relative in the industry, and would be willing to give that person a call on your behalf.

Q: *Question.* Asking a question is polite and a way to promote a two-way discussion. It is the component that will most likely change depending upon the reason you are using the 90-second introduction.

Example 1: "Do you have any other ideas?"

Example 2: "You're familiar with the industry. In what other areas do you think there might be opportunities for a person with my experience?"

Example 3: If you were looking for other career alternatives you might ask, "In what other fields might I use these skills?"

Example 4: If you were trying to see what other positions within the company use these skills you might ask, "In what other positions, besides sales, would these skills be used?"

Example 5: If you were talking to a recruiter you might ask, "What do you consider to be the most critical skills a sales person can have?"

Example 6: If you were talking to someone who knows you well or knows the field well, ask an open-ended question: "So, what do you think? How does that sound to you?"

Your 90-Second Introduction needs to be flexible -- customized and responsive to the agenda and needs of the listener. It is important to be able to expand your story when the opportunity presents itself, or to hold back if that is more appropriate. In either case, once you are comfortable with your basic story, you will find telephoning, networking, interviewing, and negotiating to be easier, more rewarding and exciting!

90-SECOND INTRODUCTION

1. Past: Write a brief career summary including (1) your *most recent* career history; (2) a snapshot of the type of work you have been performing; and (3) the type of organization, industry or functional area where you performed it.

Hello, my name is David Ponce. I hold a doctoral degree in Physics and I have most recently worked at in the optics telecommunication industry. ~~I was part of~~ part of the Research I was senior ~~optics~~ engineer and part of the ~~Hard~~ Hardware R & D Team.

2. Critical juncture: Write a sentence in a brief, matter-of-fact way, that explains why you are presently looking for work.

3. Future: Write a description of your target industry, position, function or role, mentioning the organizations you are targeting or meeting. Be specific. Identify the major points you will make.

4. Q: Asking a question is not only polite, but it is a way to promote a two-way discussion.

THE ART OF ACTIVE LISTENING

Guidelines for Active Listening

1. **Listen with your eyes** -- Approximately 80% of what is said is non-verbal[1]. This is a combination of body language (about 55%) and tone of voice (about 38%). It deals with "how" something is said, rather than "what" is said.

2. **Listen for content.** While words comprise only 7% of what is being communicated, they are still the core of the message.

3. **Listen to intent.** Listen to "why" something is said, in addition to "what" is said.

4. **Listen for emotion.** Be aware of feelings that are being expressed, and be prepared to reflect them (e.g., it appears that you are ...).

5. **Monitor your own nonverbal communication.** Be aware that you are also sending signals about this particular interaction -- the person, the question, the topic, etc. People instinctively read body language before they hear anything. Remember, 80% of what is said is non-verbal!

6. **Listen non-judgmentally**. Do not prejudge the speaker. Listen with an open mind. You do not necessarily have to accept the other person's ideas or points of view, but you do need to respect his or her right to an opinion.

7. **Monitor your emotional filters.** Each of us filters information through biases, past experiences, assumptions and expectations, and then we respond accordingly. While you may not be able to eliminate your emotional filters, you can control them.

8. **Listen with empathy.** Put yourself in the other person's shoes and try to understand what is shaping his or her feelings.

I-SPEAK Your Language®

In the Discovery stage of this course, you completed the I-SPEAK® exercise. Recall its purpose was to identify your communication style as well as *to identify the style of others so that you could communicate more effectively*. It is to your advantage to be aware of the communication style of the person with whom you are speaking and adapt your own style to his/hers to increase compatibility.

Knowledge and use of I-SPEAK® styles, when combined with active listening skills, will greatly help to build relationships and enhance your communication capabilities during interviews or networking meetings.

---

[1] These numbers vary according to which university study one reads, however, the point is that more is communicated through body language (e.g., non-verbal cues) than through the spoken word.

YOUR "AUDIBLE PICTURE"-- THE TELEPHONE

Two very important things to remember about telephone communication:

1. The body language portion of communication (55%) is missing.

2. You need to compensate for the lack of this important element of the feedback loop.

The tone of your voice (38%) and the words you use convey an over-the-phone image of you. We have all had the experience of hearing someone on the phone and creating a mental picture of him or her in our minds. When we do meet the person, we are often surprised. The voice, the expression.... everything about our telephone "picture" doesn't match the real person. That person may be experiencing the same phenomenon about you.

How important is an "audible picture"? Research conducted by Stanford University psychologist, Dr. Albert Mehrabien, has shown the relative importance and impact of words, tone of voice and non-verbal communication.

	In-Person	**Voice Only**
Words	7%	16%
Tone	38%	84%
Non-Verbals	55%	-

Most people ascribe the highest importance to the *words* in a communication. But we can see that when nonverbal communication is eliminated (as in a telephone conversation), *the way we say things* becomes even more important. Let's look at some techniques for strengthening phone image.

Telephone Image

What kind of image do you want to project? If your first impression with a contact is over the phone, you will need to be aware of the picture you create. Check those items that you think you project on the telephone.

DESIRABLE IMPRESSIONS	UNDESIRABLE IMPRESSIONS
Excitement	Anxiety
Warmth	Anger
Energy	Exhaustion
Enthusiasm	Annoyance
Friendliness	Fear
Confidence	Boredom
Pleasure	Distress
Hope	Sadness
Empowerment	Control
Time to listen	Abruptness
Other	Other

Next time you are on the phone, tape record your half of the conversation and see how you really sound, particularly if you are speaking to a relative stranger.

Or you might simulate a phone conversation with a friend or colleague, or tape your voice. Listen closely for the image you are presenting.

DO NOT FAIL TO DO THIS. This analysis will enable to you to produce a more positive impression over the phone.

COMMUNICATION AND NETWORKING

THE IMPORTANCE OF NETWORKING

Since the basis of networking depends on building relationships with contacts, *successful* networking depends to a great degree on effective communication skills.

Networking is <u>the most effective way</u> to discover employment opportunities. In fact, more people find work through networking than all other methods combined. According to the U.S. Department of Labor, *two-thirds of all jobs are located by word-of-mouth, informal referrals, relatives, friends and acquaintances.*

A NETWORKING IMAGE

Imagine dropping a pebble into a pond and creating a ripple effect on the water. In a similar manner, networking begins with the people you know best and expands outward in a circular motion, increasing the size and number of the circles. It is said that everyone knows at least 200 people to varying degrees. What a resource!

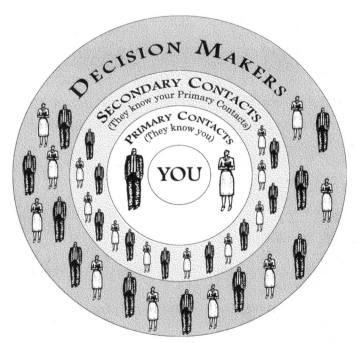

The diagram of the Networking Process above depicts this ripple effect, ultimately leading you to the decision makers. Starting in the center, "where the pebble drops," the people know you (primary contacts) provide a personalized connection to their referrals (the secondary contacts) -- where the work can be found.

WHAT IS NETWORKING?

At its best, networking means having conversations with people in your primary network to ask them for help and information about people *they* know (your secondary network), in order to seek:

- Information
- Advice
- Ideas
- Connection to others
- Support

HOW SUCCESSFUL IS NETWORKING?

Compared to the other strategies to find work (employment agencies, search firms, classified ads, targeted and mass mailings), networking has the highest success ratio.

THE NETWORKING PROCESS

Here are 5 simple steps that, in combination, will produce positive networking results.

Step 1: Build Your Network

Step 2: Prepare Your Story

Step 3: Prepare and Practice to Build Confidence

Step 4: Make Calls to Set Up Appointments

Step 5: Develop a Tracking System

Step 1: Build Your Network

In this first step, you will identify your personal contacts and build an organized list, prioritizing the names according to:

- Your most immediate needs
- People you believe will be most beneficial to your search

Your list of networking names can be drawn from personal contacts and professional contacts.

- ### *Personal Contacts*

    This list could include friends, acquaintances, relatives (no matter where they live), neighbors, doctor, dentist, banker, accountant, stockbroker, insurance agent, lawyer, PTA members, sports club/gym associates, clergy, social club members, college alumni, social service organization associates, children's teachers or scout leader, barber or beautician, contractors, local merchants, service station attendant -- even the person who sat next to you on the flight that was delayed over Chicago for two hours.

- ### *Professional Contacts*

This list might include co-workers, former managers, customers, competitors, vendors, suppliers, professional association colleagues, course instructors, your former company's ad agency, public relations firm, investment/banking affiliations.

Most people can initially think of 25-50 names. Use the form *in Exercise #5-3* to help you get started. Remember, the people in your network need not be close friends, or familiar with your work. Select people who know you and who may be willing to talk with you or others about your career plans.

NETWORKING CONTACT WORKSHEET

Directions:

In the space provided below, list your contacts for each category. Be sure to indicate after each one the kind of assistance you need: Information; Advice; Ideas; Connection to Others; Support.

PERSONAL

1. List your adult relatives.

_____   _____   _____

_____   _____   _____

_____   _____   _____

_____   _____   _____

_____   _____   _____

2. List your close friends.

_____   _____   _____

_____   _____   _____

_____   _____   _____

_____   _____   _____

_____   _____   _____

3. List the names of current or former neighbors.

_____   _____   _____

_____   _____   _____

_____   _____   _____

_____   _____   _____

_____   _____   _____

Exercise #5-3, cont.

PERSONAL, CONT.

4. List the health professionals you know.

_____ _____ _____

_____ _____ _____

_____ _____ _____

_____ _____ _____

_____ _____ _____

5. List your lawyer, accountant, brokers, insurance agents, contractors and other professionals with whom you have done business.

_____ _____ _____

_____ _____ _____

_____ _____ _____

_____ _____ _____

6. List the people you know from your involvement in religious or social organizations.

_____ _____ _____

_____ _____ _____

_____ _____ _____

_____ _____ _____

7. Others (e.g., people on your holiday greeting card list).

_____ _____ _____

_____ _____ _____

_____ _____ _____

_____ _____ _____

PROFESSIONAL

1. List the people you know from your association with professional organizations.

_____   _____   _____

_____   _____   _____

_____   _____   _____

_____   _____   _____

_____   _____   _____

2. List the colleagues (including managers) you worked with over the past five years.

_____   _____   _____

_____   _____   _____

_____   _____   _____

_____   _____   _____

_____   _____   _____

3. List others you know in former places of employment.

_____   _____   _____

_____   _____   _____

_____   _____   _____

_____   _____   _____

_____   _____   _____

4. List former vendors/suppliers you worked with.

_____   _____   _____

_____   _____   _____

_____   _____   _____

_____   _____   _____

_____   _____   _____

Exercise #5-3, cont.

5. List former customers or clients.

_____ _____ _____

_____ _____ _____

_____ _____ _____

_____ _____ _____

_____ _____ _____

6. List former competitors.

_____ _____ _____

_____ _____ _____

_____ _____ _____

_____ _____ _____

_____ _____ _____

7. List former outside consultants you worked with at your previous places of employment.

_____ _____ _____

_____ _____ _____

_____ _____ _____

_____ _____ _____

8. Others.

_____ _____ _____

_____ _____ _____

_____ _____ _____

_____ _____ _____

What you have listed are your **primary contacts** -- people who know you directly. These individuals are not likely to have positions or openings; rather, they become your publicity agents, your information sources and part of your communication system.

The people on this primary networking list will be able to refer you to **secondary contacts** who can provide you with an introduction to your target companies or others you have not yet considered. They do not have to be in your field or know your area of expertise to be helpful.

Step 2: Prepare Your Story

You will need to tell people the reason you are contacting them -- i.e., your current situation. Try creating a 90-second story for this purpose and be specific about *how* they can help you:

- Information
- Advice
- Ideas
- Connection to Others
- Support

Preparation and focus will ensure that you obtain the networking help you need. Your contacts will come away with a positive impression and a sense that you are organized and clear about your professional goals.

Step 3: Prepare and Practice to Build Confidence

Before making your first networking call, it is recommended that you try out the words you will say on a good friend or family member. To help you, here is a skeletal outline of a script that will benefit your preparation. (This script can be modified to fit your particular style.)

Script Outline:

- Your name
- Who you are (if contact doesn't know you)
- Referral name (if appropriate)
- Reason for your call (exact type of help you need)
- Inquire if this is a good time to call; if not, then when?
- 90-Second Introduction (customized)
- Prepared questions
- Thank the individual for his or her time and assistance
- Ask if there is anything you can do to return the favor

It is also important to have done your research, to be familiar with the industry or functional area of the individual you are contacting.

Following are examples of telephone scripts that you can modify and personalize.

Note: Be sure to allow time for responses, questions and small talk in your actual conversations.

Telephone Script for Someone Who Knows You

"Hi *(name of person you are calling),* this is *(your name).* How have you been? The reason I'm calling is to update you on my current work situation. Do you have a few minutes to talk?"

Response

"I recently left _____ Co. and I'm looking into new work opportunities. I'd like to set up a short meeting with you to do some brainstorming and get your feedback on my strategy. I was also hoping you might know some people to whom you could refer me who could provide me with additional information about the field."

Response

"How does next week look for you?"

Response

"Thanks for taking the time. I look forward to seeing you."

Telephone Script for Someone to Whom You Have Been Referred, but Never Met

"Good morning, *(name of person you are calling).* My name is *(your name).* A mutual friend of ours, _____, referred me to you. Have I reached you at a good time?"

Response

"I've recently left _____ Co. and *(referral name)* suggested you would be a good resource for me to talk with regarding my current search for work. S/he was clear that you may not know of any open positions, but did feel that you would be an excellent person for me to contact."

Response

"I am targeting individuals who have extensive knowledge about or connections in high tech organizations, which is why you were recommended to me. What I'd like to do is set up a 20 minute appointment to give you a brief synopsis of what I've been doing and what I'm thinking of doing in the future. I'd like your feedback on my strategy. When do you think it would it be convenient for us to get together?"

Telephone Script to Use for Making a Phone Call Following a Letter

If you are comfortable making a cold call, or if you have targeted someone for whom you have no contact name, a call following a customized letter can be quite effective. However, you will need to create a compelling reason for someone to meet or talk with you (e.g., a significant accomplishment relevant to their field or industry).

"Hello, *(name of person you are calling),* my name is *(your name).* "I'm calling to follow-up on the letter I sent last Monday, the 10th. Have I reached you at a good time?"

Response

"I was recently a Brand Manager at TruTaste Foods, and I am now pursuing a position on the agency side of the business."

"Over the past twelve years I increased revenues in the non-carbonated fruit beverage division by 75% by using a series of humorous television ads. My group won several awards for these endeavors."

"Since you are on the agency side and have the Snowgrape account, I thought it would be helpful for me if we got together."

Response

"I realize you may have a tight schedule, but perhaps we could spend a half hour for a breakfast meeting sometime in October[2]. We can share some ideas and after you meet me, you might advise me on my plans and perhaps refer me to others."

Telephone Script to Use When You Are Unable to Set Up a Face-to-Face Appointment

It is quite common to have people on your contact list who are geographically distant or who, for whatever reason, simply can't make a face-to-face meeting. As a result your networking has to be done over the phone.

If this is the case, you will make your initial phone call and use one of the three scenarios described earlier or the scenario that follows. Remember to respect the time commitments of your listener and determine a time to call back if he or she is busy.

When the time is appropriate, make sure you ask your contact if you can have 10 to 15 minutes on the phone, since you are too far away to set up an appointment. Then, conduct your networking meeting on the telephone using the following suggested outline.

"Good morning, *(name of person you are calling)*. My name is *(your name)*. Have I reached you at a good time?"

Response

"I've recently left XYZ Co., and *(referral name)* suggested that you would be an excellent person for me to talk with regarding my current search for work. While I recognize you may not have an open position at your company, *(referral name)* felt that you could be a great resource of information about ------------------- ."

Response

"I'd prefer to meet with you personally, but since you are in Chicago and I am in Tampa, I thought we could set up a 10-to-15 minute phone meeting that would be convenient for you."

---

[2] When you network, you borrow another person's time for your own interests. This means you arrive on time, pay for meals/treats, schedule yourself around their schedules and keep to the time frames allotted. One day, these very same persons may call you and you will want to be treated with the same respect.

Response

"My goal is to speak with someone with your range of experience who has knowledge of or connections in the high tech industry."

Response

"Next week, Thursday at 2:00 p.m.? That sounds great. I'll call you then. Thank you so much."

Second phone call

"*(Name of person you are calling)*, this is *(your name)*. We agreed that I would phone you for a more lengthy discussion today. Is this still a convenient time?"

Response

"Good. *(Referral name)* said you would be a great person to speak with regarding _____. Here's my background in a nutshell. I've been in information systems for 15 years. What I am particularly skilled at is using IS technology to enable managers to run the business more effectively--to actually make decisions. As I mentioned before, my goal is to speak with experts in this field who might lead me to useful contacts."

"My experience in the industry has been with XXX and YYY companies, where I've had a series of progressive positions, most recently as Director of Technology Systems."

"Here are some of my target companies. What do you think of them?"

Response

"Are there others you would suggest?"

Response

"Do you know anyone who works at these organizations, or anyone who may have worked there in the past?"

Response

"Perhaps you can suggest a good search firms in the industry? Have you ever retained a search firm to fill positions for you? Are there any I should stay away from for any reason? Is there anyone there whom I should contact in particular?"

Response

"I'd appreciate your feedback on the direction in which I am heading."

Response

"Can you think of anyone else, perhaps friends, business associates, or any others who could be helpful in leading me to decision makers?"

Response

At the end of the conversation

"May I send along my resume in case you hear of something? I'd appreciate any advice you have to offer."

Response

"Thanks so much for your time; you've been very helpful. If you hear of anything, or have any additional thoughts, would you please let me know. I will keep you posted on my progress and let you know when I accept a new position. And if there is anything I can do for you, please don't hesitate to let me know."

Step 4: Make Calls to Set Up Appointments

Once you have prepared your script and spent time practicing, you are ready to make the actual calls to set up the face-to-face meetings. Early success is based on numbers.

> **Set a goal of ten face-to-face meetings a week
> and plan to make a *minimum* of 5-10 calls per day.**

To make the best use of your time, we recommend scheduling one meeting in the morning and one in the afternoon. You can spend the time in between with research, thank you letters and telephone calls to set up future appointments. Notice, you now have a job. This job has a schedule that needs to be met if you are to be successful. You are working for yourself and your job is finding a new opportunity to use your skills and ability.

It is not unreasonable to anticipate that there may be objections to setting up a face-to-face networking meeting. Later on in this Chapter are common objections and some suggestions for handling them.

Step 5: Develop a Tracking System

You will need to develop a system for managing the information you will be accumulating:

- ◆ Phone calls
- ◆ Letters
- ◆ Informational meetings
- ◆ Interviews
- ◆ Follow-up

You will also want to keep your network alive, even after you have started in your new position, so it is important to have a storage and retrieval system for future reference. In *Chapter 12, "Campaign Action Plan,"* of this workbook there are more details on developing tracking systems.

NETWORKING: THE INFORMATIONAL INTERVIEW

What is an informational interview?

An informational interview is a meeting that you initiate for the purpose of gaining additional knowledge from a person with hands-on experience. In contrast to a job interview, you are the interviewer -- the ball is in your court as to the content and flow. You need to come prepared with questions that you want answered. **<u>Never, never ask for a job</u>** when you have booked an appointment for an informational interview. There is no quicker way to alienate this contact and the person who gave you the referral than to have a "hidden agenda." Always follow up the interview with a thank-you note in which you reiterate anything you found particularly interesting or helpful. Also, keep a record of names, dates, comments and referrals.

Why do an information gathering interview?

- to get first hand information from an expert;

- to check out if your assumptions about a career are really the truth*;*

- to get up to date information regarding trends;

- to get more specific information on just about anything;

- to get more personal and subjective information;

- to get more reflective information about the on-the-job atmosphere, demands, joys, sorrows, etc.;

- to receive an assessment of your aspirations, your skills, your strategy, your resume, etc.;

- ...and anything else you can think of.

What is the difference between an informational interview and a job interview?

- <u>Control:</u> The balance is in your favor. You know what information you want and what the questions are.

- <u>Purpose:</u> They're not interviewing you for a job (not now at least), but you are making that critical first impression which could lead to other recommendations (one of your questions should be to ask for these), or perhaps a position with the company (<u>only</u> if they initiate the subject).

- <u>Pressure:</u> There is every reason for both of you to be relaxed. This is an opportunity to investigate just what you want. The spotlight is on your contact's expertise and your interest in that expertise.

How to arrange the interview

♦ Personal referral is the most effective. Have a mutual acquaintance be the bridge for your contact.

♦ Walk in or phone call are the next best routes if you don't have a personal referral.

♦ Letters seldom work unless it includes a personal referral and follow-up by phone.

HOW TO CONDUCT A NETWORKING MEETING

I. INTRODUCTION

Establish rapport. Thank your contact for meeting with you. If appropriate, mention the name of the person who referred you again and emphasize that you are there to gather information and ask advice about your employment direction or campaign. Take advantage of this introductory time to begin building a relationship.

II. BACKGROUND SUMMARY AND PURPOSE

Give a brief description of your work history using your "90-Second Introduction" as the foundation. State your current thinking about your career and what you would like to accomplish from the meeting. This "fixes the agenda" and manages expectations.

III. QUESTIONS AND DATA COLLECTION

Use a list of prepared, open-ended questions to focus and direct the conversation. Following your research, prepare questions to reflect the kind of information you want from the meeting. Use the following list of questions as a guide.

1. Now that you know a little about my background, what do you think of my being a candidate in the _____ field?

2. What are the primary tasks and responsibilities in your work/functional area?

3. Here is a company contact list that I've compiled from my research. Is there anyone you can recommend that I network with? Would I be able to use your name as a referral?

4. Since you know the industry well, what opportunities do you envision in the near future?

5. I know the typical career progression in my former industry, but not in yours. In your opinion, where would my skills and experience best fit?

6. If you were me, who else would you talk with?

    Follow-up question: What is the best way for me to be introduced to _____?

7. I'm attending the Comdex convention next month in Las Vegas. What companies do you recommend I target?

    Follow-up question: Who should I contact ahead of time so that we can meet while I'm there?

8. Since I am making a career change, what is the best way to establish credibility?

9. Are there opportunities that I may have overlooked?

10. What advice do you have for me as I begin my career transition?

11. Please give me an honest assessment of how you feel I handled myself in our meeting today. Do you have any suggestions for increasing my effectiveness in my next meeting?

As the networking conversation unfolds, listen carefully and take notes. If your contact brings up an obstacle that stands in the way of your career transition, ask how he or she would overcome it.

IV. OBTAIN REFERRALS

Try for a minimum of three names, addresses and phone numbers. If appropriate, ask for internal referrals within your contact's company. If your contact doesn't give you any names, be prepared to ask about the appropriateness of contacting other people you previously identified.

> *For example:* "Do you know Chris Amato over at Datatron? Do you think it would be beneficial for me to call him?"

V. CLOSE THE MEETING

Keep an eye on the time. After 20-30 minutes, remind your contact that you had agreed to that time frame and you are prepared to leave. (It is fine to stay longer *if you are invited*, but don't stay on once you have completed your business.)

Summarize key points and confirm any follow-up activities.

Thank your contact for the help, advice and referrals. Ask if the contact would like to be apprised of your progress. This would be for the purpose of providing feedback on any of his/her recommendations as well as to cultivate the network. If the response is yes, use this as an opportunity to get back in touch. Things change rapidly in today's business world and you may surface more referrals.

Write a thank you note to the contact within 48 hours.

TELEPHONE TECHNIQUES

MAKING THE RIGHT CONNECTION

Communication and Telephone Skills

The telephone is a fundamental "productivity tool" in networking and in your search for work. It is your ally for contacting people you have identified as being instrumental in your search. The following guidelines may be useful in fine-tuning your over-the-phone skills.

Guidelines for Telephone Effectiveness

- **Practice.** Rehearse your scripts with friends or family members. Practice in front of a mirror or into a tape recorder.

- **Be prepared.** Have everything you need with you before calling.

- **Stand up when you phone.** Standing up gives you better breath support and helps your vocal pitch, quality and tone. It also gives you a psychological lift.

- **Relax.** Take several deep breaths to relax yourself before you dial. You will sound more upbeat and energetic.

- **Pitch.** Many people have a higher pitch to their voice if they are nervous. Be aware and try to lower your pitch.

- **Volume.** Try taping yourself or calling your own answering machine and listening to be sure you are neither too loud nor too soft.

- **Slow down.** Because you may want to get the phone call over with and your anxiety level reduced, you may naturally speak quickly. Be aware of this and try to slow down.

- **Try not to leave a message.** By leaving a message to return a call, you are giving the other person the power *not* to call you back. Keep trying to initiate the call yourself. Only after several tries (at normal and off-peak hours) should you leave a message.

- **Polish up your listening skills.** Stay attentive and interested. Ask questions of the other person, and *listen* to the response.

- **Keep it short.** When you promise to talk or meet for a specific length of time, respect the other person's agenda.

- **Remember your goal.** Your goal is to get a face-to-face meeting with the other party. At that time, you should obtain other referrals and leads. Don't have unrealistic expectations for what can be accomplished on the phone. If you can't get a face-to-face meeting don't throw in the towel; set a telephone appointment.

- **Try to avoid being interviewed on the phone.** This could diminish your chance to make a personal impression and to be at your best. You could be rejected before you get your foot in the door. On the other hand, distance may require it and many first screenings are done by telephone, so you must always be prepared to put your best foot forward.

Guidelines for Using Voice Mail

The invention of voice mail has had a tremendous impact on business, and will affect your career transition efforts. It has also changed forever the role of the assistant/ screener in most business organizations.

Here are some techniques to use it to your advantage.

HOW TO DISTINGUISH YOURSELF USING VOICE MAIL

♦ For the first few tries, don't leave a message -- simply hang up. In this way you will have more control over the placement of the next call.

♦ After many tries and before you leave a voice mail message if there is a suggested contact number given, try it. Ask the person who answers what the best time to catch *(name)* in. This may help you tactically.

♦ If you do leave a voice mail message, consider the following:

- Make your message specific, and tailored to fit each person/situation.

- Begin with your name and the reason for your call.

- When leaving your name and phone number, speak slowly and clearly.

- Keep your entire message under 45 seconds.

- Remember your goal -- to set up an appointment.

- Repeat your name and phone number.

If a great deal of time passes before your contact returns your call, be careful that the tone of your voice does not impart frustration or annoyance when calling again.

Sometimes, after trying everything you can think of to get a response to your voice mail messages, you will have to give up the idea of completing a phone connection. However, this may be a good time to *write* to the individual and follow up with a phone call at a later time.

Your Family and the Telephone

Since there may be times when you receive professional calls at home, here are a few suggestions to make the telephone process positive.

1. Invest in a second telephone line with an answering machine or voice mail system to ensure that your calls are answered professionally, and in your own voice. Other alternatives are call forwarding to an answering service or to Memory Call®.

2. Invest in a telephone system that will let you know if there is a call waiting.

3. If a family member is to answer the phone, instruct him or her on the best way to take precise, complete messages for you, and to sound professional.

4. Take your calls where you can control the environment (noise, television, other voices, etc.).

Handling Assistants and Telephone Screeners

There will be times when you will be unable to reach your contact. Although voice mail systems are being used more and more within companies, many times an assistant or receptionist will be your first point of contact. The role of an assistant or receptionist is:

- ◆ Protect the manager by screening unwanted calls.
- ◆ Save time and energy.
- ◆ Prevent unnecessary work interruptions.

Here are two techniques that have high success rates:

1. Call early or late (or during coffee breaks) when the assistant might not be there (and the contact will).

2. Take steps to build a cooperative, friendly relationship with the screener.

Build a Cooperative Relationship with the receptionist or assistant

When a receptionist or assistant shields the person you are trying to reach, take these steps to build a relationship with him or her.

- ◆ Introduce yourself, say your name clearly and spell it, if necessary.
- ◆ Use the name of your referral and tell the screener that your referral suggested you talk to the contact.
- ◆ Ask the assistant or receptionist for his or her name and use the name each time you call.
- ◆ Treat the assistant or receptionist with dignity and respect, without being evasive or condescending; this person is your "helper".
- ◆ If you cannot establish contact with your target after several attempts, ask the assistant when would be the best time for you to try the call again.
- ◆ Avoid leaving a message. You are better able to maintain control of the situation by calling at another time.
- ◆ Each time you call, maintain a friendly tone. By now the receptionist or assistant may be your new best friend.
- ◆ If possible, try to arrange an appointment directly through the assistant.
- ◆ Always remember to thank the assistant for his or her help.

Role Plays: Navigating around the Assistant/Receptionist

Example #1: Connecting to Referrals You Don't Know

1. "Good Morning. This is Jim Chang. May I speak to Mr. Rodriguez? I was referred to him by Paula Ryan."

   Assistant: "Yes, Mr. Chang, I'll connect you."

   or

   "I'll have to see if he is available. Can you tell me the nature of your call?"

2. "Yes, Ms. Ryan suggested I set up an appointment to see Mr. Rodriguez. She recommended that I get his input on a strategy I've been working on."

   Assistant: "Yes, Mr. Chang, I'll connect you."

   or

   "Is there someone else who can help you?"

3. "That might be possible, but Ms. Ryan did tell me to get Mr. Rodriguez's input. Before speaking with someone else, I'd like to be able to tell Ms. Ryan that I did speak with him. Is it possible to speak with him now?"

   Assistant: "Yes, Mr. Chang, I'll connect you."

   or

   "Can Mr. Rodriguez get back to you? He's in a meeting right now."

4. "That would be terrific. But it might be difficult for him to reach me since I'm in and out a lot. Is there a time when he does not have a scheduled meeting or appointment? When it is best to phone him again?"

   Assistant: "Yes, he'll be free tomorrow between 7 and 8:30 AM. You can try again then."

   or

   "His schedule is erratic too. Is there something I can help you with?"

5. "I appreciate your offer to help me. If you make appointments for Mr. Rodriguez, perhaps *you* would schedule an appointment for me on the basis of Ms. Ryan's recommendation."[3]

   Assistant: "Yes, I can do that for Mr. Rodriguez. How about March 14th?"

The "Never Say No" Technique

Your responses leave an impression on every person you call. The *"never say no"* technique means responding positively to whatever suggestions are made by the recipient of your call.

---

[3] (Ed. note: This is an excellent answer to a question that would otherwise end your conversation.)

Even though some suggestions may seem like barriers or diversions, the person you call will come away from the interaction with a positive impression of you. Note the caller's consistently positive responses in the examples below.

Be Assertive about Getting the Appointment

The same guidelines you used to work with the assistant or receptionist apply all the way through the process until you reach your contact.

Above all, remember your goal -- to get a face-to-face appointment with the contact or referral. If you keep that goal in mind, you can circumvent any of the attempts to divert you.

Example #2: Persistence in Making the Appointment

1. "Good Morning Mr. Boone. This is Robin Weaver. Jean Levitt from Central Bank, who is on the Chamber of Commerce Board of Directors with you, suggested I set up a meeting with you. Would you have some time next week?"

   Professional: "Yes, how about Wednesday..."

   or

   "What do you want to see me about?"

2. "I'm currently exploring new career opportunities in the marketing of new business in the banking industry. Jean thought you would be a good person to discuss my plan with and perhaps get some ideas. I should add, she gave me no reason to believe that you had an open position in your organization -- what I need is feedback. Would you have some time later next week when we could meet?"

   Professional: "Yes, what time on the morning of the 28th can you be here?"

   or

   "I'm not really sure I'm the one who can help you."

3. "I'm not sure either. But Jean spoke highly of your expertise and knowledge in the new products market, and told me you might be willing to spend some time, say 20 to 30 minutes, with me. Would you be available next week or the week after?"

   Professional: "Yes, how about Wednesday the 28th?"

   or

   "Maybe I could switch this call to Human Resources."

4. "I would be glad to talk to your Human Resources Department about employment possibilities or contracting, if it turns out my skills could be a good match for your company. But, does HR have expertise and knowledge in the new products market?"

   Professional: Well, not exactly...

5. "Jean did suggest that you could be helpful to me. I'd really appreciate 20 minutes with you to get your input on my plan and approach. I'd be glad to see you when it's convenient for you."

   Professional: "Yes, how about Wednesday the 28th?"

   or

   "I'm tied up this month with budgets and a trip to Washington."

6. "I would be happy to set up a date any time you can make it. The meeting can be short and I'll be well prepared. How about sometime the week of March 9th?"

   Professional: "All right, how about Wednesday of that week?"

Some Final thoughts..... Networking is not a ploy to afford you the opportunity to ask someone for a job. When you network, you really are looking for information; information about the job market, your field of interest, the transferability of your skills from one environment to another, how to present yourself, etc. If there is an opportunity and you make a favorable impression by just being you, the individual with whom you are networking will be "proud" to personally refer you or, better yet, hire you. After all, everyone likes to be a winner and referring the "right person" is as satisfying as being the right person. The idea behind networking is to develop reciprocal relationships.

VERY IMPORTANT SUMMARY

- ◆ Communication is the foundation of networking success.

- ◆ Networking, Interviewing and Negotiating all rely on effective oral communication.

- ◆ Everyone has an extensive network.

- ◆ Telephone skills will help determine the number and quality of networking meetings.

- ◆ Networking is the most effective method of finding employment for most people.

- ◆ Communication effectiveness is dramatically improved through planning and practice.

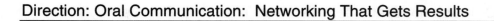

CHAPTER SIX

References

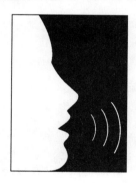

"There is only one thing in the world worse than being talked about, and that is not being talked about."

Wilde -- *The Picture of Dorian Gray*

POINTS OF INTEREST
Chapter Six discusses: ♦ The importance of references   ♦ How to develop a reference strategy that will strengthen your work search   ♦ Ways to develop a list of reference prospects   ♦ How to prepare a draft reference statement

WHAT ARE REFERENCES AND WHY DO YOU NEED THEM?

At some point in your search, usually towards the end of an interview process, you may be asked to give a prospective employer some references. You will want to be well prepared for this before the situation arises. You need to compile a reference database.

THE VALUE OF REFERENCES TO THE INTERVIEWER
I.   References provide a validity check.

What are potential employers looking for?

1.   **Resume distortion**. It is estimated that 50 percent of all resumes contain deliberate distortions. One detected misstatement can disqualify you, so do not be dishonest or stretch the truth.

2.   **Legal protection**. No one wants to hire an employee who turns out to have a violent history, criminal background, serious credit problems, or other problems that may cause harm or distress to colleagues or customers. This could turn out to be much more than simply a bad hire -- the company could become the target of a lawsuit.

3.   **Improved "hit" rate**. Hiring managers are experiencing increasing pressure to hire only those people who can make an immediate contribution. Since nearly all employers believe that past performance is an indicator of future performance, there is keen interest in exploring the accuracy of claimed accomplishments.

4.   **Psychological fit**. Hiring managers know that whether you fit in or not depends on your beliefs about work, your personality, style, behavior under pressure, flexibility and speed in adapting to their culture and environment.

5.   **Opportunity to read between the lines**. A skilled interviewer is able to get beyond what is said to what is meant. Often what references omit is as important as what is actually said. Many experienced reference checkers have an excellent intuitive sense that allows them to pick up subtleties that provide critical information.

THE VALUE OF REFERENCES TO THE INTERVIEWEE

I. References provide a final opportunity to sell yourself so
you need to be strategic in your choices.

DEVELOPING YOUR REFERENCE STRATEGY

What is Your Reference Strategy?

Even your greatest supporters may not necessarily know how to promote you in the most positive way. Prior to their being contacted by one of your potential employers, you will need to coach them and supply them with the necessary information. After, you will need to solicit feedback from them about the kinds of questions they were asked by reference checkers, and obtain their reactions to the answers. Such information could help you land your targeted position. You cannot leave it to chance. This means you must:

    I. Compile a reference prospect list.

    II. Prepare a reference statement.

    III. Contact the people on the list to seek their agreement.

I. COMPILE A REFERENCE PROSPECT LIST/DATABASE

Since references can be an extremely important element in your search, it is critical that you select people who are willing to give you a solid reference. Most of the time you will be asked to furnish five names -- three professional and two personal references. Select individuals from your **reference database** who are most likely to relate well to the specific work situation.

Potential references include:

- Former managers
- Project leaders
- Colleagues
- Customers
- Vendors/Suppliers
- External business associates
- Direct reports

I: COMPILING YOUR REFERENCE PROSPECTS LIST

Directions: Use the following form to identify potential prospects for your reference list:

1. **Former managers** to whom you directly reported. Also include managers or team leaders where you may have had a dotted-line responsibility. Include your last manager, even if he or she has retired or left the company. List only those for your last 2-3 positions.

_____

_____

2. **Project leaders** to whom you reported for the duration of a project.

_____

_____

3. **Team colleagues** with whom you worked on major projects.

_____

_____

4. **Important customers** with whom you had an excellent business relationship.

_____

_____

5. **Vendors** or **suppliers** who can vouch for your business expertise.

_____

_____

6. **Outside business people**, such as members of charitable or service organizations, who have first-hand knowledge of your expertise.

_____

_____

7. **Key individuals** who reported directly to you.

_____

_____

Getting It On Paper: Creating your Reference Database/List

Directions: Now that you have a reference prospect list, sort it selecting those who can provide different perspectives on your work, achievements, etc. Next, compile them in a format that will be easy for you to retrieve when you have a specific purpose to satisfy and that is reader-friendly for the interviewer. Be sure to check addresses and phone numbers to make sure they are current. If your reference has an e-mail address, you may wish to include it. On the following pages, write a brief summary for each reference so that a potential employer understands your relationship to each one.

Note: You need not give the entire reference database to every potential employer. Select a list that will best represent you for each given situation. You will have made sure that each person selected will support and bolster you by contacting them (see next section). The list you provide to the company interested in your services should be no longer than one page.

Reference Database

Name_____Background_____

Position/Company_____

Street_____

Town, State, Zip_____

Phone:_____

Relationship:_____

Name_____Background_____

Position/Company_____

Street_____

Town, State, Zip_____

Phone:_____

Relationship:_____

Name_____ Background_____

Position/Company_____

Street_____

Town, State, Zip_____

Phone:_____

Relationship:_____

Direction: References

Name_____Background_____

Position/Company_____

Street_____

Town, State, Zip_____

Phone:_____

Relationship:_____

_____

Name_____Background_____

Position/Company_____

Street_____

Town, State, Zip_____

Phone:_____

*Relationship*_____

Name_____ Background_____

Position/Company_____

Street_____

Town, State, Zip_____

Phone:_____

Relationship:_____

Name_____ Background_____

Position/Company_____

Street_____

Town, State, Zip_____

Phone:_____

Relationship:_____ _____ _____

Name_____ Background_____

Position/Company_____

Street_____

Town, State, Zip_____

Phone:_____

Relationship:_____

Duplicate these pages as needed

Sample Reference List

(Note: The Reference List is a selected subset of your Database)

Leslie Smith
120 Worth Street
Hartford, CT 06107
Home (860) 561-9842
Office (860) 521-6000

Reference Name	Background
James Lawford 16 Red Bank Road Winsted, CT 06999 (860) 561-6622 *Relationship: Former manager*	Jim retired at the end of 1992 as Vice President of Dickinson, Inc. I reported directly to Jim for two years; my major responsibilities were Customer Service Manager and Help Desk Manager.
Joyce Sterns, Director Dickinson, Inc. 98 Devonshire Road Boston, MA 02107 (203) 968-0103 *Relationship: Former manager*	Joyce was Director of Customer Relations, which also included managing production of the company newsletter. I worked for Joyce for three years, first as a Customer Support Supervisor, and then as Manager of the department.
Mark Walshinsky Technical Services Manager 234 Main Avenue Hartford, CT 06114 (860) 561-6000 *Relationship: Team member*	Mark was Assistant Director of Research and Production and is now Technical Services Manager of Bohman & Bohman Printing Center. I worked on a team with Mark as a customer liaison for print project production as well as on other projects in various capacities during a ten-year period.
Daniel Tremonti Director of PC Services Ames & Co. 20 Filmore Street Bridgeport, CT 06622 (203) 334-7615 *Relationship: Colleague*	Dan and I were colleagues at Dickinson, where he served as Director of PC Services. Since Dan and I know each other socially, he can also be a personal reference.
Keisha Sanders Director, Electronic Publishing Pagano Partners 35 West Avenue Stamford, CT 06902 (203) 968-0103 *Relationship: Former supervisor*	Keisha is now responsible for all corporate electronic publishing at Pagano Partners. I worked for her as a Customer Service Representative.

II: PREPARING THOSE WHO WILL PROVIDE YOU WITH A REFERENCE

Prepare a Draft of a Reference Statement

Compose a statement that your former manager or other references could comfortably give on your behalf. It should be in simple, conversational tone, much the way it would sound if discussed over the telephone. Review the points below to help create your reference statement.

- ◆ **Credibility**. How does your proposed reference know you? Cover such items as the reporting relationship and the length of time you worked together.

- ◆ **Strengths, Skills, Abilities**. A description of what you do well, and examples that illustrate them.

- ◆ **Accomplishments**. What were the things you did well for the company during your tenure? What major contributions did you make? Look back and net out your key accomplishments.

- ◆ **Personal traits**. Comment on your positive traits, especially those that relate to your work and your ability to get along with others. Cover such things as work and management style, degree of rapport with other employees, integrity and life values.

- ◆ **Areas needing development**. Make sure that your references understand that *it is customary to omit this information unless specifically asked.* If something must be said about your weaknesses, try to agree on a trait(s) that can be presented along with your efforts at improvement or the lessons you learned.

- ◆ **Reason for leaving**. This is the "official story." Keep it as simple, direct, positive and as plausible as possible.

When you have completed a draft of the reference statement, review it with each reference. It is preferable to do this in person so that you can answer questions, listen carefully, and be aware of any "signals" that there may be an issue or concern.

Remember to select the most suitable reference for each specific situation. Match the people in reference database to the interviewer, position and company, keeping in mind communication style, culture and suitability to speak about your expertise.

Sample Reference Statement Draft

Purpose: *For discussion with former manager or other references*

Remember, this is a *discussion draft* or outline. The actual words should be the words of the person acting as a referral, not yours.

On Credibility

"Chris and I worked together for eight years. We have co-managed the majority of the customer-care projects for the last seven years."

or

"Chris was my direct manager for four years. He/she led my customer service team and was responsible for reorganizing our entire division."

On Contributions

"Chris introduced new techniques in customer service: better control systems and a process to ensure adequate staffing of major projects."

or

"Chris made important contributions in organizing and managing projects which dramatically increased customer satisfaction while saving money and time."

On Personality

"Chris is able to maintain calm in the face of a crisis. And people respect his or her professional skills and integrity as a manager."

On Weaknesses (if asked)

"Chris had a tendency to become immersed in the details of a project as the scope increased. He/she often put in 50- and 60-hour weeks."

On Reason for Leaving (if asked of previous manager)

"As Chris's responsibilities became more focused on routine maintenance of the department, and opportunities for heading up new projects decreased, he or she felt it was time to move on."

III. CONTACT YOUR REFERENCE PROSPECTS

Once you have compiled your list, contact the people you have identified to solicit permission and endorsement. When each agrees to be a reference, provide him or her with:

- Details about the position you are seeking
- Information about who will be contacting them and why
- Information about the company with whom you are interviewing
- Questions he or she will likely be asked, and potential responses

In this way, each reference can speak knowledgeably and articulately about your qualifications for the position, greatly improving your chances of receiving an offer.

ADDITIONAL POINTS ON REFERENCES:

1. **Potential employers do not consider letters of reference** (collected from former employers) to be very valuable.

2. **Do what you can to prepare your references -- especially a former manager**. Even though well-intentioned, your former manager may be unskilled at handling a clever telephone inquiry. What you want is a balanced and fair appraisal from your former manager, assessing the overall service you rendered to your former company.

3. **Handling inquiries by search professionals**. Your references may be contacted by professionals from an executive search firm. These people are expert at shaping questions that will uncover inconsistencies and weaknesses. By thoroughly grooming your references, you will minimize negative comments and give them the ammunition needed to boost you toward your new position.

4. **Do not offer references until requested**. When you are asked, determine the number and type of references required (e.g., managers, peers, subordinates) and be prepared to deliver, fax or mail your list within the next 24 hours.

5. **Once someone asks for your reference list, phone your references as soon as possible**. Inform them of the nature of the position for which you are being considered, and how well you think you fit. This will give them time to think about what to say in support of your efforts. Thank them for their help and ask them to call you to let you know the results.

6. **Let your references know you appreciate their help and support**. Effective references can be a bonus in your search, so let them know you appreciate their assistance, and offer to return the favor if an opportunity arises. Be sure to keep them informed of your progress -- you will want to keep the contact alive and well for the future.

SUMMARY

A well-founded reference strategy is an important part of your employment campaign. References have the potential to make or break a positive interview process. To utilize them most effectively, you need to:

- ♦ **Identify the best reference prospects** for the positions you are interviewing for.

- ♦ **Know what needs to be included** in a reference statement.

- ♦ Understand the importance of **when and how to involve references**.

- ♦ **Prepare a concise, cohesive draft** of a reference statement that you can discuss with your references.

- ♦ **Coach references** on what to say and how to say it.

- ♦ **Maintain contact with your references** to determine what has taken place in the interview process and what was discussed. Keep them informed about the results of your search.

- ♦ **Express appreciation** for their help and offer help in return.

CHAPTER SEVEN
Research & Targeting
CUSTOMER-ASSESSMENT

"No man ever wetted clay and then left it, as if there would be bricks by chance and fortune."

Plutarch, *Of Fortune*

POINTS OF INTEREST

In Chapter Seven you will learn:

♦ That marketing yourself requires strategy, research and a new vision of your role in the workplace

♦ That today's technology-driven marketplace presents many opportunities that can be uncovered by focused research efforts

♦ How, what, where and whom to research and target

♦ How to effectively use research tools and techniques to accelerate your search, particularly the Internet

CUSTOMER-ASSESSMENT

With the same intensity you put into your Self-Assessment, you must now learn all you can about your potential customers — who they are, where they are, and what they will pay and how to appeal to them.

Conducting research will help you identify:

- The industries that need the skills you possess and the business outlook for them.

- Noteworthy companies within those industries (your potential customers).

- The qualities valued by your potential client so that you can validly compare your qualities and Ideal Work Preferences (Chapter 2) to them.

- The locations of these companies. Do they have local, regional, or national offices? Which office do you have to approach to get the job you want?

- People you know who can help you make contact with these firms (networking - Chapter 5)

- The products and services you can sell to specific customers within your defined marketplace, e.g., solutions to their business problems; innovations to improve their growth. (Chapter 2)

- The title of the individual(s) who can actually hire you or influence a hiring decision.

- The general salary range for the position you want.

IDENTIFYING POTENTIAL PROSPECTS

In this case, more is better. The more prospects you come up with, the more you have to work with. Once you have a prospect list you can refine it into a target marketing campaign. The following steps will guide you in your pursuit of prospects.

1. **Assemble a list of companies** that <u>might</u> meet your requirements. Be sure to use:

   - The information and insights you developed in the self-assessment exercises;

   - Your potential services (brainstormed with your peers, friends, acquaintances, etc., in Chapter 3).

   Your search is facilitated by asking the question, "What industries would be interested in the services I have to offer?" (See Exercise #3-1)

   For example: If you were in the pharmaceutical industry your skills might be applicable to organizations that deal in formula-made products, medical products, scientific products, FDA approval products, etc.

   In other words, you are looking for organizations that are in some way related to your skills, ability and knowledge...not necessarily the exact same business from which you came. This is the time to be a free thinker and brainstorm. Sometimes friends who know the least about your specific work can help the most. Too, you might even want to make this a family activity -- kids have great ideas as well.

2. **Look for consistency**: Companies with functional areas that are consistent with your background and experience (e.g., Finance or Human Resources) are good targets. Once you have identified these companies, cross-match them to see if any are in your preferred geographic area.

   If your career goal is more industry-defined, you will be looking for companies in your industry or others that are closely related.

   For example, a manager in pharmaceuticals would target a company that makes related products. A computer technician could target computer companies or other businesses that make extensive use of technology.

3. **Identify solid prospects** from your personal industry knowledge, including competitors, suppliers and customers. Write them down as they occur to you without pre-judging any of them.

4. **Supplement preliminary list through networking** -- ask your contacts for information about these and other companies they feel would be a good fit for you.

WHAT TO RESEARCH

You need to obtain as much information as you can about the industry, the organization, and the individuals in any organization you plan to contact. Information relevant to your search is summarized below:

- ♦ **Industry Information**
  - Historic Trends
  - Recent Trends
  - Noteworthy Companies within the Industry
- ♦ **Company Information**
  - History, Size, Growth Rate
  - Profitability
  - Products/Services
  - Financial History and Current Status
  - Top Management Players
    - – Backgrounds
    - – Tenure/Average Age
    - – Philosophy
  - Company Culture
  - Changes in Company Structure
  - Changes in Product Lines or Services
  - Have they been re-organized, downsized, TQM'ed, etc. What were the results?
- ♦ **Geographic Area Job Trends**
  - Companies moving in and out of the area
  - Compensation practices
  - Job growth in specific fields

♦ **Information about Your Specific Profession**

- The demand for persons in your profession

- The characteristics of your competition for a position

- The supply of persons in your profession

- Where are these professionals currently being recruited

- Where are these professionals gaining their continuing education (e.g., associations, colleges, universities, public seminars, etc.)

RESEARCH & YOUR MARKETING CAMPAIGN

Once you have identified some potential customers for your services, you need to develop a marketing plan. Don't go at it haphazardly, randomly sending resumes, calling every personnel department or stopping by their offices in hopes of seeing someone. **There has to be a clearly defined strategy -- a plan**. Even though you are eager to begin that new career, <u>the biggest setback to finding a new position is failing to plan a marketing strategy.</u>

The diagram below will give you a visual concept of a marketing campaign. In this chapter we will deal with the bottom portion of it, the six research steps. In the next chapter we cover the other parts.

DIAGRAM OF A MARKETING CAMPAIGN

PROSPECT FOR TARGETS	SIFT PROSPECTS	FOCUS ON PRIMARY TARGETS	MAKE THE BEST APPROACH	SELL YOURSELF
Conduct Research	Research	Your Prime Targets	Introductions	Network
Informational Networking	Analyze	(between 5-20 candidates)	Referrals	Interviews
Advertised Openings	Strategize		Phone Calls	Research
Customized Letters	Network	Secondary Prospects	Letters	First Impressions
			Search Firms	

STEP 1 Define Initial Target List	STEP 2 Screen Target List	STEP 3 Research To Obtain Interviews	STEP 4 Research To Prepare For Interviews	STEP 5 Research To Prepare For Offers	STEP 6 Research To Prepare For Negotiations

THE SIX RESEARCH STEPS

THE SIX RESEARCH STEPS:

Step 1: Define Initial Target List
End Result: To quickly generate a quantity of possible target companies (start with 20-30 companies).

Step 2: Screen Target List
End Result: To reduce original target list to 5-20 companies.

Step 3: Conduct Research to Obtain Appointments for Networking or Interviewing
End Result: To identify the appropriate functional areas in target companies where you might fit, and to make contact with influencers and/or decision makers.

Step 4: In-Depth Research to Prepare for Interviews
End Result: To become knowledgeable about the organization, the people who will be in the interview, and verify your fit.

Step 5: Final Research to Prepare for an Offer
End Result: To consolidate all research data on the company in preparation for an anticipated offer and your initial response.

Step 6: Research to Prepare for Negotiation
End Result: To gather pertinent information that supports your negotiating strategy.

THE RESEARCH STEPS

STEP 1: DEFINE INITIAL TARGET LIST

Why: To quickly generate a quantity of possible target companies (start with 20-30).

How: Start filling out Research Investigation Sheets:

♦ Write down companies you already know.

♦ Scan lists of companies and databases to expand your target list.

♦ Talk to your contacts[1] to develop more targets.

Where: Refer to DBM's *Index of Resources* for a comprehensive listing of reference resources and suggestions for how to use them for this and other research steps.

♦ Electronic databases, Internet.

♦ Directories, other reference sources (public library).

♦ Telephone listings (industry contacts, search firms, local sources in designated locations).

STEP 2: SCREEN TARGET LIST

Why: To reduce original target list to 5-20 companies using the following criteria:

♦ Does it have the potential to meet my Ideal Work Preferences?

♦ Is the company likely to have opportunities (because of expansion, growing industry, key problems) that fit my skills, interests, background, and experience?

How:

♦ Review your Ideal Work Preferences. Understand the industry/company/field growth potential and future profitability. (Chapter 2)

♦ Screen by the broadest factors first, then prioritize using other screening factors found in your IWP's. Use networking contacts to help you hone your target list.

Where:

♦ Electronic databases, Internet.

♦ Directories, other reference sources (public library).

♦ Annual Reports.

---

[1] Contacts are anyone you know: friends, neighbors, colleagues, vendors, customer, people in shops you frequent, etc.

THE RESEARCH STEPS, CONT.

STEP 3: CONDUCT RESEARCH TO OBTAIN APPOINTMENTS FOR NETWORKING OR INTERVIEWING
Why: To identify the appropriate functional areas in target companies where you might fit, and to make contact with decision-makers.
How: Use most appropriate resources to identify names and functions.
Where: ♦ Network, or use direct telephone contact, to reach decision-makers. ♦ Directories, references, electronic databases, Internet for company data and identification of functions and decision-makers.

STEP 4: IN-DEPTH RESEARCH TO PREPARE FOR INTERVIEWS
Why: To become knowledgeable about the organization and verify your fit.
How: ♦ Review I-SPEAK® notes to match up with interviewer style. Review DBM interviewing material (e.g., the "Interviewing" section of this workbook; the DBM "Interview" videotape). Review all previous research on company, decision-makers and interviewers. ♦ Prepare questions that reflect your knowledge of the company (e.g., its strengths, weaknesses, problems and opportunities). Prepare to showcase your skills and accomplishments, and match them to the company needs.
Where: ♦ DBM "*Career Continuation Workbook*". ♦ Newspapers, periodicals, financial reports, etc., to obtain current data on company and decision-makers; electronic databases (e.g., *PROMT* Articles, *DataTimes*, *DIALOG*, *Investext Reports*, *DowVision*), Internet. ♦ Network to learn about company culture, needs/styles of decision-makers, what it's like to work there, etc.

THE RESEARCH STEPS, CONT.

STEP 5: FINAL RESEARCH TO PREPARE FOR AN OFFER

Why: To consolidate all research data on the company in preparation for an anticipated offer and your initial response.

How:

♦ Determine Ideal Work Preference (IWP) issues requiring more information.

♦ Develop questions regarding what you need to know about your potential future manager and co-workers.

♦ Develop questions regarding unknowns about the components of your job, and what is expected of you.

Where:

♦ Use Chapter 2 to assist you with this.

♦ Annual Report, financial analyses, other internal information.

♦ Current and previous employees, contacts who know the company/manager, colleagues, DBM *"Career Continuation Program."*

STEP 6: RESEARCH TO PREPARE FOR NEGOTIATION

Why: To gather pertinent information that supports your negotiating strategy.

How:

♦ Evaluate offer using the results of your self-assessment analysis (e.g., Ideal Work Preferences, Satisfiers/Dissatisfiers, etc.).

♦ Determine negotiable items.

♦ Study research to develop alternatives.

Where:

♦ DBM *Career Continuation Workbook*, Chapter 11 on *Negotiating.*

♦ Books and articles on negotiation; company internal publications (policies, procedures or personnel manual).

♦ Reference material on industry (e.g., salary surveys- geographic as well as professional assn., relocation norms, cost of living).

♦ Reference material to support alternatives (e.g., articles, reports).

[Sample Research Investigation Sheet]

Name of company / Industry _____

_____

Phone number (____)___-_____   fax (____)___-____   E-Mail_____@_____

Internet Address_____

Mailing Address_____

_____

_____

Products/services_____

_____

_____

_____

Reasons for adding to target list_____

_____

_____

_____

_____

_____

_____

Key contacts (names, titles, addresses & phone numbers)

_____

_____

_____

_____

_____

_____

_____

_____

_____

_____

_____

SUMMARY

Final Thoughts on Research

The benefits of research are to:

♦ Provide you with the necessary information to target appropriate employment prospects

♦ Help you become the candidate of choice for opportunities that fit your interests and skills

♦ Provide focus

♦ Create significant competitive advantage

♦ Shorten your search for work

It is important to:

A. Balance action and research by not getting mired in unnecessary data collection

B. Work efficiently by *learning how to use* the sources available to you. Spend time in the public library or other research libraries to learn about what is available; learn how to use the Internet effectively; learn how to review financial information efficiently, etc.

Remember: The main purpose of research is to gather enough information to make informed, intelligent choices; develop contacts; and network.

CHAPTER EIGHT
Methods & Strategies
to Find Work

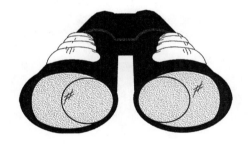

"If you wish in this world to advance
Your merits you're bound to
enhance;
You must stir it and stump it,
And blow your own trumpet,
Or, trust me, you haven't a chance."

W. S. Gilbert -- *Ruddigore*

POINTS OF INTEREST

Chapter Eight will help you to:

♦ Understand how work search strategies integrate into the new work environment.

♦ Develop and select appropriate work search strategies.

♦ Make the distinction between the types of work opportunities and how best to find each.

♦ Effectively deal with search firms and agencies.

♦ Respond effectively to ads.

INTRODUCTION TO SEARCH

DIAGRAM OF A MARKETING CAMPAIGN

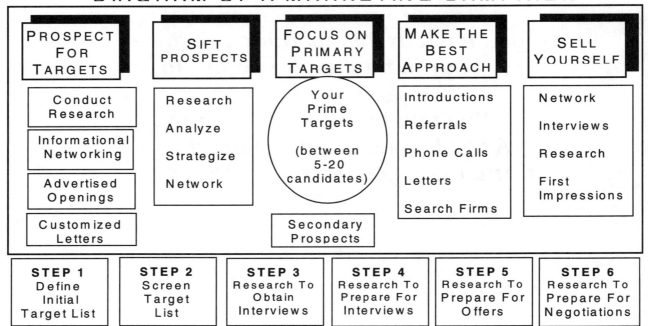

PROSPECT FOR TARGETS	SIFT PROSPECTS	FOCUS ON PRIMARY TARGETS	MAKE THE BEST APPROACH	SELL YOURSELF
Conduct Research	Research	Your Prime Targets	Introductions	Network
Informational Networking	Analyze	(between 5-20 candidates)	Referrals	Interviews
Advertised Openings	Strategize		Phone Calls	Research
Customized Letters	Network	Secondary Prospects	Letters	First Impressions
			Search Firms	

STEP 1 Define Initial Target List	STEP 2 Screen Target List	STEP 3 Research To Obtain Interviews	STEP 4 Research To Prepare For Interviews	STEP 5 Research To Prepare For Offers	STEP 6 Research To Prepare For Negotiations

THE SIX RESEARCH STEPS

Exercise #8-1

TEST YOUR UNDERSTANDING OF THE JOB MARKET

Check if the statement is true or false.

		True	False
1	It is not a good practice to ask friends and family members for employer contacts and leads.	☐	☐
2	If you mail cover letters and resumes to enough companies, it is likely to produce excellent work prospects.	☐	☐
3	Contacting executive search firms is a good way to get your resume to the right people in companies that are hiring.	☐	☐
4	On average, a potential employer will take between one and two minutes to read a resume for the first time.	☐	☐
5	The majority of positions are filled through ads and search firms.	☐	☐
6	Senior-level managers are not likely to talk with job seekers who call them on the phone.	☐	☐
7	The average work tenure in a company is less today than it was ten years ago.	☐	☐
8	The so-called "hidden job market" accounts for 35 percent of the available work for most individuals.	☐	☐
9	Networking and developing of personal contacts are by far the most effective methods of locating employment today.	☐	☐
10	Many employers are looking for individuals with broad experience in several functions rather than technical experts.	☐	☐
11	The best companies expect you to go through "formal channels" if you are to be seriously considered as a candidate for employment.	☐	☐
12	DBM will probably find work for you.	☐	☐

TESTING YOUR UNDERSTANDING OF THE MARKET

1. *It is not a good practice to ask friends and family members for employer contacts and leads.*
   False. Friends and relatives can be excellent resources and are usually glad to help. More importantly, they know other executives and professionals who know other people, etc. Use their help and you will quickly begin building a list of valuable contacts who can, if asked, lead you to opportunities.

2. *If you mail cover letters and resumes to enough companies, it is likely to produce excellent work prospects.*
   False. Mass mailings of unsolicited resumes are usually a waste of time and postage. Every day, companies across the country receive countless letters and resumes which are ignored. The odds are extremely low that you will find employment through mail campaigns.

3. *Contacting executive search firms is a good way to get your resume to the right people in companies that are hiring.*
   False. Executive search firms work for the client company, and are paid to find a nearly perfect match for an opening. Search firms work on a small number of searches at any given time and would only have an interest in you if you happen to be the perfect match for a search they are currently working on.

4. *On average, a potential employer will take one to two minutes to read a resume for the first time.*
   False. The average time an employer reads a resume is less than thirty seconds. Most of the time your resume is being screened, not read, the first time around. That is why it is so important to include the "key words" for your field that will highlight your credentials.

5. *The majority of positions are filled through ads and executive search firms.*
   False. A very small percentage of positions are filled through ads and search firms. In today's business world, employers do not need to advertise heavily because of the new paradigms regarding employment. More people are looking at their careers as a series of jobs so lots of people continuously shop. Also, jobs are found on the Internet, and through networking more often than through ads and search firms.

6. *Senior-level managers are not likely to talk with job seekers who call them on the phone.*
   False. To the contrary. Even in today's time-crunched work world, executives will talk with you if you are referred to them by someone they know.

7. *The average work tenure in a company is less today than it was ten years ago.*
   True. DBM's research indicates that the median tenure in an occupation is 6.5 years, and the length of time with one employer has dropped to 4.5 years. Over a 40-year career, that means the average worker will change career and/or career directions every six years and move to another company nine times.

8. *The so-called "hidden job market" accounts for 35 % of the available work for most individuals.*
False. The "hidden job market" accounts for roughly 3 out of every 4 jobs! Many employment seekers direct their search efforts only to those positions that are made public through ads and agencies. Do not make this mistake.

9. *Networking and developing of personal contacts are by far the most effective methods of locating employment today.*
True. It is probably safe to say that networking and personal contacts are the prime methods of locating work. In addition, locating work through networking means you will have less competition and greater potential to influence the responsibilities and authority of a new position.

10. *Many employers are looking for individuals with broad experience in several functions rather than technical experts.*
True. Technical experts in many industries are more plentiful than problem solvers. American business is facing unprecedented global pressures, resulting in a need for professionals with broad exposure to business. The ability to be flexible and manage diverse and multiple projects across business functions is highly valued.

11. *The best companies expect you to go through "formal channels" if you are to be seriously considered as a candidate for employment.*
False. The higher the level, the more positions are filled through the "back door" rather than through more formal channels.

12. *DBM will probably find work for you.*
False. DBM does not find people work. DBM will provide you with their proven process of information, tools, techniques and training to help you identify and land the best work situation.

METHODS TO EMPLOY IN YOUR SEARCH FOR WORK

Your work-search campaign will have both active and passive activities:

I. Active Techniques:

    A. Networking

    B. Targeted Marketing Letters

II. Passive Techniques:

    A. Searching the Internet or registering with electronic databases and services

    B. Registering with search firms/employment agencies or approaching contracting (e.g., outsourcing) companies

    C. Answering want ads

    D. Direct mail campaigns

    E. Other Strategies

SOURCES OF INTERVIEWS	PERCENTAGE OF POSITIONS OBTAINED
Active Techniques:	
Targeted Networking	50-80%
Targeted Marketing Letters	2-10%
Passive Techniques:	
Search Firms	10-15%
Answering Ads	5-10%

For many years, DBM has tracked the ways in which candidates locate employment opportunities. The table above shows the success rate for the four most common methods of obtaining work. Don't neglect any of these techniques, but understand the success rate. **Targeted Networking is the best strategy.** Invest most of your time in it to produce results. Minimize the amount of time spent on search methods with low success rates.

GUIDELINES FOR OBTAINING WORK

A. In addition to Targeted Networking, select search methods that make sense for you.

B. Use what you learn to modify and improve your campaign.

C. Integrate your methods into a planned campaign.

D. Monitor your progress so that you are clear about what is working and what is not.

Work opportunities can be grouped by how publicly known they are. When viewed this way you can see how different search techniques will uncover them for you. Keep in mind that work opportunities can be full-time positions with benefits, consulting situations, contract work, or even entrepreneurial opportunities where a specific job or position has not yet been fully defined:

1. **Open/ published positions.** Work opportunities that are published and can be found by searching newspaper ads, trade journals, job banks, databases, state and federal job listings. In the DBM Index of Resources you will find a wealth of resources in which to search for these positions. Of these, the most efficient method is the Internet. It will give you the most current and wide ranging information on job openings as well as electronic means to apply.

2. **Partially hidden positions.** Positions known inside a company or industry but not published or listed externally. Only **networking** will alert you to the existence of these positions. Or if you are reading newspapers or professional publications you may notice trends for particular kinds of positions. Use this information to anticipate where other positions might exist that are not advertised.

3. **Hidden positions.** Work opportunities that are not published or widely known inside a specific company or industry. This category also includes jobs that don't exist until you define the position yourself based on your skills and your assessment of a company's needs. These are positions you have to "sell" to the buyer by identifying the "hidden need" for your services. It is no different from selling any new product; you must first educate the buyer that s/he has unfulfilled needs. Again, **networking** together with research will make these kinds of opportunities known to you.

◆ S8-9 ◆

I. ACTIVE TECHNIQUES TO FIND POSITIONS

A. Networking:

Networking means systematically talking to people you already know in order to connect to the people whom they know. This is the fastest way to reach the appropriate individuals who can provide the links you need to connect with your ideal work situation. The Internet is the world's largest network, so use its reach to your advantage. Get to know people both near and far, because sometimes those distant contacts can be much closer than you think.

Initially when you network, you are seeking information, advice, ideas, names and referrals. These contacts will lead you to other people, who will lead you to other people, until you make the connection to your desired work situation.

Even though networking is the most effective method of finding work, many people resist using the technique. Although it may be easier to work within the comfort zone of answering ads and sending out resumes, the fact is that **the most effective way to tap into the hidden job market is through networking.** DBM has an entire chapter dedicated to this most important subject; Chapter 5.

B. Targeted Marketing Letters:

The most successful direct mail campaigns are with "targeted" mailings. These are **letters targeting a company or individual within a company who may require your set of skills or background.** You select your targets through research and networking efforts. They work best when you have a referral name. (See Chapter Nine of this workbook and your Index of Resources for samples of targeted marketing letters.)

II. PASSIVE TECHNIQUES

A. Using The Internet/Registering With Electronic Databases

The Internet gives you access to current information. Why wait for the information you need to make it into print, even into the newspaper? Go on-line and see if it's already available. As the Internet grows and expands, so do the number of participants and the resources for finding jobs. The Internet is available to you when you are ready to use it, 24 hours a day, seven days a week, regardless of time zones. Once you have gotten access to the Internet, you can access thousands of free resources with job listings, help for writing resumes and constructing cover letters, and even planning your career path on-line. If you are moving across the state, across the country, or out of the country, there is no need to wait until you actually arrive in your new location to begin your search for employment. Save on long distance phone calls and subscriptions to out-of-town newspapers. Organizations, especially businesses, are rushing to get onto the Internet. They see opportunities for advertising, possible commercial markets, and a vast wealth of information that they can tap. Using the Internet in your job search demonstrates to an employer your familiarity and skill with this new market area. Check a company's public web server to see what they have listed, or just see how to get in touch with them about a need you believe they have, and be the first in line with a resume. There are several places where you can post your resume at no charge. And it is an effective way to get your resume seen by recruiters and employers. For example the Internet address for DBM is **http://www.DBM.com**. See the Index of Resources for a list of Internet Search Engines to aid your job search.

B. Search Firms, Employment Agencies and Contract Companies

There are hundreds of executive search firms ranging in size from one-person operations run from home to large international firms. (For a complete listing of country-wide search firms, see *The Directory of Executive Recruiters,* Kennedy Publications, updated annually.)

Companies are more likely to use search firms for higher level positions and in situations where confidentiality is essential. **Search firms work for client companies**, not for prospective employees.

There are two primary types of search firms — retainer and contingency.

- **Retainer Search Firms**. Retainer firms are paid by employers to locate qualified people for specific positions; their fee is approximately one-third of the annual starting salary. Their assignments are exclusive, meaning that no other firm is competing with them to fill the position. *Important Note: Be sure that the search firms you target are appropriate for your salary range.*

- **Contingency Search Firms**. Contingency firms do not work on an exclusive basis. They agree to fill positions for client companies, knowing that there may be several other firms that will also be referring candidates. That means they are paid their fee (20-30%) only when the company hires an individual they have presented.

How to Make Contact with a Search Firm

First of all, make sure that you are contacting a search firm and not a marketing company. Unless a search firm contacts you, the best way to contact them is by mail. Since they work on commission and time is money, they cannot make money talking on the phone or setting up appointments with people who are not good matches for assignments they are trying to satisfy. Send a brief cover letter that includes the following:

A. A brief background of your experience.

B. Titles of the positions for which you qualify.

C. The geographic area you prefer.

D. The salary range you desire.

E. A copy of your resume.

While the odds are slim that the search firms you contact will be working on an opening that is an exact match for your background and skills, it may still be worthwhile to forward a letter listing your qualifications and objectives. Sample search firm letters are included in your Index of Resources and discussed in *Chapter Nine* of this workbook.

If a Search Firm Contacts You

The following guidelines will help you if you are contacted by a search firm:

1. **Extract as much information as you can about the nature of the position and the company**. This might include company size, industry and geographic location, why the position is open, what happened to the last 2 persons in that job, etc.

2. **Do not go around a search firm by directly contacting the potential employer**. This might tend to alienate the search firm.

3. **Be prepared to present yourself well**, with interest and enthusiasm.

4. **Don't try to retrofit your skills to meet the requirements of a position that is not right for you.** A better strategy is to become a resource for the search executive by offering names of colleagues who might be a better match.

5. **Use the search executive as a method of obtaining feedback** about how well you were received by the client company. This will provide useful information for your next interview.

Types of Contingency Firms and Who Pays the Fees

Executive Search — Compensation Above $40,000

Work for client companies, usually at the mid-management level. There is no fee to the candidate, and they may send multiple candidates to interview for the same position.

Private Employment Agencies — Compensation below $40,000

Many employment agencies require you to sign an application that constitutes a contract, committing you to pay a certain percentage of your new income if you take a position they find for you. In other words, **they work for you**, because you are paying them.

Contracting/Interim Search Companies — Compensation can range from hourly to daily, monthly, or yearly.

Contracting companies are hybrids, often functioning as temporary employment agencies. Fees can be paid by candidates or by employers, and many times the contracting agency is itself an employer.

Many contracting companies have specific expertise in particular industries, such as information systems or engineering. (In the past they were often referred to as "job shops" where people who had particular technical skills were placed in temporary assignments.)

Employers often work with contracting companies when they need skilled, trained people for a particular project or function. The contracting company will negotiate a rate to provide workers for the assignment for a specific period of time and will pay the people it recruits for the assignment, sometimes even paying for benefits, such as medical insurance and/or vacations.

More often the contract company pays a daily, monthly or hourly rate with no benefits. If an employer decides to hire a contract person as a full-time employee, the employer pays a fee to the contract company, just like a search firm.

Contract employment is a growing business, and is reflective of today's business trends. As organizations become more "virtual " they increase the use of contract employees. This allows the organization to expand and contract as the market demands without having to downsize or layoff. It is thought that this may be more cost-effective over time. Too, it parallels the idea that people will have more than one career and will work for at least 9 companies in their lifetime.

Summary: Search Firms, Employment Agencies and Contract Companies

HOW SEARCH FIRMS WORK	
RETAINER	**CONTINGENCY**
Work for Client Organization	*Work for Client Organization*
Fee structure — 1/3 of first year's compensation.	Fee structure — 20-30% of first year's salary if they fill open position.
Must replace individual if situation doesn't work out within 12 months.	Must replace individual if situation doesn't work out within 3-6 months.
Produce a profile, not your resume, to make a presentation.	Stamp your resume with their company name.
Usually control the interview process.	Send you on interviews with some coaching.
Usually work on 8 to 12 searches a year.	Usually work on multiple openings, as many as 15 to 25 at a time.
Act as a consultant to the company, make staffing recommendations.	Volume business based on speed. Work with many companies.

C. Direct Mail Campaigns

In the past, most employment advice included instructions about how to conduct a mass market letter campaign. No matter how effective they may have been a few years ago, today mass mailings are very tenuous.

Mass mailings, even those that are narrowly targeted, often consume valuable search time with little likelihood of success. The time wasted is not in generating letters or sending them, but in the inactivity that occurs while waiting for replies. These could be replies that never come.

In summary, do not send out cold marketing letters. Doing so is as unproductive, costly and frustrating as a cold marketing call. It is not recommended by DBM, unless you have done considerable research to refine the list of companies. Then they become "targeted" marketing letters.

D. Answering Ads

Major newspapers have pages of employment ads that usually require written responses. Ads that include the company name are called *open ads*. Sometimes the name of the company is concealed — only a box number is given. These are called *blind ads*.

Open Ads

Companies publicize openings through ads that not only include position requirements, experience and education, but also include company name and a contact person. These ads are usually placed in the newspaper by the Human Resources department. The benefits of responding to an open ad are:

◆ It is a valid, open position which the company is trying to fill.

◆ You can follow up with the contact name in the paper if you do not receive a response to your reply.

Blind Ads

Although there may be some advertisements that are particularly suited to your talents, because of the low response rate you need to restrict the time you spend on answering blind ads. There are a number of reasons to explain the low response rate of blind ads.

◆ Advertisers use blind ads specifically to avoid the burden of replying to hundreds of applicants.

◆ Advertisers avoid unwanted phone calls and drop-ins.

Agencies or search firms may place blind ads to build candidate bases (called "sourcing"); they may not have any openings.

Companies use blind ads to:

◆ "Sample the market" without any requirement to acknowledge letters and resumes, or to interview anyone.

◆ Maintain privacy.

◆ Research availability of candidates and current salaries.

◆ Save agency or search firm fees (an advantage open ads also offer).

What can you get from an ad?

- Key words

- A feel for market trends: competencies, functions, even companies that are growing

- Ideas

- Possibly a position

Sources of Ads

- The local Sunday newspaper "Help Wanted" ads.

- *The Wall Street Journal*, the *Sunday Chicago Tribune*, *The New York Times*, and other major city papers. Because of their size and audience, these papers sometimes list nationwide positions.

- The *National Business Employment Weekly* and *The National Ad Search* are two weekly compilations of ads drawn from around the country.

- Employment sections of professional journals.

Ads often draw thousands of replies, dramatically lowering the odds of generating an interview. Don't spend much time on one ad unless the job is a perfect fit for you. Screeners often look at resumes and separate them into three stacks: "*Yes,*" "*No*" and "*Maybe.*" You have a better chance of getting into the "yes" or "maybe" groups if your background and experience clearly and immediately match their needs, both stated and implied.

Most ads ask for salary history or salary desired. If you do not fall within their range or if you ignore the request, it may be viewed as a disqualifier. Indicate a broad range of acceptable salary, (e.g., $45K - $60K) or give an indication (e.g., in the high $50s) and mention your willingness to discuss it in more detail at the time of the interview.

What to Expect

Companies that place blind ads will not acknowledge your letter or resume unless they wish to talk to you.

Open ad companies are not concerned about being identified, and usually give at least a form reply — although it may be weeks later — after they have made a decision.

The advantage of open ads is that you can check the company before you reply to determine if it is right for you.

Answering Ads

To avoid spending excessive time on ads:

♦ **Skim the papers in a few minutes**. Make copies of the ads you want to examine more closely.

♦ **Select the employer's most notable needs**, especially the ones your skills can meet.

♦ **Concentrate on their needs at the start of your letter** and match them with your skills and experience.

♦ **Maintain records** of your ad replies.

Sample ad response letters are included in the Index of Resources and in Chapter 9 of this workbook.

E. Other Work Search Strategies

In addition to the methods listed, there are a few other sources to find suitable work:

♦ Local or regional job fairs

♦ College alumni offices

♦ Networking at professional organization meetings

♦ Federal and state government positions

SUMMARY

The effectiveness of the various work-search strategies is as follows:

Active Techniques: 50-80%

    A. Networking

    B. Targeted Marketing Letters

Passive Techniques: 15-35%

    A. Internet/Electronic Databases[1]

    B. Search Firms/Employment Agencies

    C. Classified Ads

    D. Mass Mail Campaigns

As a result of these percentages, the following points are essential to remember:

    A. Because of changes in the working world, employing companies have changed the way they recruit professionals.

    B. The new competitive marketplace calls for more creative work search techniques.

    C. Networking continues to be the most effective strategy for most DBM Candidates.

Use a marketing plan -- do not wing it!

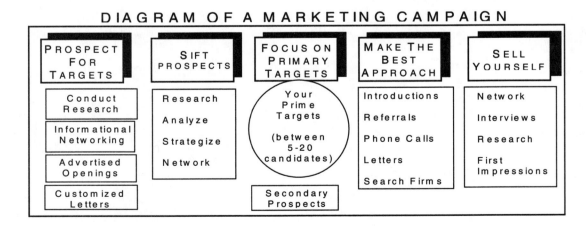

DIAGRAM OF A MARKETING CAMPAIGN

---

[1] The Internet is growing by leaps and bounds so its effectiveness is in a constant state of upward change. Whereas you may not directly land a job via the Internet, you can amass valuable research and networking information.

CHAPTER NINE

Written Communication

> *"A writer is rarely so well inspired as*
> *when he talks about himself."*

Anatole France

POINTS OF INTEREST

In Chapter Nine you will learn that:

♦ Written communication can be grouped into two major categories:

- Customized letters

- Non-Customized letters

♦ High impact written communications have a structure that hooks and holds readers' attention.

♦ Well designed, targeted, customized letters, especially those with a referral name, can lead to interviews.

HIGH IMPACT LETTERS

Letters are excellent tools for connecting with people or companies where you believe you would be a good fit, and where you may not have a direct contact. A well constructed letter can replace your initial networking phone call, but it will not replace the follow-up telephone call that must be made.

Benefits Obtained By Writing Rather Than Phoning:

♦ You may secure an interview.

♦ You have an opportunity to think through and express what you have to offer in a concise and relevant way.

♦ You are better prepared to talk about yourself one-on-one after you have written down your thoughts.

♦ It puts you into a selling mode -- ready to demonstrate your capabilities and aim for more responsibility and higher pay.

♦ It eases anxiety that may be associated with making phone calls.

♦ It creates a written, lasting document.

What Makes Letters Effective?

An effective letter is one that:

1. Is read by the appropriate, targeted person.

2. Produces a response leading to a face-to-face meeting.

3. Emphasizes the *skills* of the writer that are most relevant to the *needs* of the person or organization addressed.

4. Uses a format specifically designed to induce reader interest and initiate the face-to-face meeting.

GENERAL FORMAT OF A LETTER

The following is a recommended format for producing high-impact letters:

Opening Paragraph: Hooks the reader and holds his or her attention.

Answers the Question, "Why read me?"

What you can do:

♦ Use a referral name

♦ Write something (tastefully) humorous or creative

♦ Demonstrate something dramatic (an outstanding accomplishment)

♦ Give examples of how you: increased sales/revenues/savings; created new business opportunities; decreased expenses or reduced costs; streamlined processes or production

♦ Cite special industry or functional expertise

Second Paragraph: "Who/What/How"

Answers the Question: What have you done lately?

What you can do:

♦ Describe your most recent work experience (including title, scope of responsibilities and organizational function)

♦ Describe 2-3 relevant accomplishments, based on your knowledge of the company, your network, and research you conducted

---

Third Paragraph (Optional): More "Who/What/How"

Answers the Question: What else have you done?

What you can do:

♦ Describe your previous relevant work experience

♦ Describe 1-2 relevant accomplishments

Final Paragraph: "When"

Answers the Question: What comes next?

What you can do:

♦ Action step (meeting or interview)

♦ Follow up

The Result You Want

BENEFIT
TO SEE YOU

YOUR SKILLS &
EXPERIENCE

SELF
ASSESSMENT

CUSTOMER
ASSESSMENT

THEIR BUSINESS
NEEDS

WORK
OPPORTUNITIES

Additional Guidelines for Letters

◆ **Keep letters to one page** wherever possible.

◆ **Keep paragraphs to no more than five lines in length.** Use white space and bullets to make your points.

◆ **Keep your stationery simple** -- size, color, texture.

◆ **Do not explain your work situation** unless appropriate.

◆ **Omit salary information** -- past or desired. *Exception -- include salary range in search letters*.

◆ **Omit personal data,** e.g., age, marital status, number of children, hobbies (unless they relate directly to the position).

◆ **Omit references**.

Exercise #9-1

Take 5 minutes to draft a letter to one of your networking contacts who:
- has information you need or
- whose company has a position available.

Do that now.

CATEGORIES OF LETTERS

At this point we will examine in detail the following categories of letters:

1. **Customized letters.** Aimed at a specific person, a specific company, or tailored to address a specific objective.

2. **Non-customized letters.** Designed to deliver the same message, with no personalization, to multiple individuals or organizations.

We have included a **section of sample letters from both categories in the Index of Resources.**

1. Customized Letters

A. *Pre-Networking Letters*

Pre-networking letters are written *before* an attempt to telephone for networking appointments. They indicate that you will be calling soon to schedule a face-to-face networking meeting. They do not usually include a resume.

If you are hesitant to phone for appointments with people you don't know or to whom you have not been referred, you may choose to send an *introductory* letter first. If possible, let the individual's assistant know that you will be writing, and try to solicit cooperation in calling attention to your letter.

B. *Target Marketing Letters*

Customized target marketing letters, aimed at specific individuals or companies you have researched and who might be able to use your skills, can be as significant and influential as a resume. Although these letters were once intended to stand alone *without* an attached resume, this is not necessarily true in today's business climate.

Because people are busier (and organizations are leaner), they want to see what you have to offer immediately, so attach your resume.

Target marketing letters, *especially those with a referral name*, have the highest success rate of all correspondence.

When Target Marketing Letters Are Appropriate

♦ The individual you have targeted is not available (after several previous phone tries).

♦ You have identified a promising target company, but you have not been able to obtain a personal referral to the decision-maker.

♦ You have been unable to identify the decision-maker, so you send a letter to an individual in the appropriate functional area.

♦ You have identified the decision-maker and are sending a focused, customized letter.

Guidelines for Target Marketing Letters

Review your accomplishments and skills to better focus on the many strengths you have to offer. Then, determine how to integrate them into a letter. Here are some guidelines for effectively presenting your unique skills and capturing the reader's attention.

• **Be sure the letter is sent to someone at the appropriate level,** (i.e., a decision-maker for your particular job classification)

• **Highlight your accomplishments**, *relevant* experience and skills that relate to their specific organization. (This is why you did your research)

• **Keep the data current**; don't go back in time more than 5 to 7 years.

• **Limit your letter size** to one or, at most, two uncrowded pages.

• **Verify mailing information** (name and correct spelling, title, address, internal mail code, zip code). Verify that the person you are addressing is the appropriate addressee.

• **End the letter with the statement that you will call the person in a week or so.** Do not expect the person to call you.

Remember, your goal is to address your letter to the *best* person -- one who will take a keen interest in hiring your type of talent, or who is willing to refer you to the person who does. To the extent you can, relate your skills to the needs of the organization addressed.

The Response You Should Expect

Companies and professionals receive many letters and resumes. While some firms are conscientious about responding, others are simply too busy. Don't take it personally if you do not get responses to your written communications. While some letters and resumes are handled personally, many are delegated to a screener. Here are some of the responses you can expect.

1. Nothing.
2. A standard rejection letter (thank you; we're not interested).
3. A post card acknowledging receipt.
4. A phone call requesting clarification or additional information.
5. A phone call as a pre-screening interview.
6. A phone call to set up a face-to-face meeting.

Categories 1 - 3 are not very encouraging. These responses seldom have anything to do with you. Generally they mean there are no vacancies at this time. If the organization was

one that really did interest you then you might want to try calling the person to whom you wrote your letter and follow up using your networking skills.

C. *Search Firm Letters*

Search firms receive large numbers of unsolicited resumes. They search for their own candidates and are not a placement agency, as many people believe. Search executives only look for individuals to fill open positions they are currently retained to fill.

Unless contacted by a search firm, the most appropriate way to contact them is by letter, using a referral name if possible -- either a client company that has used them, or an individual who was placed by them.

There are several ways to obtain lists of appropriate, reputable search firms.

♦ Bloomberg's listing of Executive Search Firms by region on the Internet (http://www.bloomberg.com/fun/jobs/recruit/recruit.html).

♦ *The Directory of Executive Recruiters*, published annually by Kennedy Publications, Fitzwilliam, NH. This book is available in the reference section of most libraries.

♦ Professionals who have used search firms.

♦ Contacts in your network.

Once you have compiled your list, write a brief, concise cover letter (send with your resume) that includes the following.

♦ The titles of positions for which you are qualified.

♦ Your geographic preferences.

♦ Industries where you are a fit.

♦ The salary range you require.

♦ Your availability for work.

♦ Any major restrictions (e.g., relocation).

When Search Firm Letters are Appropriate

♦ If the search firms handle assignments in your industry, functional or geographical area.

♦ If you have the name of a search executive from a referral.

♦ If you know they have an opening that is right for you.

(For further information on search firms, refer to **Chapter 8, Methods and Strategies.)**

D. *Ad Response Letters*

Select ads that fit you well. Today there is so much competition that companies immediately screen out those candidates who do not closely fit their requirements.

Customize each ad response letter. If you are familiar with the company and can also include a referral name, your chances increase significantly.

Guidelines for writing this type of letter:

♦ Craft a letter that illustrates how you fit the key requirements listed in the ad.

♦ Include a resume with each ad response.

♦ Respond to ads that request salary history by providing the *salary range* you are seeking or by stating a round figure, e.g., salary was in the $60s.

♦ Keep ad responses to one page.

Before mailing your letter, you might consider waiting a few days after the ad appears. By doing so you can avoid the initial crush of respondents and your materials might be looked at when screeners are not so overloaded.

Emerging trends*. You can fax a resume if you have the correct name and fax number. Faxes often are put directly on the desk of the person to whom they are addressed. Since a fax does not create the same impression as a letter sent on quality stationery, it's a good idea to follow up with a hard copy of your resume.*

More and more companies are using e-mail to screen job applicants. If the ad specifies an e-mail address and you have the capability, use it. Since most executives read their electronic mail without it being screened by someone else, there is a higher likelihood that your letter will actually be read by the person you targeted.

E-1. *Follow-Up Letters When You Haven't Heard Anything after an Interview*

These letters must be well-timed and carefully written. You certainly don't want to be perceived as:

♦ Desperate

♦ Impatient

♦ Annoyed

Two Reasons Why You May Not Have Heard

Reason #1

When company representatives say they will make a decision in a specified amount of time, it rarely happens. Illness, business trips, or work crises may cause a delay in the decision-making process or a change in the original schedule.

> **Remember**, although this is *your* number one priority, it is often not the number one priority of others.

Reason #2

You were not selected. Although it does not reflect well on an organization to invite people to interview and not give them the courtesy of a response, this happens.

E-2. *Follow-Up Letters after a Turndown*

These are letters to thank an individual in an organization for considering you and to request that they keep you in mind if conditions change or if they have another opening in the future.

Keep these letters short and the tone friendly, yet professional. Don't suggest that you think you were the best candidate; instead, respect their decision to select someone else and suggest they feel free to contact you if anything changes.

F. *Thank You Letters*

Send thank you letters shortly after your networking meetings or interviews, but not so quickly that recipients receive them the next day. Thank you letters are the only letters that may be handwritten, but they must be legible. These letters convey your thanks for the interview or networking meeting and can be addressed to:

- Networking contacts
- Human Resource interviewers
- Search executives
- Hiring managers

Finally, use thank you letters to:

- Make a favorable impression

- Get closure regarding the next step

- Expand on a subject discussed during a previous conversation

- Clarify a point or misunderstanding

- Restate your interest

A method for keeping your thank you note schedule organized is to address the thank you note when you have the appointment scheduled. In this way, it acts as a reminder after the appointment has been concluded.

G. *Letters Related to Interviewing*

Following an employment interview, an articulate, well-expressed letter can support your candidacy. Here are some suggestions.

♦ Reinforce the skills or accomplishments you felt were the most important to meeting the needs of the position, the decision-maker and the company.

♦ Use white space and bullets to make your letter easy to read and get your points across quickly.

♦ Use words that sound as if you are convinced that you would be a great asset to the organization. (If you touch base with your emotions as well as your intellect this should not be too difficult -- remember, enthusiasm and conviction are emotions!)

    A. "I feel certain ..."

    B. "I know..."

    C. "I am convinced..."

♦ If you interview with a Human Resources individual *and* a hiring manager, send letters to both. <u>Do not send the same letter.</u>

♦ If you interview with three or more people, only send letters to the decision-makers and the Human Resources professionals.

♦ This is a good opportunity to clarify anything you feel might have been misunderstood or to add something you may have forgotten.

♦ End your letter reiterating to the recipient your understanding of the next steps.

♦ If you are referred by a search professional, *phone* the search person to debrief and *write* letters to the people in the organization with whom you met.

Remember, *do not* mention what you need, what you want, or "what's in it for you." Companies hire you because of "what's in it for them."

H. *Acceptance Letters*

These are the letters you send when offer negotiations have been completed and you have decided to accept the position. There are two types:

♦ *Detailed*, in which you reiterate the agreed-upon points.

♦ *Abbreviated*, when the negotiated conditions have already been detailed in an offer letter or written agreement.

Letters of Offer and Letters of Acceptance are legal agreements. Make sure you review them carefully.

I. *Withdrawal from Consideration Letters*

This type of letter expresses thanks for an interview opportunity with a request to be removed from the candidate list. Do this diplomatically and professionally so that you do not damage any relationships with individuals within the company. With multiple careers becoming the norm, you don't know when you will want to make contact again.

2. Non-Customized Letters

A. *Broadcast Letters*

These are mass mailings to companies, usually prepared from lists or databases. The letters are all the same and include resumes. They are addressed to an actual person whose name is in a book or on a list.

Note: These letters are rarely used today because of their low return on investment (1-2%). Since they include no referral name or research to grab the reader's attention, they are usually discarded before they are read.

You would be better off to broadcast your resume via the Internet. Resumes are searched using key words and at least have the possibility of being read. Check out the Internet resources in your Index of Resources.

B. *Progress Letters*

Writing to your previous networking contacts to let them know that you followed up on their suggestions and to keep you in mind is a strategy that often produces great results.

When your earlier contacts receive a letter from you, it keeps your name in mind so they will think of you when they hear of an opportunity. Sometimes it prompts them to review their contact names for referrals for you.

Even when your career transition is complete, **stay in touch with your network and add to it continuously.** There is simply no way of knowing when you may need to tap this valuable asset again.

C. *Announcement of New Position Letters*

These letters are meant to inform or thank your contacts and to let them know that you have accepted a new position.

You may wish to write these on your new organization's letterhead.

If you have a new business card, it is a good idea to enclose it. You may want to hand write notes to those who did something special for you. Using announcement letters is a solid strategy to keep your network "fresh."

SUMMARY

Customized marketing letters are excellent tools for connecting with people or companies where you believe you would be a good fit, and where you may not have a direct contact.

Here are important points to keep in mind:

- ◆ **Written communication can result in face-to-face interviews** when it is well conceived, planned and executed.

- ◆ Marketing letters are more likely to elicit a positive response when they are **narrowly targeted** and **customized to specific company needs**.

- ◆ Narrowly targeted, customized letters with a **referral name** produce even better results.

- ◆ Marketing letters that offer **evidence that you can impact business results** are most likely to result in a meeting.

CHAPTER TEN
Interviewing

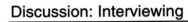

"To know when one's self is interested, is the first condition of interesting other people."

Walter Pater, *Marius the Epicurean,*
Chapter 6

POINTS OF INTEREST

Chapter Ten details critical information, such as:

♦ Interview preparation and practice

♦ Answering frequently asked interview questions and recommended responses

♦ Marketing yourself by asking questions: Sample questions to ask the interviewer

♦ Handling inappropriate interview questions

♦ Presenting yourself successfully in any interview

♦ Managing your interview image

UNDERSTANDING INTERVIEWING

Directions:

Check "T" in front of those statements that you believe to be true and "F" in front of those you believe to be false.

T   F

❑   ❑   1. The person who would be your future manager is always the decision-maker.

❑   ❑   2. The interviewer often feels as much anxiety as the interviewee.

❑   ❑   3. The more prepared you are for the interview, the better impression you will make.

❑   ❑   4. You should let the interviewer take the lead and ask the questions. Your role should be answering those questions in detail.

❑   ❑   5. You should continually sell yourself during the interview.

❑   ❑   6. First impressions can make you or break you.

Notes:

Let's see how well you did.

1. The person who would be your future manager is always the decision-maker.

   False. At the professional level, most employment decisions are consensus decisions among key executives, and one of the decision-makers may be your future manager. Although this individual may have the "official" yes or no vote, decisions concerning the staffing of key positions are usually a group decision.

   For non-exempt positions, sometimes the Human Resource Department selects the new employee.

2. The interviewer often feels as much anxiety as the interviewee.

   True. In this era of downsizing and cost reduction, executives are under increasing pressure to hire only top performers. Also, many executives are not professional interviewers and are uncomfortable interviewing a prospective employee.

3. The more prepared you are for the interview, the better impression you will make.

   True. Preparation is all important and includes presenting yourself in an organized, professional and collaborative manner. Although substance is far more important than style, in the short time an interview lasts, time may limit your ability to overcome a sloppy presentation.

4. You should let the interviewer take the lead and ask the questions. Your role should be answering those questions in detail.

   False. An employment interview is an opportunity for mutual exploration between the potential employer and employee. While the interviewer may initially take the lead, the interview should be a two-way conversation.

5. You should continually sell yourself during the interview.

   False. This is one of the most common mistakes. Selling yourself before you have taken the time to thoroughly understand the company's issues may indicate that you are more interested in yourself rather than in the company's needs. You would be better off to remember that the quality of your questions indicates your interest in the company and, at the same time, indicates your professional expertise...all of which are selling points.

6. First impressions can make you or break you.

   True. Clothing, haircut, polished shoes, resume quality, note-taking materials, voice quality, enthusiasm, etc., are very important. Most interviewers will make a visual assessment in the first fifteen seconds, and an auditory assessment within two minutes.

INTERVIEW FORMATS:
STRUCTURED VS UNSTRUCTURED

Today, most companies use structured interviews. They have defined the competency requirements for each position in the organization so they *know* what they want. Also, structured interviews are best for insuring compliance with fair employment practice guidelines such as those defined by the Americans with Disabilities Act or the Equal Employment Opportunity Commission.

Structured Interviews are conducted with a predetermined set of questions. A common structure is:

1. Greetings/small talk
2. Introduction
3. Education
4. Work Experience
5. Activities and interests
6. Summary of strengths and weaknesses
7. Description of position; candidate questions
8. Close

The trained interviewer conducting a structured interview will be likely to do the following:

♦ Ask open-ended questions and focus on past performance, e.g., Behavioral Interview.

♦ Encourage the candidate to talk 70-80 percent of the time.

♦ Give limited specific information about the position until the candidate's qualifications have been confirmed.

♦ Maintain eye contact.

♦ Be comfortable with silences and wait for the candidate to speak.

♦ Not ask personal or illegal questions.

Unstructured Interviews - Unstructured interviews are non-directed and are geared to be more casual and open. Often the interviewers have had little or no training about the process, and may have done little to prepare.

These can be difficult situations, particularly when the interviewer does not know what to look for or how to direct the interview. It is important for you to take the initiative and lead without appearing to dominate; the person asking the questions usually controls the interaction.

SELECTION INTERVIEWING

A selection interview is a planned, formal, and focused interview. It provides the interviewer with sufficient information to evaluate whether or not a candidate has the ability and motivation to perform successfully and fit into the organization. At the same time, the candidate is gathering enough information to make his/her **decision** -- "Does this company and position offer the opportunities and satisfactions I am seeking?" You will answer this question by the criteria you defined earlier in your Ideal Work Preferences. (See Chapter 2)

Selection interviews include everything from pre-screening to the encounter with the decision-maker. They are conducted by search company professionals, internal Human Resources professionals, teams or the ultimate hiring manager. *The purpose of these interviews is to screen you in or out,* based on predetermined qualification criteria. Interviews differ in terms of the amount of time scheduled, the number of people being seen at one time or sequentially, and the positions of those people. You will probably be told or be able to tell what type of interview to expect ahead of time when arrangements are being made. Regardless, make sure to get the names and positions of each of the people you will be seeing so you can follow up with a thank you note or other correspondence.

Types of Selection Interviews (Screenings):
Note: These categories are not mutually exclusive.

PRE-SCREENING
Resume screening -- Do you meet our basic criteria? Do your key words match ours? This step may be done by computer before any human ever sees it. To make this hurdle you must have taken the time to "fine tune" your resume, used terminology (key words) appropriate to the field in which you are looking for a job and formatted your resume properly. **Telephone pre-screening -- Is what I see on your resume true? How do you sound?** You may not know the hiring significance of the person you are talking to on the telephone so "assume" this person has the final word on whether or not you get a position. <u>Key Points:</u> A) Answer all questions directly and to the point -- most telephone screeners do not want to get into the details...they want to verify information. B) Ask questions that will verify for you that you want to continue the selection process.

THIRD-PARTY SCREENING INTERVIEWS

Third-party screening -- Are you who you say you are and can you do what I think <u>they</u> need? Screeners may be outside parties such as an executive search firm consultant, employment agency representative, or even an independent psychologist. Often these interviewers are more expert in extracting information and evaluating people than the company interviewer who will eventually make a decision about you.

Many companies have internal screening interviewers who sort out applicants and candidates, deciding whether to pass them along to the decision-makers. These screeners are usually from Personnel or Human Resources and have titles like Placement Director, Manager of Recruiting or Employment Manager. Keep in mind that although they often cannot hire you, they can eliminate you from consideration.

<u>Key Points:</u>

A) Never underestimate what they know about the job. Some of these folks spend a great deal of time "qualifying" the position. That means they understand the demands of the work, the tough parts of the job, the people with whom you will work, etc.

B) It is important to relate to them as individuals who have a vested interest in "selecting" the right candidates for the position. If they send on too many "losers" they will lose their jobs.

C) Engage them in a dialogue. Answer their questions directly. Ask them questions that will help you to decide whether you want to continue the exploration into that company.

SEQUENTIAL INTERVIEWS

These are a series of interviews scheduled one after another at specific intervals over a period of time (half or full day). Sequential interviews can be conducted with a reporting chain of supervisors, peers or team members.

It is important to **consider each new interviewer the most important person you are meeting**. Focus on style adaptation, active listening and thoughtful responses for that individual. I SPEAK® techniques can help you make these adjustments. Often you will find that there is little coordination among the interviewers and they will ask you the same questions over and over again. Always answer as enthusiastically as if you were hearing the question for the first time -- *it will be the first time they hear your answer.*

BEHAVIORAL INTERVIEWS

The majority of companies use the **Behavioral Interview** to select a new employee. Here, the interviewer asks how "you" acted, performed, handled a certain situation in the past. The assumption is *how you have acted in the past in a given situation, will predict how you will act in the future*. The interviewer might make up a situation and ask you how you would deal with it. They might ask you to relate a time when you had a problem with a co-worker or when you had difficulty with a project, how you handled it, what steps did you take and what was the outcome. The interviewer generally has been trained in this methodology. Some interviewers create mini-scenarios that will show them how you work under pressure...for example: irate customers, deadlines, changing specifications, etc.

PANEL OR TEAM INTERVIEWS

Vested interest party screening -- What do you know? Is it what I need? Do you fit <u>our</u> culture? These are interviews conducted by a number of interviewers (usually three to five) in the same room at the same time. You will be meeting co-workers, team members, persons with whom you would work and possibly the decision-maker. This is where you get "business intimate". They will want to know what you can bring to the job, how you've approached particular tasks in the past, what makes you excited or mad, what it would be like to share time and space with you. You will want to know the same things about them. This is an opportunity for you to get to know "your team".

Key Points:

A) Be open, honest and natural.

B) The questions you ask are indicative of what you know about the industry, the position, the challenges, etc. Hence, as you "qualify your interest in the position" recognize that you are not being offensive...you are actually selling yourself while you gather information.

C) You need to make each individual feel that you are paying particular attention to him or her. Be sure to maintain eye contact as you address each one, and try to apply the I SPEAK® techniques to communicate with each in a way that he or she is likely to respond positively.

D) Remember to call people by their names.

INTERVIEWS WITH DECISION-MAKERS

Decision-maker screening -- In what ways can you make me a winner and can I work "easily" with you? This interview is with the candidate's future manager, the person who "owns the job" and who may make an offer. If you have done well with the screeners and other interviewers, you will have some positive momentum when you meet the decision-maker, because favorable evaluations will precede you.

The decision-maker needs to find out if you will be an asset to the team. You need to find out whether this person can or will provide you with the opportunities you need to be successful. Remember the two of you will be spending a lot of time together. Ultimately, the decision-maker has the keys to your IWPs.

Key Points:
A) Be open, honest and affable.
B) Make no judgments for the first 5 minutes. Job-owners are not necessarily delighted with the opportunity to interview people. They would rather be doing "real work".
C) Notice the decision-maker's style...is s/he task-oriented, pleasant, people-oriented, gruff. What is on the desk/walls -- family pictures, baseball mementos, work stuff -- that can tell you about this person.
D) Ask what the challenges associated with the job are and what criteria s/he uses to determine success/failure.

If you see a task that is particularly interesting to you, **identify** it and use the word "we". For example: "We could try doing _____?" Or "Have you tried _____ before?"

STAMP-OF-APPROVAL INTERVIEWS

These are final interviews. Depending upon the job level these can be conducted by supervisors, department heads, senior executives or company presidents. While the hiring decision may already have been made, this is an opportunity for the candidate to meet potential new key players and vice versa.

Key Points:

A. This is an opportunity to find out what the executive thinks about the contribution your new functional area can make to his/her organization. Ask questions in this area.

B. S/he is probably interested in "who was selected" so put your best, most professional and affable character forward. Make sure you are interested in how this person got to where s/he is today and ask if s/he has any tips for you. Ask about the direction of the company, department, etc.

STRESS INTERVIEWS

In this situation, the interviewer deliberately creates a stressful atmosphere, possibly arguing with or contradicting the candidate, or creating tension.

The purpose of this type of interview is to assess how a candidate responds under pressure. (Candidates should keep in mind that the "stress interviewer" may also be a "stress manager.")

Key Points:

A. Assume that stress must be a part of the job, hence, your ability to stay calm, cool and collected is important.

B. Silence while pondering is an excellent way in which to handle the argumentative or attack questions/responses. After you have pondered for a while and collected yourself, respond thoughtfully but directly to the situation.

C. If you do have a clearly defined position on a situation that has been posed, make sure you say it. Vacillating from "yes" to "no" to "maybe", is not a desirable quality.

D. Take the offensive and reflect as an observer on the interview method, e.g., "Am I correct in assuming that this position carries a lot of stress with it?" If the interviewer was intentionally doing a stress interview to assess how you respond to stress, this is not a bad tactic. If, on the other hand, the interviewer is a stressful person, his/her response will provide you with that information.

Summary: Interviewing is a mutual process. You are not there to ask for a job. Both parties are there to determine if a mutually beneficial exchange, trade, or contract can be struck. Keeping this in mind is critical for the right mental attitude -- You are an equal with something of value to offer, not a supplicant with your hat in your hand. At each level of the interview process you are being selected and **you are doing the selecting**.

DEVELOPING YOUR INTERVIEWING SKILLS

Interview Preparation

Preparing and practicing for interviews will insure that you handle them well. So you've lined up a job interview -- now what? The first thing to do is to continue investigating the company.

- Read the newspapers.
- Talk to your broker.
- Search the Internet for information on the company or its homepage.
- Check to see if your local library maintains a press clipping file on them.

In short, know as much about the company, the position and the interviewer as possible.

GETTING THE INTERVIEW STARTED

At some point during a selection interview you will probably be responding to the question, "Tell me about yourself." In the networking chapter you developed **Your 90-Second Introduction**. It is the best initial response to that question and is your opportunity to introduce your product. You have prepared for this moment -- you know the company, you know the position. Make sure you refine **Your 90-Second Introduction** to reflect this information.

Or an interviewer might ask you an "ice-breaker question" to get started. This type of question may be quite bland, for example:

1. "Where were you were born and raised?"
2. "Where did you receive your basic education?"
3. "Where did you receive your post-high school/college/graduate school education?"

These questions are difficult to really glow-in-the-dark over unless you were raised in a unique place, went to a remarkable school, etc.

Meaningful ice-breakers

To avoid being asked a lackluster ice-breaker question, you might initiate the conversation yourself. Use information you've learned about the interviewer from:

- The secretary with whom you scheduled the interview (if there was one),
- Looking up the interviewer in Who's Who,
- Looking around the person's office.

For example, you might say, "I see you were a basketball player in college. So was I." Or,

"I see you have daughters. I have one myself." Or,

"Where did you do your deep sea fishing?" Or,

"I see you went to Purdue. I graduated from their school of business. What was your field?"

Meaningful ice-breakers are easier to manage than pot luck. They help you get down to business quickly and smoothly. You can then segue into **Your 90-Second Introduction**.

For example: "I see you played basketball in college. So did I until I joined IBM as a programmer. From there....." Spend about 15 seconds talking about personal history and then wait for the interviewer to respond.

Sometimes an interviewer may focus on a single point he found in your resume or application.[1] It may not be something you prepared for and has the potential of making your feel uncomfortable. To avoid embarrassment, it is a good idea to practice managing discomfort. What follows is an exercise to provide you with some laughs and enough experience to avoid finding yourself in the HOT SEAT.

---

[1] This can happen when you have "holes" in your resume. Hence, you are well advised to be proactive and practice problem avoidance by reviewing and having others review your resume. Otherwise, you may end up problem solving in real time.

Exercise #10-2

If an interviewer asked you any one or more of these questions, would you be prepared?

Hot seat questions:

1. I see here that you have had quite a few jobs...can't you hold a steady job?

2. Tell me all about your education, starting with grammar school.

3. I see you studied physical education in college. What makes you think you can be a _____ now?

4. You've spent many years with your former employer...what makes you think you can modify your thinking to join our organization?

5. Where were you born and raised?

6. Hmm...did you actually graduate from college or take a few courses?

7. Some organizations have a casual day, while others are always casual...what's your opinion on that?

8. I see here you were with ___XYZ Corp.___ and never got a promotion.

9. Tell me what it was like when you really had to work the entire day with no time for breaks.

10. Tell me about your worst performance review.

✂ Supplement the list above with your own repertoire of dreadful questions.

ANSWERING INTERVIEW QUESTIONS

The Interview and Your Ideal Work Preferences

Recall from Chapter 2 that your Ideal Work Preferences specify the competencies, skills, motivators and preferred work environment you want in your next position.

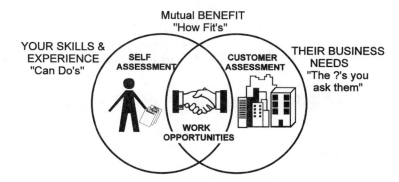

During the interview process, you will want to mentally evaluate what the company has to offer against your Ideal Work Preferences. See if your basic tangible and intangible criteria are met by the position and company culture. In other words, you are looking for the overlap in the above diagram.

You might encounter many of the interview questions on the following pages. (A list of inappropriate questions and possible responses is also included.) If you do your research and conscientiously practice answering these questions, you will be prepared for most interviews. We have suggested ways you might wish to respond to each question. Personalize each of these suggestions because there is no substitute for your own good judgment in determining how best to respond during an actual interview. As you go through each of these questions, **jot down next to it what you would ask the interviewer in return.** Remember, the interview is a process of mutual discovery.

Frequently Asked Interview Questions/Suggested Responses Arranged in Sub-Groups:

- ♦ **"GENERAL"**-- generic questions that may be asked in any type of interview.

- ♦ **"CAN DO"**-- self-assessment questions regarding your skills, abilities, experience, accomplishments, interests, motivation, and values.

- ♦ **"HOW FIT"**-- questions that determine if you are a good match for the company.

CATEGORY: GENERAL

INTERVIEW QUESTION	RECOMMENDED RESPONSE
1. Tell me about yourself.	The best initial response to that question is **Your 90-Second Introduction** <u>Approx. Time</u> Education/Military 5 sec Accomplishments/Work Experience 50 sec Current Situation 5 sec Future 30 sec
2. What can you offer us (that other candidates cannot)?	Use your research about the company to help you make your answer meaningful to the interviewer. Respond by emphasizing your unique qualities and capabilities. Relate them to the position at hand whenever possible.
3. What do you know about our company?	If you have done the research, you can include: products, services, revenues, current business issues, people, history. You might also state that you would like to know more -- from the interviewer's vantage point, and then be prepared to ask further questions.
4. What other types of work or companies are you considering?	Don't feel obliged to reveal details of other interviews or negotiations. If you are interviewing elsewhere, refer to them in a general way, but concentrate mainly on this specific position.
5. If you could begin your career again, what would you do differently?	"While hindsight is 20/20, I am pleased with the choices I have made in my life." If there is something specific you can mention (e.g., your desire to have completed college, or started your education earlier), it would be appropriate to mention it here.
6. How have you kept up in your field?	Discuss reading, seminars, courses (in or outside work), association meetings, or discussions with colleagues or other professionals.
7. What are your strengths?	Enumerate three or four of your key strengths with examples that are relevant to their needs. Base your response on the position, your research, and other data you have gathered about the company.

CATEGORY: "CAN DO"	
INTERVIEW QUESTION	**RECOMMENDED RESPONSE**
8. What are your weaknesses?	Offer only one, and emphasize what you learned and how you changed as a result.
9. What have been your most significant accomplishments so far?	Refer to your accomplishment statements you wrote in *Chapter 2* selecting ones relevant and specific to the position for which you are interviewing and the challenges you would be facing.
10. How successful have you been so far?	Be prepared to define success for yourself and then respond. Try to select accomplishments that relate to the organization's needs and values (if you have been able to determine them from your research).
11. How did you do in school?	Emphasize your best and favorite subjects; leadership activities; working to finance your education, etc.
12. What qualifications do you have that you feel would make you successful here?	If this question is asked after you have sufficient information about the position, talk about two or three of your major skills (supported by accomplishments) which you believe will be useful in the position. If the question is asked early on, talk about two or three of your major skills and, to the extent you can, relate them to the company. Or, suggest that you postpone answering that question until you have or information about the position.
13. How long would it take you to make a meaningful contribution to our firm?	More and more companies are looking for people who can "hit the ground running." If you know enough about the specific position to give a convincing response, talk about your accomplishments and related experience, and then make selections that are indicative of the kind of work you can do. Or, suggest that you postpone answering that question until you have or information about the position.
14. How do you feel about assuming the responsibilities of a supervisor or manager (if no previous experience)?	If this is not an interest for you, emphasize your strengths as an individual contributor. If you want to manage others, say so with enthusiasm and give examples of why you feel you would be successful.

CATEGORY: "CAN DO," cont.	
INTERVIEW QUESTION	**RECOMMENDED RESPONSE**
15. Describe a situation in which you had a difficult management problem and how you solved it.	Relate an accomplishment that had to do with this kind of situation. Depending on the company's culture and needs, highlight conflict management, team building, communication skills, or staffing.
16. As a manager, what do you look for when you hire people?	"Their skills, initiative, accomplishments, creativity, adaptability -- and whether their chemistry fits with that of the organization."
17. As a manager, have you ever had to fire anyone? If so, what were the circumstances and how did you handle the situation?	If you have fired someone, say so, as well as how it worked out to the benefit of both the individual and the organization. Also say you followed the company's disciplinary procedures carefully before proceeding to termination. (The company may be concerned about discrimination and legal issues.) If you have never fired anyone, say so, but talk about how you would utilize progressive discipline before resorting to termination, in order to protect the company's interests.
18. What do you see as the most difficult task in being a manager?	Managing multiple priorities between: various workgroups, individuals, budgets, etc.; maintaining high ethical standards; or other management issues relevant to the interviewing organization.
19. Do you prefer working with figures or words?	Base your response on the position requirements.
20. Describe a situation in which you have worked under pressure or met deadlines.	Refer to your accomplishments. Discuss one or two in which you were especially effective in meeting deadlines or dealing with high-pressure situations.
21. Tell me about an objective in your last job that you failed to meet, and why.	This question assumes that you failed to meet one of your objectives. If you can honestly state that you met all your established objectives, say so. If there was an objective that you were unable to meet for legitimate reasons, discuss it with an explanation of the obstacles over which you had no control. Above all, state what you learned as a result of the experience.

CATEGORY: "CAN DO", cont.	
INTERVIEW QUESTION	**RECOMMENDED RESPONSE**
22. What have you done that helped increase sales or profit? How did you go about it?	This is your opportunity to describe in some detail a business accomplishment that is relevant to the proposed new position. Be specific about the numbers.
23. How much financial responsibility have you had in previous positions?	You can answer this in terms of your budget, head-count, or the size of the project or sales team that you directed. If you haven't had this type of responsibility, refer to an accomplishment that demonstrates a related skill.
24. How many people have you managed?	If you have not managed others, refer to those over whom you had influence (including subordinates, teams, contractors).
25. Give examples of times when you were a leader.	Draw examples from accomplishments that demonstrate your leadership skills.
26. If I spoke with your previous manager, what would he or she say are your greatest strengths and weaknesses?	Use on-the-job examples of strengths. Position any weakness in a positive way. (Your former manager would probably want to give you a good reference, so recount some of the positive things you did for him or her.)
27. Give one or two examples of your creativity.	Refer to accomplishments and creative solutions or insights that relate to the company and the position.
28. What are your goals or ambitions for the future?	Indicate your desire to concentrate on doing the immediate work well -- and your confidence that the future will be promising. You do not want to convey that you have no desire to progress, nor do you want to appear to be using this position as a stepping stone.
29. Why are you seeking a position with our company?	Indicate that from your research, the business issues they face are the kind that excite you and match up well with your skills, abilities and past experiences. If you can do so honestly, express what it is about the company that appeals to you.

CATEGORY: "CAN DO," cont.	
INTERVIEW QUESTION	**RECOMMENDED RESPONSE**
30. What things are most important to you in a work situation?	Use information developed from your Satisfiers /Dissatisfiers and Ideal Work Preferences, and relate it to what you know about the position.
31. What kind of hours are you used to working?	"I'm willing to do whatever it takes to get the job done."
32. You might be over-qualified for the position we have in mind.	Sometimes this question means: "I am concerned that you are willing to take this position because you need to work and you will leave as soon as you get a better offer." Your answer must address this concern. "At this point in my career, I am looking to do the kind of work that gives me the greatest satisfaction. And what I enjoy doing most is ..."(describe the contents of the position). It is also possible that you are getting the message, "Your salary may be too high for the salary range of this position." Respond by mentioning your ability to "hit the ground running" and be up to speed quickly.
33. What do you feel you should earn in the proposed position?	Postpone answering this question until you know the scope of responsibilities. When you do know, you may want to answer this with a question, such as "What is the typical compensation range for similar positions in your company?" If there is no range in the company, give the range that is local to the city. Or say, "I consider myself to be a stronger than average candidate, so I anticipate an offer that is higher than the midpoint of the salary range for the position."
34. What motivates you the most?	Use the results of your career assessments and your life experience. Do keep your answer fairly general: (e.g. the satisfaction of meeting the challenges of the position; working with individuals or team members; meeting organizational goals.)

CATEGORY: "HOW FIT"	
INTERVIEW QUESTION	**RECOMMENDED RESPONSE**
35. Describe a situation in which your work was criticized. What were the circumstances? How did you respond?	Discuss one mistake or area of criticism, emphasizing what you learned and how your behavior changed. Do not offer additional detail, or defend your position. Criticism does not have to be a negative.
36. How would you describe your personality?	Mention two or three of your most beneficial traits; highlighting those that would be a valuable asset for the position under discussion, and what would be a "fit" in the company.
37. How would you describe your management style?	If you have management experience, you might want to talk about how you set goals and get people involved in them. Also, describe the techniques that you like to use to bring out the best in people, motivate them, and help them grow.
38. Tell me about a work situation that irritated you.	Talk about this type of situation in terms of the skills you used to manage and improve the situation. Stress your ability to remain calm under pressure.
39. Why are you leaving your present job?	This question must be answered briefly. Do not get defensive or explain excessively; simply state the circumstances, for example, a forced reduction, a merger or acquisition, etc. If possible, explain how your termination was not a single layoff, but part of a large group reduction. When you have finished answering, look the interviewer in the eye and stop.
40. Describe what you feel would be an ideal work environment.	This is an opportunity to mention insights from your Satisfiers and Ideal Work Preferences, and relate them to the company and position.
41. Looking back, how would you evaluate your previous employer?	Be positive. Refer to the benefits you have derived: "It is an excellent company which has given me many valuable experiences and opportunities to perform successfully."

CATEGORY: "HOW FIT," cont.	
INTERVIEW QUESTION	**RECOMMENDED RESPONSE**
42. Had you thought about leaving your previous position before? If yes, why did you stay?	Refer to the positive aspects of the position, the company; to the knowledge and experience gained.
43. How long would you stay with us?	"For as long as the work situation is mutually satisfactory, I am making a meaningful contribution and the contribution is recognized and acknowledged."
44. How would your co-workers describe you?	Refer to your skills, strengths and personality traits.
45. How did your subordinates perceive you?	Be positive and honest, referring to your strengths, skills and traits.
46. What do you think of your previous manager?	If you liked the individual, say so and describe why. If not, think of something positive to say.
47. Why do you want to work for this company?	Match your skills, strengths, experience, Satisfiers and Ideal Work Preferences to the position and the company profile.
48. Why should we hire you?	Relate past experiences to current position; cite relevant accomplishments; describe industry or functional knowledge -- all benefits to hire you.
49. What sort of outside reading do you do? What are the recent movies you have seen?	Mention some of the things you read to keep current in your professional field, balanced by recreational reading and viewing.
50. What was your previous salary? What kind of compensation are you seeking?	Organizations usually try to uncover your previous salary to determine if the position is the right fit, and to save themselves some money. Your best response is to answer with a question, "What is the range of this position?" Or "What kind of dollars does an outside contractor performing this work typically earn in your company?" If asked to elaborate further, you can say, "During the last three years, my compensation ranged from $ _____ to $_____."

Inappropriate Questions and Possible Responses

What do we mean by inappropriate questions? Based on laws such as Equal Employment Opportunity (EEO) and Americans with Disability Act (ADA), these are questions that are *not legal* for potential employers to raise. As an interviewee, you have the option not to answer these questions, or to answer them in a way that protects your privacy and integrity.

You must decide *before the interview* whether you will answer these questions directly, or deflect them in order to remain neutral in your response.

Most importantly, you do not want to be caught off guard. Here are some examples.

INAPPROPRIATE QUESTIONS AND POSSIBLE RESPONSES	
INTERVIEW QUESTION	**RECOMMENDED RESPONSE**
1. What was your maiden name?	This is a discriminatory question, since the response can indicate ancestry and simultaneously confirm marital status. Whether or not to answer is your choice, since there are only discriminatory questions, not answers. You can avoid answering it by asking, "How would my name relate to suitability for this position?"
2. Do you plan to have a family?	Because this question is usually asked of females, usually those of child-bearing age, it is also discriminatory and you can refuse to answer. However, a non-disclosing response might be: "I don't have any plans in that area." Or, you could say, "I have a family" and not say whether that is a sister/brother, spouse or children.
3. Are you a Christian?	The interviewer is asking for information that is not job related. You could come back with a rhetorical question such as, "I'm sorry, I don't understand your question. Could you rephrase it?" If the interviewer continues then you can point out that your religious persuasion does not affect your ability to do the job.

INAPPROPRIATE QUESTIONS AND POSSIBLE RESPONSES, cont.

INTERVIEW QUESTION	RECOMMENDED RESPONSE
4. What year did you get your bachelor's degree?	While this question may seem innocuous, the answer can easily be used to calculate age, since most people go on to college directly from high school. If your resume does not reference a degree, it may be a subtle means to determine whether you have one. You can circumvent a direct answer by focusing on a related fact, such as, "I'm very proud of the fact that I finished my undergraduate work in only 3 years." Or, "I continued into graduate school right after college." Or, if you don't have a degree, "I enjoyed engineering so much, I've continued taking courses ever since college."
5. We have many social activities here at XYZ. Do you and your spouse/partner enjoy going to company functions?	The interviewer is asking for confirmation that you are married -- and you may decide that your marital status is off limits. If you are married, if you and your spouse/partner enjoy company functions, and if the question does not bother you, feel free to answer with a simple "Yes, very much" and move on. If not, you can respond along these lines: "Oh, how interesting! What kinds of activities do you provide?" — And let the interviewer expand on the subject without revealing your own position.
6. How is your credit rating?	If you choose, you can simply respond "Fine." If you prefer not to answer, you could say, "My credit rating will not affect my ability to make a contribution to this company."

Remember, the interview is a two-sided process. You want to be asking as well as answering questions. Throughout the last section, you identified questions you might want to ask the interviewer. Here are a few more.

SAMPLE QUESTIONS TO ASK AT THE INTERVIEW

Select questions that are *most appropriate* for your situation and to the position at hand:

1. Why is this position open?

2. How often has it been filled in the past five years?

3. Why did the person most recently in this position leave?

4. What would you like done differently by the next person who does this work?

5. What are some of the objectives you would like accomplished -- short-term and long-term?

6. What is most pressing? What would you like to have accomplished in the next two or three months?

7. What freedom would I have to determine my work objectives, deadlines and methods?

8. What kind of support does this position receive in terms of people and budget?

9. What are some of the more difficult problems facing someone in this position? How do you think these could best be handled?

10. Where could a person go who is successful in this position, and within what time frame?

11. What significant changes do you foresee in the near future?

12. How is one evaluated? What accounts for success?

13. What are the most critical factors for success in your business? (Note whether or not he or she mentions that people matter.)

14. Where do you see the company (department or functional area) going in the next few years?

15. How do you win support from top management?

16. How would you describe your own management style?

17. What are the most important traits you look for?

18. How do you prefer your staff to communicate with you, e.g., orally, in writing, informally, in meetings, only when necessary?

19. What are the success factors for a person to be effective in this position?

20. What does above-average performance look like?

MOCK INTERVIEW

Instructions: Select a partner with whom you have had little to no contact as yet. Copy your Work Objective and Summary Statement (written in Chapter 2) to this page and exchange information with your partner. Each of you are to read your partner's information and imagine a position that you have open in your company. Jot down a few notes for yourself so that you can interview your partner.

Work Objective:_____

_____

_____

Summary Statement: _____

_____

_____

Notes_____

_____

_____

_____

_____

_____

_____

_____

_____

_____

Here are five steps that will sharpen your interview interaction skills.

Step 1

Review your assessment results: accomplishments, skills, I-SPEAK® style, research data, and resume.

Step 2

Study the interview questions and "Your 90-Second Introduction" and plan how you would respond.

Step 3

Review the DBM pre-recorded "Interviewing" videotape.

Step 4

Practice by role-playing -- by yourself/with a partner and with audio/video recording.

Step 5

Obtain feedback by reviewing your audio or videotape. Ask a spouse/partner, close friend or business associate to review it as well and give you feedback about your skills and presentation style.

WHAT ELSE DO YOU NEED TO DO IN ORDER TO BE PREPARED?

What to Bring to the Interview

There are a few basic items that are essential for your interview:

- Extra copies of your resume

- A pad and "good quality" pen

- A briefcase or portfolio, preferably leather

- Your list of references (to be offered only when asked and which are appropriate for this specific position)

- Your best self

Managing Your Image

Since you will have only one opportunity to make that all-important first impression, keep the following in mind.

- **Physical presence**. Dress appropriately for the culture where you are interviewing and, when in doubt, dress on the conservative side. Be sure your grooming and hygiene are immaculate, and that your posture is neither too relaxed and sloppy, nor too tense or forward. Avoid smoking or chewing gum.

- **Movements and mannerisms**. Use natural gestures; do not clench your fists, fidget, or fuss with objects such as a pen, glasses or change in your pocket. Move around naturally; avoid looking stiff or awkward.

- **Manner of speaking**. Make sure you can be heard; be aware of the interviewer's reaction to your voice. Don't mumble or drop your voice to a whisper toward the end of your sentences. Avoid sing-song or monotone recitations, which will give the impression that you are over-rehearsed. Also, avoid slang, jargon and colloquialisms like "You know," as well as grunts, ums, ers, or other verbal "fillers." Try to match your word choices to that of the interviewer.

- **Demeanor**. Convey an appropriate amount of enthusiasm, warmth and sincerity to suit the dynamics of your interviewer. Express your energy and fitness. Be positive, avoid negative topics and don't vent hostility. Smile! I-Speak® is helpful here.

- **Listening skills**. Listen with full concentration and maintain eye contact 75 percent of the time. Eye contact does not mean staring at the interviewer, it means " to look interested and involved." Indicate attention and acceptance with nods and smiles. Avoid interrupting, and allow silence when thought and reflection are needed.

- **Communication skills**. Mirror the style and pace of your interviewer. Use straightforward replies, be credible, and stop when you have answered the question. If you don't know something, say so, and clarify a question you don't understand before answering it. Listen before you respond and think before you speak.

Marketing Yourself

During the interview process, the product you are marketing is YOU -- with all your unique features, functions, and capabilities. The company/interviewer is your potential customer. In this context, keep in mind the following points to increase your success at marketing your candidacy:

♦ Understand your customer's needs, desires and expectations. (You do this by researching the company, department, etc. See Chapter 6)

♦ Know your product and the benefits it will provide. (See Chapter 2)

♦ Know how to strategize potential areas of opportunities for your customer. (You imagine some opportunities they might not have explored yet.)

♦ Solve or avoid incurring customer problems. (You think of how some of your knowledge and experience can solve or avoid some potential problems the organization might have.)

♦ Provide added value and become a resource. (Imagine how your value-adding service would benefit the company you are interviewing. Once the conversation gets going, fine tune these thoughts so they become useful information during the interview.)

To meet these requirements you have to be prepared. You have to visualize the discussion you will be having with the interviewer and imagine how you fit within the organization.

Using I-SPEAK *Your Language*® to Prepare for Interviewing

Re-read the material on I-SPEAK *Your Language*® and view the I-SPEAK® videotape again. This will help you to focus on other people as you strive to analyze their style and adapt your own. Be aware of your own dominant, back-up and least-used styles as well. On the next page, the chart, *"Modifying Your Interaction Style,"* will help you to apply the I-SPEAK® concepts to your search.

You will obtain most of your information about the preferred style of the interviewer by listening analytically. If you can identify the interviewer's communication style, you can tailor your responses to meet his or her needs and expectations. However, it is even more important to listen to what is being said and to present yourself well.

Final Tips for the Interviewee

♦ If there is an opportunity to take control of the interview by getting the interviewer to talk, do so. It gives the impression that you are a good listener, and you can learn a great deal about the interviewer and the company.

♦ If specific job criteria can be elicited from the interviewer early on, you can gear your responses to meet those criteria.

♦ Maintain external calm in a stress interview or when you are asked questions that you consider to be uncomfortable or inappropriate.

♦ The more embarrassing or sensitive a question is, the shorter your answer should be. For example, if an interviewer asks why you were let go, you can respond with: "Our industry has been experiencing difficult economic times, and my company had to eliminate many positions -- including mine"; then, stop.

♦ Obtain names and exact titles of everyone you meet.

MODIFYING YOUR INTERACTION STYLE (Applying I-SPEAK Your Language® in your work search)			
INTERVIEW FOCUS	**WHAT THE INTERVIEWER NEEDS**		
	Intuitor	Thinker	Feeler	Senser
Preparation for Interview	Allow ample time for strategizing and discussion. Think through your beliefs and philosophy. Read about company patents and articles. Study company technology. Study future of company, industry.	Have specific facts ready. Be organized and to the point. Have chronological presentation outlined. Think through logic of story. Dress conservatively, business-like.	Prepare a few topics for "small talk." Set stage for informal discussion (maybe lunch?). Find shared friends, activities. Read company history. Study its traditions.	Prepare succinct answers. Be ready to state what you can do for them. Have facts ready (as with Thinker). Assume interviewer may run late. Indicate a sense of immediacy to their business issues.
Your Interview Style, Content	Start with the broad picture. Stress long-term planning and technology. Discuss their creative work and yours.	Emphasize your analytical skills. Be logical, orderly and systematic. Quantify! Be precise.	Recall the human issues you faced. Mention positive impact on people. Explore mutual friends, bonds.	Give crisp answers, don't ramble. Use ACTION words (achieved, ran, directed, initiated). Focus on their bottom line, P/L.
Written Communication, Including Follow-ups	Begin with a summary. Narrative format.	Use outline or structured format. Complete, terse.	Personal touch! ("Enjoyed our evening.") Not too stiff.	Be brief, to the point. Keep to one page.

Closure

For your own peace of mind, pay attention to closure at the end of the interview. Because there is usually a great feeling of relief, many people do not ask the few simple questions that can remove some of the anxiety from the weeks ahead.

Take note of the following questions. Bring them with you and make sure you leave enough time at the end of the interview to collect this information. These questions can also be asked as you are walking out with the last interviewer or preparing to leave.

- ♦ What are the next steps?

- ♦ What is the timing?

- ♦ Where am I in the interview sequence?

- ♦ Will there be additional (rounds of) interviews?

- ♦ When will you notify the candidates?

Follow Up

It is **mandatory to write a thank you note within 48 hours,** expressing your pleasure and interest. Unless it is an unusual circumstance, thank you letters should be no longer than one page. They should contain something that causes the recipient to remember you, weaving in information that is work-related or drawing on a particularly interesting event during the interview.

If you noticed that the interviewer had an issue with something you discussed, bring it up in the thank you letter with a possible solution or verification. You can start the paragraph with "Upon further reflection, I feel that...."

Send thank you letters to everyone with whom you interviewed on a one-on-one basis. Don't send copies -- make sure you say something a little different to each person. It is not necessary to send individual letters to each of the people in a panel interview. However, you should know through your closure questions which individuals you need to follow up with. Send a letter to these individuals and also to the decision maker (if they are different people).

Interview Post-Analysis

Post-analysis is important in assessing your need for further practice or training. Be honest with yourself. It is possible to invest months in preparation and sacrifice the position during the interview. Learn from each experience and use your cumulative learning to continuously improve your interviewing skills.

Use the following questions as a post-analysis check list.

1.   What went well? Why?

2.   What did not go well? Why?

3.   What would I do differently if I were to repeat the interview?

4.   What key facts did I learn?

5.   What interview skills must I further develop?

6.   How well did I listen to the responses I got?

7.   How does this company/position meet my IWPs?

8.   In what ways do I meet their needs?

SUMMARY

To increase the success of the interview process, keep the following points in mind:

♦ The quality of your **pre-interview research** will strongly impact the success of your interviews

- Matching your strengths to the company profile

- Planning questions to ask

- Planning answers to questions you will be asked

♦ **Manage first impressions** by maintaining confidence, vitality and an appropriate physical appearance.

♦ **Control the content and flow of the interview** by following an agenda, using a sales approach, and managing your responses and stress level.

♦ Use awareness of your **I-SPEAK® communication style** and that of your interviewer to communicate even more effectively.

♦ **Follow up with a thank you letter** to the appropriate individuals within 48 hours.

CHAPTER ELEVEN

Negotiating

> *"Everything is worth what its purchaser will pay for it."*
>
> — Publilius Syrus, *Maxim 847*

POINTS OF INTEREST

Chapter Eleven discusses:

- ♦ The Negotiating Process
- ♦ Important negotiating points
- ♦ How to recognize when an offer is forthcoming
- ♦ What to do when you receive an offer
- ♦ Analyzing and evaluating the offer
- ♦ Planning your negotiating strategy
- ♦ Accepting the offer
- ♦ Negotiating as an Independent Contractor
- ♦ Types of contracts

THE NEGOTIATING PROCESS

Today, the average American worker will change work situations approximately every six years. Consequently, you may find yourself using negotiating skills on an ongoing basis.

What is Negotiating?

Any time two parties come together to exchange goods or services there is an opportunity to negotiate. You don't always get exactly what you want but neither must you always pay the "sticker price." Negotiation is a process in which the parties come to an agreement concerning the terms and conditions under which they are willing to do business. It requires open and honest discussion, flexibility, and the ability to avoid making potentially erroneous assumptions about what the other party wants or is thinking. Time spent learning to be a savvy negotiator has universal application.

Although the negotiating "window" opens *after* an offer has been made, you need to have evaluated your critical requirements *before* the negotiating process begins.

Important points about negotiating:

- Establish your criterion *before* the offer is made (e.g., compensation, benefits, etc., you defined in Exercise #2-9) so that you can assess it against your IWPs (Best Fit Analysis as seen in Exercise #2-1).

- Create a list of the benefits you would bring to the organization, i.e., "What's in it for them to hire you." (Refer to your PARS, skills and key words Exercise #2-3.)

- Negotiating begins during your *first contact* with a potential employer.

  For example, if there are criteria you feel strongly about (rated as "Musts" or very high "wants" in Exercise #2-9), you should make such positions known early in the discussions, rather than have them arise later and result in a lost deal. If it becomes clear that a "Must" will not be met, the only point in continuing the negotiations is for practice.

- Money left on the negotiating table is lost forever.

- Every situation is unique.

What If You Are Not Good at Negotiating?

Use the information in this section to help you become a more proficient negotiator. In addition, strategize with colleagues and other professionals, read books or listen to audiotapes on the topic. Remember, there is no such thing as a "bad negotiator." There are only people who haven't taken the time to prepare.

THE NEGOTIATING PROCESS OVERVIEW

This is the general flow of the negotiation process. On the succeeding pages we will examine each step in detail, relating them back to previous exercises you did to prepare for this time.

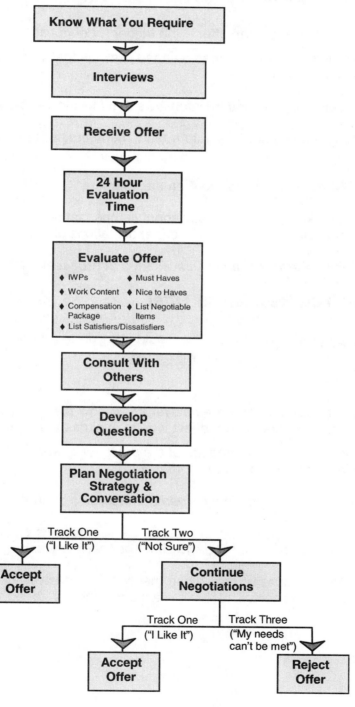

RECEIVING OFFERS

Recognizing Offer Signals

Here are the signals that indicate that an offer -- the trigger for negotiation -- may be forthcoming.

- ♦ The interview takes more time than planned -- a sign that your interviewer considers you to be a viable candidate.

- ♦ You are invited to second or third interviews that include decision-makers.

- ♦ You are interviewed by potential future team members or put through the company testing program.

- ♦ Your interviewers begin to "sell you" on the company.

- ♦ The decision-maker talks specifically about compensation, perhaps exploring your previous compensation package, or your expectations of future earnings.

- ♦ They talk about references, a physical exam or a drug test -- all final steps.

What to Do When You Receive an Offer

An offer might sound something like this: "We would like you to join our organization as (title and function). The yearly salary (or monthly rate) will be ($$$)."

Ask for Evaluation Time

The first thing you want to do is to let the employer know how pleased you are to receive an offer. Be gracious, in both words and tone, and request time to evaluate the offer. An approach might be:

"Thank you for this offer. I am excited about the prospect of working with your organization in a position where I feel I can make a real contribution."

"There are a few items I'd like to clarify -- perhaps we could do that now...(Q and A)"

"Thanks for answering my questions, ____name____. Since this is a very important decision for me, I'd like a day or two to think it over. Can I get back to you on __date__?"

The company may give you a specific date when they want an answer, or they may tell you to take all the time you need. Be sensitive to their reactions, and try to adjust your decision-making schedule accordingly.

There are sound reasons why you need time to respond to an offer.

1. You may require time to study and understand the total package.

2. The salary may be lower than you expected and you need to decide how to deal with the situation.

3. You want to discuss the offer with your family, colleagues or network contacts.

4. It takes time to plan and execute a successful negotiation.

5. You need "transition time" to move from the high of getting the offer to the level-headedness required to negotiate.

6. You think you are going to get another offer shortly and you don't want to limit your options.

ANALYZING AND EVALUATING THE OFFER

1. Begin with the mind-set that *every element is negotiable*. Then, determine whether there are issues you need to clarify, and define what additional information you will need.

2. Return to your Ideal Work Preferences (Exercise #2-9), Work Objective (Exercise #2-7) and Best Fit Analysis[1] (Exercise #2-10) to evaluate the offer and compare it to the considerations you previously identified as important. For example, if one of your preferences is a position that requires no more than 20 percent travel, and this position requires 50 percent, then you must consider whether this is the right position for you. Can a compromise be reached?

There are three key areas to analyze and evaluate.

1. The work content

2. Your Satisfiers/ Dissatisfiers

3. The compensation package

---

[1] Best Fit analysis was completed in Chapter 2 so that you would have an objective method for evaluating any and every offer. Do not change your mind now regarding Must Have items or any of the weights you assigned. This will diminish the value of the assessment it will provide.

1. WORK CONTENT

Questions you can ask regarding work content might include:

♦ What are the company's mission and principal goals?

♦ To whom will I report?

♦ What will be the scope of my responsibility?

♦ What will be the scope of my authority (budget, salaries, staffing)?

♦ Is the authority sufficient to fulfill the responsibility?

♦ What are management's expectations regarding performance?

♦ Within what time frame must those expectations be accomplished?

♦ Are the necessary resources in place (staff, equipment, programs)? If not, are they budgeted?

♦ How is performance measured and rewarded?

♦ Who will conduct my performance review and when?

♦ What will the company do to help me (and my staff) maintain and improve our professional growth?

♦ Are there full details (preferably in printed form) on the organization's benefit programs and how they work?

♦ What will the travel requirements be?

2. SATISFIERS/ DISSATISFIERS

Satisfiers and Dissatisfiers are **negotiables** and are discussion points with potential employers.

Examples of Satisfiers	**Examples of Dissatisfiers**
Travel	Commuting
Managing employees	Direct sales
Managing change	Working in teams
Dealing directly with customers	Long hours (including nights and weekends)
Working on commission	Status
Working with little direction	Unrealistic deadlines
Moral/ethical standards	Routine
Dealing with budgets/numbers	Job security
Workaholic culture	Conflict
Structured environment	Managers

Now is the time to pull out the list you created in Exercise #2-8.

3. THE COMPENSATION PACKAGE: SALARY, BONUS, ETC...

Since salary negotiations begin before you receive an offer, take the time to research salaries in your field and region[2] by questioning your contacts, talking to executive recruiters and looking at salary surveys and advertisements. Take time to learn everything you can about what the market will bear, and how valuable your skills are in that market.

The script below illustrates a suggested way to handle some of these compensation issues.

> *"As you know, my package at ABC Co. was equivalent to about $60K, and I'm anticipating that joining your firm will be a progressive step. I wonder if we could put the compensation issue aside until we have worked through some of the other factors -- particularly job scope and future opportunities. Is that agreeable?"*

If the salary you want is outside the norm, or the salary question is difficult to resolve for some other reason, consider how your skills can positively impact the company's results.

If bonus or pay for performance is an important component in your future package, you should agree on the **criteria upon which bonuses will be determined** and what range is likely, based on history and current profit trends. In fact, you should **explore *how and when* all salary, bonus and other compensation matters are reviewed and decided**. If you come to a negotiated agreement, get it in writing or include it in your acceptance letter.

Relocation Costs

The out-of-pocket expenses of packing, moving and traveling can easily run into the high five digits. The major costs come with:

♦ Selling a house, especially in a depressed local market.

♦ Refinancing, if new mortgage rates are higher than the rate you are currently paying.

♦ Buying a new house in a higher cost area.

An organization's willingness to help you with such issues depends on its established policies and how badly it wants you. Your key strategy is to study these factors thoroughly, including a visit with a Realtor to the new location, before you make any commitments in the negotiation. As with all items you plan to negotiate, you must know the facts and be prepared to offer a reasonable solution that will satisfy the needs of all parties. Each and every item is a separate negotiable.

---

[2] There are regional variations in salary/wages due to cost of living differences. Thus $60K in Chicago may be equal to $40K in Little Rock and $80K in L.A. Adjust any and all compensation figures to reflect the cost of living difference if you are relocating to a new city so you can properly evaluate them and compare them to your former pay levels.

Quality of Life Issues

There have been significant shifts in the emphasis on personal values in recent years. Many professionals now value their family time as much as their work time, share equally with their partners in household responsibilities, and are requiring concessions from their employers to support these priorities. As a result, vacation time may be a flexible item to negotiate since many organizations cannot see an immediate bottom-line impact.

As you prepare your own negotiating strategy and wish list, keep in mind the issues described below that may be important to you.

- ◆ Working at home, usually with computer ties to the office.
- ◆ Time off or a flexible schedule to be with family members.
- ◆ Child or eldercare assistance.
- ◆ Job sharing.
- ◆ Tuition reimbursement/sabbaticals.
- ◆ College tuition assistance.

Other Items that May Be Negotiable

Depending on the position, the following items may be negotiable:

Base Salary	Relocation Expenses	Miscellaneous Expense Allowance
Bonus/Commission	House Hunting Trips	
Pension*	Purchase of Home	Savings Plans
Life Insurance*	Lodging Between Homes	Tax Assistance
Profit Sharing*	Housing Differential	Bridge Loans
Stock Options*	Closing Costs	Professional Association Dues
Medical Insurance*	Home Visits	Club Memberships*
Disability Insurance*	Legal Assistance	
Company Car*	Financial Planning	
Vacation	Annual Physical	
Business Travel	Equipment (car phone, laptop)	

* Less likely due to legal restrictions and tax implications

PLANNING YOUR NEGOTIATION STRATEGY AND CONVERSATION

While every situation is different, here are some basic tenets to keep in mind when developing your negotiating strategy.

- ♦ **Attitude**. Maintain a positive attitude and visualize the positive results you are striving to achieve.

- ♦ **Keep the atmosphere congenial**. This individual could be your next manager, so it is important that both of you get off on the right foot.

- ♦ **Need**. Assess your strengths in relation to the marketplace. How much do they really need you? Are you the only candidate? How long has the position been open? Have others refused it? Are your skills rare in the marketplace, or can they readily find someone else if they don't like your conditions?

- ♦ **Put all points on the table at the same time**. Otherwise, you create the suspicion that there will always be one more item about to be disclosed, and the other party will be unwilling to negotiate on any issue.

- ♦ **The person who sets the agenda controls the discussion**. Develop an agenda for the negotiation and prioritize it, beginning with the most important item.

- ♦ **Negotiate in person, if possible**. While offers are frequently communicated by telephone, you should make every attempt to conduct negotiations on a face-to-face basis. Factoring in non-verbal cues and I-SPEAK® style is also crucial to successful negotiation.

- ♦ **Obtain salary data from sources within the industry**. Do not rely solely on nationally published statistics. Industry and location are the best determinants of salary.

    For example, you could respond to the company's $60,000 offer with information about comparable positions in the industry and area. You might say:

    "I understand that $60,000 is the area average for a similar position in a smaller company with narrower responsibilities and requiring only a few years' experience."

    "Yours is a significantly larger organization. Since the kinds of challenges we have been discussing will require my level of experience and broad expertise, I would hope the company might be able to increase that offer."

- **You can negotiate on almost any basis except your own personal needs**. What you need for your children's education, mortgage payments, etc., are *your* problems, not the company's. Relocation is the one possible exception. A working spouse whose relocation must match yours is a valid negotiating point. Finding your spouse a job could frame one basis of the negotiation. On most other matters, you still must have a valid, work-related rationale to support your position.

- **Do not make an impromptu decision during a negotiation**. You must decide the limits of your flexibility *before* you begin negotiation.

- **Contingency plan**. What can you do if your initial requests are denied? Suggestions might include: negotiate a shorter merit increase period (e.g., a performance review and salary action in three months rather than the traditional six-month period), amount of vacation time, sign-on bonus vs. higher base salary, and waiving or reducing non-compete arrangements.

- **Turn down the offer**. If things do not proceed in your favor, are you prepared to walk away from the offer?

Planning the Negotiation Conversation

In planning the negotiation conversation, consider the following points.

1. Make notes of key issues.

2. Start with the positives -- what is right about the position, company and the offer.

3. Use questions, not demands. For example, "Is this salary negotiable?" "How much flexibility does the company have in ...?"

4. Don't push too hard unless you are willing to walk away.

5. Do your research first.

ACCEPTING/REJECTING OFFERS

Getting to Win-Win

The negotiating process is similar to selling your home. You want to get the highest price possible and make the most profit; the buyer is aiming for the lowest price possible. Each of you knows what you *must* have and what you *want* to have. In the best of scenarios, a compromise is reached wherein both parties feel that most of their needs and wants have been satisfied. This is called a "win-win" situation. The following diagram will illustrate:

Accepting the Offer, "As Is"

You may be inclined to accept the offer "as is" for the following reasons.

♦ You are pleased with the offer -- it contains everything you want.

♦ The work market is tight right now.

♦ Your search for work may have taken longer than you anticipated.

> You do need to exercise caution and not appear desperate, or too eager. Your worth will be lessened if your actions imply, "I'll do anything to get this position."

Wait at least 24 hours before you render your decision. During that time, discuss this opportunity with professional colleagues and family.

Accepting the Negotiated Offer

Once all the details of an offer have been ironed out, *it is important to get the final offer in writing.* Most companies make it a practice to provide written offers. If there is no written offer, you can send a letter expressing gratitude and confirming all major aspects of the offer. (See *Chapter 9, Written Communication,* in this workbook for a description and the Index of Resources for sample letters.)

Following your verbal acceptance and receipt of a written offer from the company, it is a good idea to send a letter of acceptance. This letter should contain the following:

- ♦ Your thanks for receiving the offer and your enthusiasm about starting work.

- ♦ Statement of your agreed-upon compensation, your title, department, start date, and any other special conditions that may have been negotiated.

Rejecting the Offer

If it appears that you are not going to reach an agreement or accept the job from a company you have negotiated with extensively, be sure to sign off on a pleasant note. If the lack of agreement was over some condition of employment such as salary, it is not uncommon for a company to come back later with an offer of a higher salary. Or, it could happen that, six months from now, they will remember you favorably when an even better opportunity arises.

You should also send thank you letters to companies that made offers to you that you declined. Make sure you compliment the company, but do not necessarily give them any details about the offer you finally accept. Samples of these letters are also in your Index of Resources.

Multiple Offer Strategy

If you are fortunate and have pursued several opportunities concurrently, you may have two or more offers at the same time.

Playing two or more offers against one another can be tricky, but it can be done. The recommended strategy is to select the company you would prefer to join and negotiate the best deal you can.

If an offer is made but your dream position is waiting in the wings, what are the options? This is the time to get on the phone and obtain an up-to-date reading on all your other potential opportunities that may be close to reaching the offer stage. A possible approach might be:

> *"I've been extremely interested in your firm and in our discussions so far. My early impression was that I could make a worthwhile contribution, and that working at XYZ Co. would be exciting and rewarding.*

> *I must make a decision soon on another opportunity, and I'm wondering about the current status on the position with your company. Is there anything I can do to further your consideration of my candidacy?"*

You will usually find that if Company #2 is sincerely interested in you, they will "move mountains" to get the process accelerated and make you an offer. If they are more interested in other candidates, they will probably suggest that you go ahead and take offer #1. If they don't get back to you, then a decision "has been made" and you can assume that you are no longer in the running with that firm.

If this gentle push accelerates negotiations with one or more of your prospects, you need to determine whether it would be practical and prudent to delay your response to offer #1 while you bring one of the others to closure.

Effective Stalling Tactics

Waiting a week or two to render your decision is not unusual. Asking specific questions that will require some research on the part of the interviewer (e.g., company policy on a particular issue) can be an effective stalling tactic. House-hunting visits prior to acceptance can also buy time, as can working out specific questions about benefits.

One way to explore their feelings on the subject would be to ask a direct question.

> *"I appreciate your offer very much. I have one other serious negotiation in progress which I am also obliged to see through to conclusion. I was wondering if you could give me until the end of the month (or week) so that I can finalize my decision process. Would this be agreeable to you?"*

You have just given them an option, plus an opportunity to show concern. If they agree, you will have time to evaluate and negotiate other offers. Remember, you are a "product"-- possibly a scarce resource -- and if the buyer wants a specific product, s/he will wait or improve the offer.

NEGOTIATING AS AN INDEPENDENT CONTRACTOR

Negotiating your fee is a major intangible of contracting. Since the service you provide is not the same as a store-bought product, there is no universal standard to guide you, because pricing can vary by profession, geographic region or individual assignment.

Here are two important points to keep in mind.

♦ Your fee needs to be high enough to take into account overhead and profit.
So if, for example, you feel you should be earning $300 a day, you might have to bill out at $500 in order to cover your costs and make a profit.

♦ There is a formula that can be used as a pricing guideline, especially for the starting consultant. Establish a targeted annual salary; divide the desired annual pre-tax income by 260 days (or 52 five-day weeks). Multiply that by 2 to allow for 50% non-billable time.

That result would be further multiplied by a percentage to cover "profit." (For a 15% profit multiply by 115%, for 20% by 120%.) The resulting formula looks like this:

$$\left(\frac{\textbf{Annual Salary}}{\textbf{260 days}} \times 2\right) \times 120\% = \frac{\textbf{Rate}}{\textbf{Day}}$$

For Example:

$$\left(\frac{\textbf{\$60,000}}{\textbf{260 days}} \times 2\right) \times 120\% = \frac{\textbf{\$553}}{\textbf{Day}}$$

Use a pricing model as a *guideline* in setting fees, since no formula will fit every situation.

♦ Don't forget to factor in the cost of medical and dental benefits; they may be of paramount concern. You will need to "round up" your fee to take these items into account (which are roughly 20-30% of salary).

Daily Rates

Daily rates, a standard for pricing in the contractor environment, must be established and tested in the market. Here are some guidelines to take into consideration.

♦ You may need to customize your pricing depending on the client and the type of service you will be providing.

♦ Use your judgment about what to charge, keeping in mind your client and the competition.

♦ Some fields command higher fees than others; consider what the traffic will bear in your area of specialty and geographic region.

♦ Some larger companies have established fixed daily rates for services provided by contractors and consultants.

Professional organizations, as well as executive recruiters and outsourcing agencies, can often provide helpful pricing information. Nearly every field has societies or professional groups with this type of data, and many organizations keep detailed demographic and financial data about their members and their costs of doing business. The marketplace will provide the parameters for you.

Hourly Rates

You can negotiate your hourly rate by dividing your daily fee by eight hours.[3] Hourly rates are sometimes used at the beginning of a project, as you become acquainted with a company.

Project Fees [4]

A project fee, also known as a "fixed contract" fee, can be useful when tailoring work to fit a company budget. In setting project fees, it is extremely important to establish clear expectations, with targets and timetables for completing the work. It is also extremely important for you to make sure you have identified all the parts and pieces of the work required of you before setting a price. You don't want to short-change yourself or surprise the customer with an override.

Many contractors prefer to bid exclusively on a project basis because they feel they have more latitude in how and when the job is done; the company only pays for the results.

---

[3] If hourly rates are not the general norm for your profession then add a small percentage to your hourly rate to cover inconvenience. This is a sales technique to indicate purchasing your services by the day is a better deal.
[4] In some instances, your customer will want an accounting of how you spent your time and their money.

THE WRITTEN CONTRACT

It is not unusual for independent contractors to operate on a contract basis. Contracts can be written to cover hourly rates, daily rates or projects.

The contract is a legal document that protects your interests, and it reflects in explicit language the terms that you and your client have agreed upon.

Why is it important to confirm terms in a written contract? A contract gives both sides the opportunity to ensure that the project is clearly defined and approved by the appropriate sponsor in the client organization. A contract:

♦ Confirms all the important terms and arrangements.

♦ Clarifies ambiguities.

♦ Can act as a guide once the project is underway.

Types of Contracts

There are many types of contracts, each with a different purpose. They can be as simple as a letter of agreement or as formal as a contract filled with clauses and subclauses. To familiarize yourself, look at the following overview of the major types of contracts and how they apply to independent contractors.

Letter of Agreement

The letter of agreement is the simplest and least formal of all contracts. You will find it sufficient for most of your contracting jobs. The letter clearly defines the terms, outlines the conditions of the project, and establishes a pay scale and schedule for the contractor. Letters of agreement can also specify special arrangements, such as the kind of support you will receive on the job, performance expectations and how to handle any problems.

Although the tone is usually less formal than a general contract, the letter of agreement is actually considered a legally binding contract when signed by both parties and when it includes scope, terms and other special considerations. By ending your proposal with the term "Accepted and Agreed" and signature blocks, you can save time and effort by converting your proposal into a letter of agreement.

General Contracts

General contracts are formal, detailed and elaborate documents in which every relevant condition of an agreement is specified. These contracts are most appropriate for large or complex projects, and usually are drawn up by an attorney.

Commission and Retainer Contracts

These are variations of general contracts. If your work is directly linked to company performance, e.g., a sales representative selling products, you may be paid on commission.

Commission contracts require greater detailing of the client's responsibilities and your access to the company's records to enable you to determine the amount of sales or production upon which your commission is based.

The retainer contract usually indicates the time you allot to the client in return for the retainer, as well as billing and payment procedures for work in excess of the guaranteed amount. For a contractor, a retainer agreement makes sense when you can predict the amount of time that the client will need and are able to fit it into your own schedule. For the client, the main advantage of having you on retainer is that your services can be quickly and easily tapped.

Daily/Monthly Rate Contracts

Many contractors prefer daily or monthly rate agreements, particularly in situations where the work is repeatable and well defined by the client. Daily rate contracts are also preferable in situations where time overruns are likely. In a daily rate contract, the contractor gives an estimate of time and expenses but is not responsible for overruns. For example, if you are working on a daily contract and the work extends beyond an eight-hour day, the company must pay for the extra time.

Monthly rate contracts are used by clients to "lock in" a rate for a specified time -- in one-month increments and to ensure that the contractor will devote all available time to the client's project.

ELEMENTS OF GOOD CONTRACTS

The introductory section, or opening of the contract, always identifies the contractor and client parties to the agreement. The rest of the contract may include the following:

- ◆ A definition of the services that will be performed.
- ◆ Clearly defined objectives.
- ◆ A breakdown of the client's responsibility.
- ◆ Scope of services.
- ◆ Specified time frame for delivery of services.
- ◆ Provision of equipment and supplies.
- ◆ A fee payment schedule.
- ◆ Terms of ownership of the project.
- ◆ The dates for which the contract is in effect.
- ◆ Conflict of interest/exclusivity/non-compete provisions.
- ◆ Insurance requirements.

Contracts are signed and dated by both parties at the bottom of the document. Not every agreement includes all the features listed above, but these are features that should be carefully considered.

A sample *Monthly Contractor Agreement* is included in the Index of Resources.

Employment Contracts

In some industries, employment contracts are the rule rather than the exception. But in much of the industrial and commercial world, they are not common.

If a contract appears to be feasible, find the right attorney to protect your interests, someone who is experienced with professionals at your level and who is in the same or related industry.

The contract should include all of the items that you would negotiate in an ordinary hiring situation, with the addition of items that are suggested by the nature of your particular employment situation.

- ♦ It should provide a contingency if the company decides to back out of the contract. How long would your salary and benefits continue? Can you keep your company car and club memberships? Do you get a lump sum at the end of the period?

- ♦ If you are the one who wants to leave, what prohibitions or penalties will prevent you from joining a competitor or doing something else deemed harmful by your former employer?

- ♦ If the contract provides for termination "for cause," what would constitute adequate cause?

- ♦ With the current trend toward mergers and acquisitions, you may want to protect the longevity of your contract.

A sample *Employment Contract* is included in the Index of Resources.

SUMMARY

Receiving a position offer is an exciting time, one that requires pre-planning, thorough research, and a consideration regarding how the decision will fit into your life plan.

Effective negotiation requires the following:

- ♦ Before beginning the interview process, **have a clear idea of what you are looking for** from this position.

- ♦ **Research the company, industry, comparable salary, and region** before the negotiating begins.

- ♦ **Ask questions during the interview** to gather as much as information as possible to effectively evaluate position and compensation package.

- ♦ Once the offer has been made and you have all the information you need, **ask for time to consider the offer.**

- ♦ **Use your IWPs, *"Best Fit Analysis"* and other self-assessment information** to develop your negotiating priorities.

- ♦ **Get an agreed-upon offer in writing** before notifying any one of your new position.

- ♦ **Do not discontinue your search for work** until you have accepted the offer.

- ♦ If you decide not to accept the offer, **be sure to leave relationship on good terms.**

CHAPTER TWELVE
Campaign Action Plan
And
What To Do If Your Search Stalls

"It is a rough road that leads to the heights of greatness."

Seneca, *Epistles Chapter 84, 13*

POINTS OF INTEREST

Chapter Twelve presents tools and techniques to help you:

♦ Organize your career search activities.

♦ Manage your time efficiently.

♦ Establish work patterns that will increase the likelihood of success.

♦ Set up the necessary records and systems to track all the details of activities associated with your search.

♦ Create ways to measure your productivity and effectiveness.

♦ Revitalize your employment search if it becomes "stalled."

BUSINESS STRATEGY

Exercise #12-1

DBM considers the following list of exercises from your workbook to be mandatory preparation for your job search and therefore constitutes an initial "Action Item List" for you. Check them off as you complete them.

EXERCISE #: TITLE	INPUT	OUTPUT	Min. TIME Rqt.	[
#1-3: Budgeting for Transition	Personal Finances	Financial Assessment: Expenses vs Income/time	1-2 hr.	
#2-3: Writing Your Own *PARS*	Personal Experience	Accomplishment Statements (PAR & S)	1 hr.	
#2-4: Skills And Knowledge	Review list	Skills & Knowledge ID'ed	15 mins.	
#2-5: Identifying Your Specific Skills embodied in your PARS	Exercise #2-3, #2-4	Accomplishments, Skills and Key Words for use in Resume	20-30 mins.	
#2-6: The Summary Statement	Personal Knowledge	Resume-quality Summary Statement	20-30 mins.	
#2-7: Work Objective (W.O.)	Personal Knowledge	Resume-quality W.O.	20-30 mins.	
#2-8: Your Satisfiers/ Dissatisfiers	Personal Knowledge	Information for IWP's, Best Fit, and Negotiations	20 mins.	
#2-9: Defining Your Ideal Work Preferences (IWPs)	Exercise #2-7 & #2-8	Tangible & Intangible Ideal Work Preferences for use with Resume	30 mins.	
#2-11: I Speak®	Self Knowledge	Identify your speaking style & understand style of others.	40 mins.	
#4-1 or #4-2: Resume	Exercises #2-3, #2-6, #2-7	Rough draft of a Resume	1 hr.	
#5-1: 90-Second Introduction	Exercises #2-3, #2-5, #2-6	Introductions for all circumstances	30 mins.	
#5-2: Analyzing Your Telephone Image	Self knowledge, others' assistance.	Knowledge of how you come across on a telephone	30-60 mins.	
#5-3: Networking Contact Worksheet	Personal knowledge and address book	Initial contact list for Networking	variable	
#6-1: Compiling Your Reference Prospects List	List contacts from business experiences	Potential References for any circumstance	20 mins.	
#6-2: Creating your Reference Database	Exercise #6-1	Information for each Potential Reference	1 hr minimum.	

RECORDKEEPING

There are several reasons for establishing and maintaining accurate and complete records.

1. You will be accumulating a great deal of information during the course of your activities.

2. The information you are gathering is valuable, and will be useful to keep for future reference.

3. The contacts you make and letters you write may require follow up for completion.

4. You may be in different phases of the career continuation process at the same time, requiring many activities. Recordkeeping and tracking are vital to remain organized and in control.

5. You will want to measure results of your efforts; to assess what is working well for you and what is not (e.g., Are you getting interviews? Is answering ads, or some other strategy, sufficiently productive?). Recordkeeping allows you to analyze current events and outcomes, make modifications, and plan future actions.

6. Writing things down while the data and impressions are fresh in your mind will help ensure that you do not forget important information.

RECORDKEEPING FORMS

DBM recommends using the following forms to track events and activities, and to maintain records during your search. Samples appear at the end of this section and are also found in your Index of Resources.

Weekly Action Plan (Item #12-1)

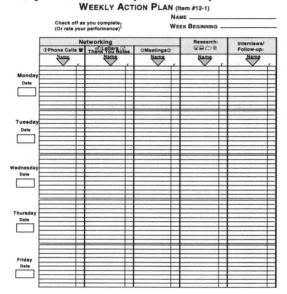

The information you write in your Weekly Action Plan will be based on activities, outcomes and follow-up from the previous week, and goals you set for the upcoming week.

It is organized vertically by days (Monday to Friday), with horizontal columns for:

- ♦ Networking Activities:
    - ♦ Phone Calls
    - ♦ Letters /Thank you notes
    - ♦ Meetings
- ♦ Research Activities:
    - ♦ Company to investigate
    - ♦ Resource to check
- ♦ Interviews /Follow-up Actions:

As you carry out your job search, you will be generating a large amount of information, contacts and obligations that you need to manage. If a new contact will be on vacation for two weeks you need a system that will remind you to contact him in two weeks. There are several specific record sheets for detailed notes but your Weekly Action Plan is the summary to manage it all. There are spaces under each column for listing the names of individuals or organizations that you will be contacting and a column to check off after you do it.

Use this form to plan and accumulate weekly activities; at the end of each week, you can compare it against your expectations or estimated targets to analyze how you are meeting your goals. (See Daily Performance Review Item #12-6)

Networking Contact Records (Item #12-2 A/B)

Networking Contact Records are shown in two formats, index card (2A) and full page/notebook (2B). This form will help you keep track of all the networking information you gather: whom you meet, what transpired and follow-up activities. You can file these alphabetically by individual or company name in a card file and flag those requiring further action. You can take them with you to appointments/meetings. Be sure to cross-index them to your correspondence.

Name	Office Phone/Fax		Home
Company	**POSSIBLE TYPE OF ASSISTANCE**		
Address	☐ INDUSTRY INFO. ☐ INTRO. To TARGET ☐ TARGET CO. INFO. ☐ JOB LEAD ☐ SECOND CONTACTS ☐ FEEDBACK ☐ FUTURE REFERENCES		
Contact	Mode	What Happened?	Follow-up
	☐ Phone ☐ Letter ☐ Interview		☐ Required ☐ Completed
(List referral on back of card)		Referred by	

NETWORKING CONTACT RECORD (Item #12-2B)

CONTACT NAME	Follow-up _____ Status:_____	REFERRED BY:
Title/Function: Business Phone #: Business Fax #: Company Name: Street Address: City/State/Zip:		Contact Name: Title/Function: Company Name:

Background Information On Contact

Relationship to referring
Family: spouse, children, pets:
Age:
Hobbies:
Interests:
Other:

DATE	STATUS/COMMENTS:

If you have a personal computer, you may prefer to automate your tracking system, rather than maintain it manually, using software for a personal information management system (e.g., Rolodex, Day Timer, Franklin Day Planner, ACT or Lotus Notes).

Whichever format or system you select, it is vital to maintain current and accurate records of all your networking contacts for present and future use.

Interview Logsheet (Item #12-3)

INTERVIEW LOGSHEET (Item #12-3)

F I L L O U T P R I O R T O I N T E R V I E W

Name: | Phone #: | Fax #:
Title: | Interview Date:
Company Name:
Address:
Background Information on Individual:

Information on
• Scope of Work
• Compensation Package
• Names & Titles of Key People
• Organizational Structure
• Key Locations
• Products/Services/Lines of Business

Desired Outcome/Next Step:

A F T E R I N T E R V I E W

What Worked Well:
Areas for Improvement:
Reactions to/from Others:
Main Interests in My Background:
What Happens Next (What, Who, When):

The Interview Logsheet form can be used to summarize information and results from employment interviews.

Prior to the interview, be sure to note:

♦ Scope of the work.
♦ Compensation.
♦ Names and titles of key people.
♦ Organizational structure.
♦ Locations of operations.
♦ Products, services, lines of business.
♦ Any other relevant data.

After the interview, debrief yourself by filling out the bottom half of the sheet. Then transfer any follow-up activities or thank you note to your Weekly Action Plan.

Correspondence Logsheet (Item #12-4)

This form will help you track all of your correspondence (e.g., target marketing letters, thank you letters, letters in response to ads, etc.).

Correspondence Logsheet

Type of Correspondence	Name/Address/Phone/Fax	Mail Date	Phone Date		Result of Follow-up	Written Reply Rec'd	Further Action
			Sched'd	Actual			

To be efficient, you will need to keep:

♦ A copy of the original letter (be sure that any attachments are specified on the letter and on the logsheet).
♦ A copy of the name/address list (plus phone numbers).
♦ A notation of the actual mailing date.
♦ A date reminder for following up with a phone call or other required action.
♦ A note of the dates that you called, whether or not you connected with the person and the end result.
♦ A copy or notation of any written reply you received to letters.
♦ A copy of your handwritten thank you notes following interviews and networking meetings.

This too can be automated if you have ACT or Lotus Notes or perhaps some other software program for this purpose.

Advertisement Record (Item #12-5)

```
          ADVERTISEMENT RECORD  (#12 - 5)

  THE AD:                    Appeared in: _____
                                            (Publication)

                             _____  _____
                              (Edition)    (Date)
  _____ Sent attached letter with _____ attached
  _____ Phoned number given, spoke to _____
    ◆  Result:


    ◆  Follow up required:


  _____ Researched/networked for more information on company
  _____ Plan to follow up by _____
  with _____
  Notes from research:
  _____
  _____
  _____
  _____
  _____
```

For ad responses, keep a copy of the following:

- ◆ The ad (including newspaper and publication date).

- ◆ Your response.

- ◆ Notes about company from research.

- ◆ Notes from phone calls to you by the company that placed the ad.

DAILY PERFORMANCE REVIEW (ITEM #12-6)

Throughout the Career Continuation Program, we have talked about the necessity of keeping on track if you are to make the best transition in the shortest amount of time. A helpful tool is your personal performance review. DBM recommends that you use it to evaluate your own daily performance. It will help you to stay focused on your task

Instructions: At the end of each day, take out your Weekly Action Plan (Item #12-1). The items you listed for that day are your performance objectives. They are what you will evaluate. Answer the question: How well/completely did I perform each task? **It is not good enough to have simply accomplished them**.

Assign a rating to each of your daily goals on a scale of 1- 100 with 100 being the best. You are your own best judge of personal quality.

74 or less means that you have not faced up to your situation as yet or are choosing to remain unemployed. You might benefit from talking to a mentor.

75-84 means that you want to find a position but are choosing a leisurely route. Time is not a concern. On the other hand, if time is a concern, review the chapter(s) in this workbook that are relevant to the tasks on which you gave yourself low scores. Talk to your mentor and refine your skills at the job of finding a position.

85-94 means that you are giving it your best shot, but there is room for improvement. You need to evaluate the quality of your interactions; review your letters, your networking for information activities and get a little coaching to further enhance your deliverables. Talk with your mentor or network for coaching assistance.

95-100 means that you are sincere in your efforts, professional in your deliverables and relentless in your pursuit of a desirable future.

After you have reviewed the day's activities, go through those for tomorrow and refine them with any insights you may have gained from what happened today. In this way, each day can build on the last until you reach your goal. In addition, this review time is an opportunity to pause and enjoy the experience.

MANAGING YOUR TIME

With the number of events, meetings and activities associated with an energetic campaign, it is important to maintain time management strategies. The forms mentioned above will go a long way to help you stay on target. Below are some guidelines for managing your time.

- ◆ **Assess the amount of time you have to find a new position.** This will depend on your program, and your individual financial situation. It is critical to know exactly how long you can manage before you **must** find work.

- ◆ **Design a system based on your own personal style** and work habits. What is most important is to have *some kind of system.*

- ◆ **ASAP.** Keep the process *As Simple As Possible:* you are more likely to stick with a time management plan that is simple to use, simple to maintain and comfortable for you.

- ◆ **Create a daily, prioritized** *"To Do List"* by making use of the Weekly Action Plan form. Carry forward any items that did not get accomplished.

- ◆ **Perform a *daily assessment*** of how your time was spent. What did you accomplish? What didn't you accomplish? Adjust the next day so that by the end of the first week you will have established a workable system. In addition, look at where most of your time is being spent in relation to your goals. Remember Pareto's Law, 20% of the activity yields 80% of the success.

Exercise #12-2

We would like you to leave here with a concrete plan of action so you can hit the ground running. To make that happen you need to fill out a Weekly Action Plan for the first week after leaving the DBM course. Make ample use of the various lists of people (networking contacts, references, etc.) you have created prior to this point.

☆Also, when you get home this evening, create a Business Notebook subdivided into sections corresponding to the forms on which you will store your business records and any other category that will assist your data organization.

OBSERVATIONS

It takes time to get a position. Sometimes longer than you had originally hoped. On these occasions it is easy to become dejected and to lose your cutting edge. You know you are blue when:

- You stop cleaning up in the morning before going to "your office";

- Rather than making networking calls or writing letters of introduction, you bake bread or go golfing;

- Rather than answer your phone, you let your phone machine or answering service take the calls;

- You prefer to play computer games rather than review your action plan and define the next steps;

- You stop your social activities and begin to nap, drink, smoke, or eat at inappropriate times;

- You withdraw from other human beings and feel terrible.

If you have a plan of action that you are following and continuously renewing to keep your business afloat, you are in continuous search for a customer. This is true in any business. Sales organizations set quotas, production lines set output expectations, every business has to find their customers, so why should yours be different.

> NOTE: If you are feeling blue, you cannot hide it. Any encounter you have with a potential customer, networking associate, peer or old friend will be shadowed with the color of blue. When blue comes across, people are not inclined to be attracted to you. By catering to blue, **you** will be limiting your success. Hence, along with your business plan, we suggest that you also put together your physical, spiritual and social plan of action. No matter what, make a commitment to participate fully in physical, social and spiritual activities. These activities will keep you "pink" enough to continue your search.

PROFILE OF A CAMPAIGN IN NEED OF A CURE

How does a doctor know what is ailing you? Answer, "By asking about your symptoms." Similarly, your campaign to find work may experience some problems from time to time. Here are some signs that your campaign may be getting off track.

- ◆ **Procrastination.** You find many things to do *other* than work on your campaign: fix the roof, plant a garden, read a book, paint the house, or take the dog for a long walk. In other words, do things that were at the bottom of the pile anyway. Procrastination may be the symptom of a larger issue, so it is important to talk to your DBM colleagues, other professionals or a family member if procrastination becomes a way of life.

- ◆ **Sickness.** "I can't look for work, I have a (headache, backache, etc.)." Again, ongoing symptoms of malaise may be an indicator of other issues.

- ◆ **First meeting rut.** You are consistent at getting a first informational networking meeting, a first interview, a first anything -- but that's all.
  This may be a symptom that you may not be presenting yourself in a way that invites the second round.

- ◆ **"My resume isn't finished."** If this all-important document is in its fourteenth revision and it is week six of your campaign, this may be another version of procrastination.

- ◆ **People aren't taking you seriously.** You may appear unfocused, your research may not show sufficient depth, or your presentation skills may not be as keen as they could be. Be sure that you are truly focused and ready to move on in a demonstrable way.

- ◆ **Negative attitude or state of mind.** A negative attitude about your search, for whatever reason (e.g., anger, fear), is a symptom that you need to examine some personal issues that may be getting in the way.

- ◆ **"The dog ate my homework."** You are unprepared for meetings with your contacts or interviewers. This is another symptom to be examined.

It is likely that if you are able to talk to someone about these "symptoms," you will discover and be able to address the root of the problem. There are often legitimate reasons or concerns that can delay or derail a search for work. What is most important is to be aware of the situation and then do something about it -- <u>**quickly**</u>.

WHAT TO DO IF YOUR EMPLOYMENT SEARCH STALLS

It is not uncommon for candidates to launch their campaign with a flurry of activity and then experience a slowdown at some point. While we know that candidates who set goals, seek support and stick to their plans tend to be the most successful, even the most ardent candidate may experience some "dips" in activity level.

If a lull continues for more than a couple of weeks, it should alert you that it is time to re-assess your campaign strategies and activities before becoming discouraged or unfocused. This is why you have Exercises #12-1 and #12-2 plus all of the items for recordkeeping.

A Real World Example

Listen to the words of a manager in the communications industry, whose position was eliminated last year.

> *"After the initial shock of leaving my former company had worn off, everything happened almost too easily. I put together my resume and game plan, all of my industry contacts were fresh and everyone seemed willing to help.*
>
> *I went out and networked like crazy, and everything looked promising. I even had two interviews within the first few months (which did not turn into offers).*
>
> *Then I reached a stage where nothing seemed to work. People I had known for years didn't return my calls. Letters I wrote went unanswered, and all the creativity and enthusiasm that marked the first three months of my search seemed to evaporate. I felt like the air had leaked out of my balloon and I was sinking."*

This individual's experience is not unusual. Many job hunters find that the first phase of their search is not as difficult as they had anticipated. However, as opportunities fail to materialize or are discarded, and the candidate exhausts his or her initial list of contacts, the search for work can move into a more difficult phase.

Just as marathon runners "hit the wall", many candidates find themselves discouraged or losing the momentum they need to move forward in their efforts to find a new position. However, don't assume that your game plan is off target because it has taken longer to achieve your objective than you thought it would. Success is also dependent upon market conditions.

The Rationale

Why do candidates hit the wall? Here are some explanations. One possibility is that well meaning friends/family can create the mistaken impression that finding a new position takes only a few weeks and is a simple process. Their comment, "I can't imagine that anyone with your background and skills will have any trouble finding a job," might be offered during early conversations. In fact, it may be hard to resist believing it!

Hitting the wall can also be a reflection of how you interpret "feedback" from the outside world, and the assumptions that are made as a result. Calls that are not returned, a promising interview that did not seem to go anywhere, or a position that failed to materialize; these events might cause you to question your self-worth or doubt your marketability. In the absence of information to the contrary, emotional judgments might be made. As the search time lengthens, the most rational, thorough candidate may abandon the very factors that created a successful career.

So, what are the solutions? The strategies listed below are straightforward and often have the side benefit of preparing candidates to cope with *any* personal crisis they may face.

Maintain Your Perspective

When finding work is not as easy as it seemed early on, don't assume the worst -- get the facts. Base your actions on real information whenever possible, and spend as much time as you can evaluating what has worked and what hasn't.

It is also helpful to take short breaks from your search to clear your head and regain your perspective. Work a month and then take a three day weekend.

Use Your Support System

Sometimes the discomfort of not having found work creates a tendency to withdraw from friends, associates and family. The truth is that people do want to help, but you need to tell them how. Talk to a friend or mentor, consider joining a support group, or take advantage of the built-in support network provided by other candidates.

Stick To Your Plan

Hopefully, your search for work began with an evaluation of your past experiences, and an assessment of your skills, interests and values, which led you to develop a personalized marketing plan with goals and objectives. Stick with it! Review the plan regularly and make adjustments based on what you have learned.

Take Control

Take charge of your search by maintaining regular work habits and full work weeks. Implement task planning, keep up-to-date records of your activities and results, and evaluate your progress regularly.

Since networking continues to be the number one effective strategy for finding the next position, spend most of your time out of the office meeting with people and getting feedback on your strategy and activities.

SUMMARY

♦ Your career transition requires **a goal** and **a plan** for organizing and prioritizing necessary tasks.

♦ Transitioning to your next career position requires an understanding of the **Phases of Transition** and the **development of skills** necessary to accomplish the required tasks.

♦ The specific recordkeeping system you use is not as important as having and **using a system that works for you.**

♦ **Your mental preparation and attitude** are the foundation on which an effective campaign strategy and action plan are built.

♦ **Be vigilant in assessing your campaign.** If you suspect you have "hit the wall," review the relevant pages in this chapter and discuss your situation with someone whose opinion you respect and who supports your situation. You do not need sympathy. You need objective guidance and support.

RECORDKEEPING FORMS

WEEKLY ACTION PLAN (Item #12-1)

NAME _____

Check off as you complete ✓
(Or rate your performance)

WEEK BEGINNING _____

	Network Activities:			Research:	Interviews/ Follow-up:
	☾Phone Calls ☎	Letters ✉ Thank You Notes	☺Meetings☺	💾💻📂📄	
	Name	Name	Name	Name	Name
Monday Date					
Tuesday Date					
Wednesday Date					
Thursday Date					
Friday Date					

NETWORKING CONTACT RECORD (ITEM #12-2A)
INDEX CARD FORMAT

Here is an example of a good tracking method for your networking contacts -- using index cards.

Name	Office Phone/Fax	Home
Company		
Address		

POSSIBLE TYPE OF ASSISTANCE

☐ INDUSTRY INFO. ☐ INTRO. TO TARGET
☐ TARGET CO. INFO. ☐ JOB LEAD
☐ SECOND CONTACTS ☐ FEEDBACK
                   ☐ FUTURE REFERENCES

Contact	Mode	What Happened?	Follow-up
	☐ Phone		☐ Required
	☐ Letter		☐ Completed
	☐ Interview		

(List referral on back of card)   **Referred by**

You can file these alphabetically by individual or company name in a card file and flag those requiring further action. You can take them with you to appointments/meetings. Be sure to cross-index them to your correspondence.

NETWORKING CONTACT RECORD (Item #12-2B)
FULL PAGE/NOTEBOOK FORMAT

CONTACT NAME	Follow-up _____ Status:_____	REFERRED BY:

CONTACT NAME

Follow-up _____
Status:_____

REFERRED BY:

Contact Name:

Title/Function:

Company Name:

Title/Function:

Business Phone #:

Business Fax #:

Company Name:

Street Address:

City/State/Zip:

Background Information On Contact

Relationship to referring

Family: spouse, children, pets:

Age:

Hobbies:

Interests:

Other:

DATE	STATUS/COMMENTS:

INTERVIEW LOGSHEET (Item #12-3)

**F
I
L
L

O
U
T

P
R
I
O
R

T
O

I
N
T
E
R
V
I
E
W**

Name:

Phone #:   **Fax #:**

Title:

Interview Date:

Company Name:

Address:

Background Information on Individual:

Information on
- **Scope of Work**
- **Compensation Package**
- **Names & Titles of Key People**
- **Organizational Structure**
- **Key Locations**
- **Products/Services/Lines of Business**

Desired Outcome/Next Step:

**A
F
T
E
R

I
N
T
E
R
V
I
E
W**

What Worked Well:

Areas for Improvement:

Reactions to/from Others:

Main Interests in My Background:

What Happens Next (What, Who, When):

CORRESPONDENCE LOGSHEET ITEM (#12-4)

| Type of Correspondence | Name/Address/Phone/Fax | Mail Date | Phone Date | | Result of Follow-up | Written Reply Rec'd | Further Action |
			Sched'd	Actual			

ADVERTISEMENT RECORD (#12 - 5)

THE AD: Appeared in: _____
                                                                      (Publication)

                                             _____ _____
                                                  (Edition)   (Date)

_____ Sent attached letter with _____ attached

_____ Phoned number given, spoke to _____

   ♦   Result:

   ♦   Follow up required:

_____ Researched/networked for more information on company

_____ Plan to follow up by _____

with _____

Notes from research:

_____

_____

_____

_____

_____

CHAPTER THIRTEEN
Transition/Summary

> *"Rivers are highways that move on, and bear us whither we wish to go."*
>
> — Blaise Pascal, *Thoughts, Chapter 9, 38*

POINTS OF INTEREST

In Chapter Thirteen you will:

♦ Learn the key components to transition into a new position, including:

- Formally accepting the offer
- Informing your network about your new position
- Creating a working relationship with your new manager
- Planning for the future

♦ Recap your successful transition process and learn to use those same skills in future endeavors

FORMALIZING YOUR ACCEPTANCE

The first step in moving into your new job is to formally accept the offer. The offer was probably made verbally and may have been followed with a letter confirming the offer. For many companies, it is standard procedure to confirm a job offer in writing, especially for middle to upper managers. For other positions, or in smaller, less formal companies, this may not be their practice. Nevertheless as we recommended in Chapter 9 -- Written Communication -- it is always good to confirm in writing.

Draft an acceptance letter that outlines the key items agreed upon -- salary, vacation, job title, scope of responsibilities, location and start date. Be sure that any components of the package that are outside of normal company policy or precedent are clearly defined. (See sample acceptance letters in Index of Resources.)

Before you terminate your other search efforts, you will need to get clarification on whether there are any **contingencies to the offer**, such as passing a physical exam or completing a reference or credit check, and if the offer is subject to internal approvals at higher levels.

If the company gives you a written offer, you should respond with a short letter of thanks and acceptance. This will allow them to begin the paperwork to get you on the payroll, and also to notify other candidates that the job has been filled.

The formality of a written letter of acceptance does provide *some* assurance against the following occurrences:

- The person who hired you did not have full authority to create the position or fix the salary, and someone countermanded his or her offer.

- Your employer has a different understanding of what you have agreed upon.

- Someone else in the company made an offer to a different candidate, or the candidate they really wanted suddenly said "yes."

- A hiring freeze has just been declared by top management.

Starting Date

Once you have officially accepted the position and clarified all the details, it will be to your benefit (financially and emotionally) to start work as soon as possible.

Take note of effective dates of internal programs: group insurance coverage (which is often tied to the first of the month); vacation (some define eligibility in terms of the quarter or half of the year in which an individual commences employment); profit-sharing or savings plans (which may define eligibility by month of employment); and other programs with special eligibility qualifications.

Spreading the Good News

A well-organized company may want to announce your addition to the staff. Be sure to give your new company a chance to announce the news in its own time and manner, and be prepared to cooperate by furnishing whatever biographical data is appropriate.

Once you have assurance that you have been hired (you have met/passed any outstanding contingencies), you will need to:

♦ Notify any firms with whom you have been negotiating that you have accepted a new position.

♦ Inform and thank any search consultants who have assisted you, and let them know where you will be located.

♦ Inform your network contacts, offering special thanks to those who helped you during your career transition.

Teaming with Your New Manager

It is important to meet with your new manager soon after joining the organization in order to be clear about his/her goals and priorities. Identify areas in the department or function that are in need of improvement.

Below are suggestions for a start-up plan.

♦ **Agree on a schedule of activities for approximately the first thirty days**. To the extent possible, detail meetings, trips, introductions and orientations.

♦ **Spend time becoming acquainted with new colleagues and staff members**. Where appropriate, solicit their views on the goals defined by the manager.

♦ **Discuss start-up plans**, long-term, interim and short-term goals with your manager and then with your staff.

♦ **Do not implement any changes** until you know what is going on.

♦ **Manage expectations;** yours, your managers and those who work for you.

THE TRANSITION PROCESS

Do you remember the reactions you experienced and the emotions you felt adjusting to the loss of your former position? Gradually, by talking about what happened, exploring your feelings and working through the phases of transition, you made a personal commitment to move ahead with your career and your life.

Looking back at what you have accomplished during your search for work, you can see how you successfully navigated your way through this transition process:

- Experienced an **Ending** (the loss of your previous position, relationships, your work responsibilities), processed your feelings and reactions, and began to look ahead to the future.

- Entered the phase of **Exploration**, in which you examined possibilities and options, while challenging some existing assumptions about your life and career.

- Moved into the phase of **New Beginnings**, characterized by personal renewal and realignment with your decisions and goals.

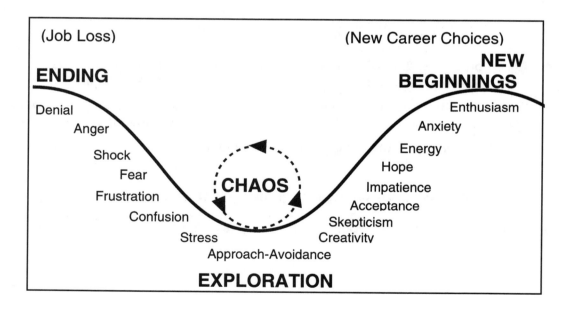

If you were to look back at Chapter 1 and reflect on where you were in the transition process, you might recognize that you have come a long way down the path. You will experience this transition process over and over again as you encounter the many changes life has in store.

The difference between then and now is that you are more able to quickly identify where you are, solicit the support and information you need, and move on when you are ready.

You have an advantage over your competitors in the employment market. You have successfully surmounted a major life change, learned a great deal about yourself as well as valuable and life-long self-marketing skills. You have taken control of your situation, planned a strategy to move your career to the next step and, in the process, emerged stronger than before.

This is a challenging and rewarding time, during which you can enjoy the fruits of your labor and be proud of your efforts and accomplishments. You are prepared with the skills to meet these challenges, and you are sensitive to the needs of others who may also be experiencing change and transition. Enjoy this success -- you have earned it!

BE PREPARED -- STAY PREPARED

First Year Planning

Now that you are in your new position, you need to think about how to maximize the benefits of your situation. Think through the following.

- ♦ What have you learned about yourself that will help you in your new work?

- ♦ What potential obstacles to success do you foresee in the new job (culture, relationships, etc.), and how do you plan to handle them?

- ♦ How do you plan to build on your strengths and become a better manager or professional?

- ♦ What improvements or changes in your behavior or (management) skills do you plan to make?

- ♦ What career plans do you have in mind beyond this immediate move?

Should your job be similarly affected at some time in the future, be prepared with a plan. Use what you have learned about yourself, your objectives and your market to develop contingency plans for the future.

PLANNING FOR THE FUTURE

In today's fast-changing business world, the ability to recognize the need for change and adapt quickly are essential career skills. Toward that end, here are some things you can do.

♦ **Maintain the business records notebook you created to find this job for your future.** Think of it as a "Marketing Plan Book." Periodically review and add your written accomplishment statements as you achieve new successes. Record information on new networking contacts you make, and information on companies that come to your attention that you may want to target sometime in the future.

♦ **Stay in touch with your network.** Have lunch, share information of mutual interest or refer a prospect. As you continue to network, add new and important names to your list.

♦ **Continue to "sell yourself"** within your new organization when the opportunity presents itself.

♦ **Use the active listening skills and questioning techniques** you studied, practiced and observed to gather information from subordinates and other colleagues.

♦ **Cultivate relationships with professionals other than your manager.** If staffing requirements change or new opportunities open up, you will be visible and known to the decision-makers.

♦ **Focus on getting results** that mean something to your company and make sure that key decision-makers are aware of your contributions.

♦ **Use and refine your negotiating skills** whenever you can -- they apply in many business and personal situations.

♦ **Maintain the good work habits and effective planning and monitoring techniques** you used during your campaign for maximum utilization of your work and personal time.

♦ **Develop the capabilities of those who report to you.** Be a model leader. Collaborate, share department dreams and visions and invite their innovations. Above all, listen.

♦ **Develop relationships outside your company** in trade associations and professional groups.

CAUTION SIGNALS

Continue to be aware of what is going on inside and outside your company. Be sensitive to subtle signals of forthcoming change or shifts within the organization and your work environment.   For example:

- ◆ Increasing numbers of confidential upper-level management meetings.

- ◆ Your manager becomes less and less available to you.

- ◆ Employees appear inexplicably anxious.

- ◆ Communication channels seem to be collapsing.

- ◆ Your company's stock price falls sharply.

- ◆ A shift in focus to cost cutting.

- ◆ Talk of an impending merger or acquisition.

- ◆ Sudden changes in the company's senior management team.

- ◆ Your industry has started to decline.

If you get in the habit of staying in touch with what is going on, you will be prepared to activate your contingency plans before an upheaval.

By all means, begin your new position with great optimism and enthusiasm. But also be aware that in today's marketplace the best job security is your own competence and foresight.

SUMMARY

As your transition period comes to a close, you will need to plan and prepare not only for your new position, but for the future as well. Here are some points to keep in mind:

♦ **Clarify the details of your new position** with a written agreement.

♦ **Review what you have learned** from past work experiences and identify areas you can strengthen to enhance your future success.

♦ **Use insights from the self-assessment process,** the work search process, friends and family to guide your behavior in the new work environment.

♦ **Confirm details of your first day**, and prepare for it by reviewing company literature, work requirements and travel logistics prior to the start date.

♦ **Learn what is important to your manager**, and communicate in a style that is comfortable for him or her.

♦ **Develop relationships with colleagues** and allow time for those to solidify.

♦ **Continue to upgrade your skills and knowledge,** and maintain networking activities and relationships, both in and out of the workplace.

♦ Recognize that **career planning and management have become your *personal* responsibility,** not your company's.

Career Continuation Program Evaluation

Company:_____ **Program Instructor:**_____

Program Date: _____

DBM would like to thank you for your feedback and wish you early success in your career continuation efforts. Will you please take a moment to thoughtfully answer the questions that follow.

To what degree:[1]	Excellent...Poor							What would have helped?
With regard to YOU, the participant:	**7**	**6**	**5**	**4**	**3**	**2**	**1**	**Comments?**
1. Did the program enhance your ability to get your career on track?								
2. How did you feel your chances were for finding a good position before taking this workshop?								
3. Do you feel prepared to negotiate for a new job?								
4. Did you have a clear picture of where you were going in the course and why you were doing the various activities and exercises?								
5. Do you feel the course prepared you for the job search?								
6. Do you feel that you have been sufficiently prepped to ask the right questions during your interviews?								
7. Did the course improve your self-confidence and/or orient your thinking in an optimistic way?								
8. Did the course provide you with a realistic notion of the time it would take to find a position?								
9. Did the course provide you with sufficient alternatives and action plans to reduce the emotional distress of peaks and valleys?								
With regard to the Content:								
1. Was the information timely and current?								
2. Was the program suited to your needs?								
3. Was the program well organized?								

_____

[1] Every question should begin with the phrase, "To what degree......"

To what degree:	Excellent...Poor	What would have helped?
With regard to the Instructor:	7 6 5 4 3 2 1	**Comments?**
1. Was the instructor knowledgeable and well prepared?		
2. Was the instructor interesting?		
3. Were questions answered clearly and completely?		
4. Was the presentation adjusted/adapted to match the make-up of the class?		
5. Did the instructor provide support and understanding?		
6. Did the instructor show knowledge of local job market?		
7. Did the instructor provide assessment and feedback that was helpful?		
With regard to the Materials:		
1. Were the course objectives reinforced with materials and handouts?		
2. Was the Index of Resources a useful item?		
3. Did the video demonstrate skills you need to know?		
4. Was the video realistic?		
	Yes No	**Comments?**
1. Do you plan to refer back to your workbook as a resource?		
2. Do you plan on completing the exercises in your workbook?		

3. What aspects of the program did you find most valuable?

4. Please offer any general comments, thoughts or feelings you might have regarding the program.

9212 Berger Road
Columbia, MD 21046
T 443. 259. 6836.

Vera Orsova
Technical Recruiter
vorsova@opticalcoptalgroup.com